TALES OF THE HEART

Affective Approaches to Global Education

Tom Hampson
Loretta Whalen

Friendship Press

for
Church World Service and Witness

a web of global ecumenical partnering

widening the world
of its U.S. constituency
through
global education

for
Ronald E. Stenning
who enkindled & sustained
the vision

We are here to awaken from the illusion of our separateness.

Thich Nhat Hanh

Most Bible quotations in this book are from the new Revised Standard Version, copyright 1988 by the Division of Education and Ministry of the National Council of the Churches of Christ in the United States of America.

Book design and typesetting by Patricia Kellis

Editorial Offices: 475 Riverside Drive, Room 772, New York, NY 10115
Distribution Offices: P.O. Box 37844, Cincinnati, OH 45222-0844

Manufactured in the United States of America on acid-free paper.

Library of Congress Catalog-in-Publication Data

Hampson, Tom.
Tales of the heart : affective approaches to global education / Tom Hampson, Loretta Whalen.
p. cm.
Includes bibliographical references
ISBN 0-377-00223-2
1. Christianity and justice—Study and teaching. 2. Peace—Religious aspects—Christianity—Study and teaching. 3. International education. 4. Worship programs. I. Whalen, Loretta. II. Title.
BR115.J8H36 1991
261.8'07—dc20

91-37173
CIP

CONTENTS

Appreciations

Spring promises. Word of forsythia filters from the South. A project named The *Tales* Seminar ("seed plot") catalogues its yield. A tale of abundance. Our thanks embrace special persons, accompanists all in a unique experiment:

- the **Global Education Committee of Church World Service** superbly chaired by Norma Kehrberg, supporter of the seminar vision; colleague, sounding board, advocate and evaluator through its four-year tenure.
- **Church World Service and its Unit Committee,** architect of the Office on Global Education in 1980 and underwriter of the seminar project. May its new life as Church World Service and Witness be fruitful.
- our superb colleagues in the Office on Global Education, dedicated midwives who labored over the birth of this project and volume. **Susan Soohoo** gathered, tended, and weeded the many resources found at *Tales'* end. Foremost in "floppy files." **Rose Downing** doggedly tracked permissions, enabling us to cite the work of others in the field. Draft layout suited her too. **Rita Johnson**, and her NCR processor "Blitzen," entered much of the material before you. Each proofed and corrected, faxed, FedExed and ferreted out. It would have been an untold *Tale* without them. We mark gratefully such competent and amiable companionship.
- those many individuals and groups whose collaboration, recruiting, and plain hard work made possible wide field-testing of the seminar model. Their often feisty oar-in-the-water approach made design an adventure, decision a consensus, and decentralization a well-practiced art! The cast of characters:

  Church World Service Regional Staff, cornerstone of CWS life in communities across the U.S. These persons were primary collaborators:

  Carolinas—**Ed King, Joe Moran, Dilys Hale, Yvonne Harris**
  Greater Chicago—**Janet Young, Janice Fielding**
  Iowa—**Russ Melby, Doris Knight**
  Illinois—**Dennis Metzger, Kristy Knappmeyer**
  Ohio—**Les Sauer, Dan Coster, Loretta Swanson**
  Pacific Southwest—**Casey Howell, Thomas Leschefsky**
  Upstate New York—**Doug Anderson, Pat Lambert**

There are no passengers on Spaceship Earth. Everybody's crew.

Marshall McLuhan

Other valued partners:
The NCC/DOM Africa and Latin America Area Offices
The Church Federation of Greater Chicago
Church World Service staff: **Larry Hixon** and **Hugh Wire**

NCC Division of Education and Ministry:
Professional Church Leadership Program, **Jim Gunn**

NCC Division of Church and Society, **Mary Ellen Lloyd:**
Working Group on Domestic Hunger and Poverty
Genesee Ecumenical Ministries (Rochester, NY)
Ghost Ranch, NM—Presbyterian National Adult Study Center
Las Palomas de Taos (Taos, NM)
The Illinois State CWS/CROP Committee
Iowa Interchurch Forum
The Ohio State CWS/CROP Committee
The Presbyterian Hunger Program
The Stanley Foundation (Muscatine, IA)
Union Seminary, New York: **William Bean Kennedy**
NCC Women's Portfolio Network
First Congregational Church of Santa Barbara, CA

- Witnesses who shared their tales of faith and struggle:

Jane Adams: Illinois South Project
Burgess Carr: Africa Secretary, The Episcopal Church
Jim Jarvis: Teacher, York High School; Global Education Consultant, Greater Chicago CWS Region
Mikel Johnson: AFSC, Midwest Region
June Keener-Wink: potter
Maghan Keita: Assoc. Director, NCC/DOM Africa Office
Stephen & Tessie La Boueff, Antonio Medina, Cipriano Vigil: The Rio Grande Institute
Ben Magubane: South African expatriate, Professor of Sociology, University of Connecticut/Storrs
Mutombo Mpanya: Zairean, Kellogg Fellow/University of Notre Dame
Dan Nagengast: Longtime Africa development worker, Iowa CWS Regional Director
Dave Ostendorf: Founder and Director, PrairieFire
Roz Ostendorf: Staff, Iowa Interchurch Forum

This is what Yahweh asks of you, to act justly, to love tenderly, and to walk humbly with your God.

Micah 6

Bernard Spong: Media Director, South Africa Council of Churches
Gene Stolzfus: Director, Synapse
Jim and Jean Strathdee: Musicians, troubadours, composers, lovers of earth
Tomas Telez: Executive Sec'y, Baptist Convention/ Nicaragua

We are grateful to our evaluators for bringing fresh, discerning eyes to the work. They challenged and encouraged.

Ann Dubois: Staff, Women's Division, Presbyterian Church (USA)
Rev. Ed McMahon and **Peter Campbell:** Directors, Institute for Bio-Spiritual Research
Jill Roth: Faculty, Immaculate Heart College Center
Ronald E. Stenning: Former Associate Director, Church World Service
Tom Thomas: Ph.D. Cand., Education, U. of Illinois

To colleagues who brought requested critique to certain sections: **Lowell Brown, Dick Brumleve, Kevin Kleinheksel, Barb Murock, Ruth Toomey, Mike Wessells.**

To Canadian confrères for cross-border networking which enlarges and illuminates our world: **Ten Days for World Development,** and the **Development Education Center.**

To **Audrey Miller and the Friendship Press editorial staff,** as well as their **NCC Program Committee on Education for Mission**. Your enthusiasm for this approach helped immensely in moving it to print. Thanks for listening us into speech!

To **Eunice Cudzewicz,** Medical Mission Sisters (Philadelphia, PA 19111), who crafted the hearts, making possible the *Tales*. Eunice, we rejoice in continuing collaboration, evoking your inimitable graphic gifts. We take heart from your lifelong commitment to a communal life of healing on six continents, in this your Jubilee year. Peace and grace, beloved sister.

Finally, our profound gratitude to all who participated in the seminar. Your openness, inventiveness, spirit of inquiry (and at times of mutiny!) give us stamina still. We set out to learn. You were our greatest teachers. So be it.

Tom Hampson
Loretta Whalen

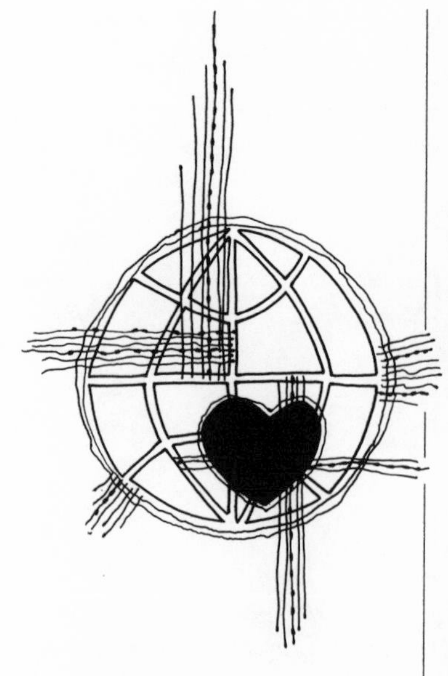

Preface

Welcome. We are pleased to introduce you to *Tales of the Heart,* a multifaceted resource. Here you will find a garden for personal reflection and renewal, a tool box of educational resources, a blueprint for community-based global education seminars. We have crafted *Tales* for education leaders who seek support in their effort to broaden the world of their constituency, and for everyone who aches for a more just and peaceful world.

You may approach Tales *to spark your own reflection.* Wander the garden paths of her margin quotes, savor the beauty of her drawings, absorb the wisdom of collected prayers and readings. If you are looking for solace in the face of our wounded world this "cloud of witnesses" reminds us that we are not alone in our longing for a world that works for all. **Preface** and chapter openings (note: other chapters are cross referenced in **bold**, particular elements are referred to in *italics*) elaborate on this theme—how may we remain open-hearted and energetic in the face of so much suffering?

You may approach Tales *as a tool box* containing a variety of well-tested global education activities including curriculum, and worship designs. Careful step-by-step instructions are included. **Elements** provides an overview. These activities can be used individually or in various combinations to fit your particular needs. Participatory, imaginative, tapping our feeling as well as thinking sides, they enkindle a deeper appreciation of connection to all persons on the planet.

The universe is made of stories, not of atoms.

Muriel Rukeyser

A word more on method. As *Tale's* title suggests we approach the challenge of educating about our present time from within the context of our personal life stories. We are persuaded from long experience that opening to our own story and that of those nearest us enables a more sustained openness to the story of our world. We are each bearers of a tale, a fragment of the world's wisdom, sorrow, delight. As we share our life-learnings, energy, creativity, and hope are generated. The tale unfolds.

Finally, Tales *can be approached as a blueprint* for organizing global education seminars. All that you need to organize a one to four-day event is included in these pages. See the *Seminar Description Sheet* page 192, and **Organizing** for elaboration.

Such seminars, offered around the U.S.A., were the womb of the book you hold in your hands. The tales of hundreds of earlier participants, and our local organizing committees, murmur between the lines of every page. By following the guidance provided here you too will be able to create a welcoming hearth around which the tales of the heart may be told, and heard, and treasured. May it be so.

Introduction

We have only begun to know
the power that is in us if we would join
our solitudes in the communion of struggle.

So much is unfolding that must
complete its gesture,

so much is in bud.

Denise Levertov

The Week of God's Passion

In this Holy Week, the Christ hands over his life as sign and sacrament, as the shape of love, as instruction in truth-telling, in the transcending of self, in the passing over from death to abundant life.

In a nuclear age, this series of seminars explores right-relation (read justice) in the global family, and ways toward equity for all of created life. These seminars empower, heighten creativity, celebrate life *in the very passage through* our common brokenness and its attendant pain.

With a people called Western and Christian, the seminars connect questions of method and of substance:

- How can we be awakened to a much-needed view of the "whole inhabited earth" *(oikoumene)* as the third millennium approaches?
- How can brutal global inequities and their causes be candidly addressed, releasing energy rather than paralyzing with guilt?
- Can we learn that to the degree we distance ourselves from our own inner pain, we flee the truth of all painful reality?
- Dare we enlarge the portrait of the hungry child to make visible the web of systemic injustice that keeps her hungry? Will making the connections indict us in ways we cannot bear?
- Can we enhance our learning in unaccustomed, even playful ways?

Dare we attend to the tales of our own hearts? A dozen years' involvement with global education in the United States has revealed these tales as teacher. What follows contextualizes almost a thousand North American Christians' reflections on the central passion of their God: ". . . that all may have abundant life." *Tales of the Heart* enables you to go and do likewise, as leader or participant, alone or in a community of learners.

We rejoice in your companionship in this life-giving work as the twenty-first century edges onto the horizon, a century that will surely intensify the clamor that we "join our solitudes in the communion of struggle."

First, a moment with the essence of our discoveries.

No one of us doubts the treacherous nature of our times. So much to recoil from. So much anger, terror, inequity, violence, death, grief and injustice, loss of love, and inability to relate. We seem without anchor. Adrift.

The text you hold suggests that *unless and until we allow ourselves to feel all that, sit with and sense it deeply, embrace it, we cut ourselves off from our power to change it.* We further suggest that this feeling/sensing task is at the heart of a global spirituality. Says Madonna Kolbenschlag, "The befriending of our anxiety is the prologue to our spiritual transformation."

For, although it is true that fear and despair can overwhelm us, hope cannot be purchased with the refusal to feel.

Susan Griffin

A litany of today's anxieties:

- We wonder at our nation's use of its power. In what cause will our sons and daughters lose their lives? What are our national priorities?
- Toxicity despoils our earth. Brother and sister creatures disappear, their wild splendor forever unavailable to our imagination.
- Ethnicity builds walls between us. A note from atop Africa's Zomba plateau last summer, courtesy of BBC and shortwave:

  Burma: Hopelessly outmatched Karen rebels struggle against the genocidal Burmese majority. Waves of cruelty, brutality, and death create 450,000 Karen refugees on the Thai border. Meanwhile, Thai teak interests make common cause with the Burmese government in a macabre drive toward extermination of a people.

- Our children numb themselves with killing chemicals.
- A woman is beaten every fifteen seconds in the United States.
- Western pressures on the International Monetary Fund manipulate the debt of already hopelessly impoverished nations. Their youngsters take to the streets (by the hundreds of millions at this writing) to "raise money" for their family's survival. Annoyed, their nation's "security police" murder them.

Our whales and sons and souls all seem endangered species.

- As for our daughters, "sex tourism" in Thailand (as only one example) destroys hundreds of thousands of bodies, minds, and spirits—at an age when finding our roller-skate key was our chief concern. Professionals,

physicians, and lawyers from half-way round the world are the "tourists." How did we lose our way?
- The global economy brinks on collapse. The Soviet Union and her proud, longsuffering peoples face years of chaos and deprivation. Sisters and brothers East, West, and South teeter on the brink of extinction from repressive armies, ecological catastrophe, urban squalor, homelessness.
- The nations of Africa have already lost 5 million human beings to AIDS. Twenty-two percent of the pregnant women in Blantyre, Malawi are infected with the AIDS virus.
- The 625 million persons who live in those same African nations have a combined gross national product smaller than that of Belgium. A statistic worth sitting with and sensing.
- And those same nations carry (proportionate to population) the heaviest debt burden in the world. Severely eroded monetary values and purchasing power become killing hunger and malnutrition. Those who survive become generations of severely compromised children, physically, intellectually, spiritually. A living death. A phantom future. A wound, an indictment in the global community.

A discomfited reader is doubtless reaching three conclusions at this juncture:

1) This book really concentrates on the "downside"!
2) So, this book is about economics, abuse, drugs, war . . .?
3) DOES THIS BOOK EXPECT ME TO WORRY ABOUT OR FIX ALL THIS?

Let's take those one at a time. First, "downside." I have experienced that acute awareness of both the beauty and brokenness of our "neighborhood" (the whole inhabited earth) assures that we are fully alive. Nobel Prize winner Elie Wiesel: "There may be times when we are powerless to prevent injustice. But we dare not ever fail to protest." Nobel Prize–winner Martin Luther King, Jr.: "Injustice anywhere is a threat to justice everywhere. We are caught in an inescapable network of mutuality, tied in a single garment of destiny."

Our "way of life" so often cited in these warlike times is not the only one. There is a rich (and enriching) tapestry out there! Our fear and insularity do not serve us well at any level: educationally, culturally, spiritually, economi-

What objectives can we set, what resources can we call upon then in the great effort to relieve suffering? First we must face it and let it in. Different orders of service and loving kindness follow.

Ram Dass

cally, psychologically. This text celebrates the vast pleasures and perils of opening ourselves—as Jesus did—to the present, to the pain, to relationship, to a risk-filled ministry to a world that works for all.

This ethic, this asceticism is what our historic moment demands. It is a vivid breakthrough to engagement, a redemption for our drifting souls. We finally "get" the vulnerability of our crucified God. Like that God, we open to full connection to Life: Resurrection. Far from a "downside," we uncover a vibrant side of the tomb.

To the reader's second possible conclusion: So, this book is about economics, abuse, drugs, war . . .?

In a manner of speaking.

It is about the economics of relationship, beginning with ourselves. About our abuse of our sensing life, our failure to heed the cries from within. About numbing ourselves, preventing the feelings that are associated with this treacherous and tender agenda. About the wars we wage in unforgiving ways on ourselves. About the war of attrition against our very capacity to feel.

Your pain is the breaking of the shell that encloses your understanding.

Kahlil Gibran
The Prophet

The third concern is that we might need to worry about or fix . . .

Neither.

This book suggests that we examine the verbs of current events, and notice their currency in our inner lives as well. Prepare for war. Toxify. Suffer deprivation. Fear. Endanger. Kill. Impoverish. Avoid.

It suggests that our communal agenda—which seizes our attention with the evening news—provides a handy mirror of the work we have to do in our inner life.

It suggests, as an example, that if we are those who long for a negotiated end to war's conflict, that we check our own ability to listen deeply to another point of view, to flex, to compromise, to appreciate difference and to move beyond its borders.

This book is meant to exercise us in self-healing as a part of peacemaking. It suggests that to the degree we are blocking global facts and the feelings they evoke we are blocking our power to make a difference. Blocking our hope of right-relationship (justice).

It suggests that more facts on global madness are to no

avail. The deep dis-ease that our complicity engenders in us needs an "intervention." You hold one in your hands.

You'll be amazed at the resurgence of joy and energy as you hear yourself and are heard; as you listen, connect, and reclaim the power you handed over to numbing. This re-connection is at the heart of the seminar. It is at the heart of genuine religion, which in its Latin root *(re-ligere)* means to re-link.

Colleague Joanna Macy says it this way, "Whether we make it or not, whether our efforts to heal our world succeed or fail, we live then in so vivid a consciousness of our community that the most obvious and accurate word for it is love. And that seems, in and of itself, a fulfillment."

You can't imagine how many borders and boundaries you cross, again and again and again, and you don't even see them. . . the thing is a whole and it's so beautiful.

Russel Schweikart
Astronaut

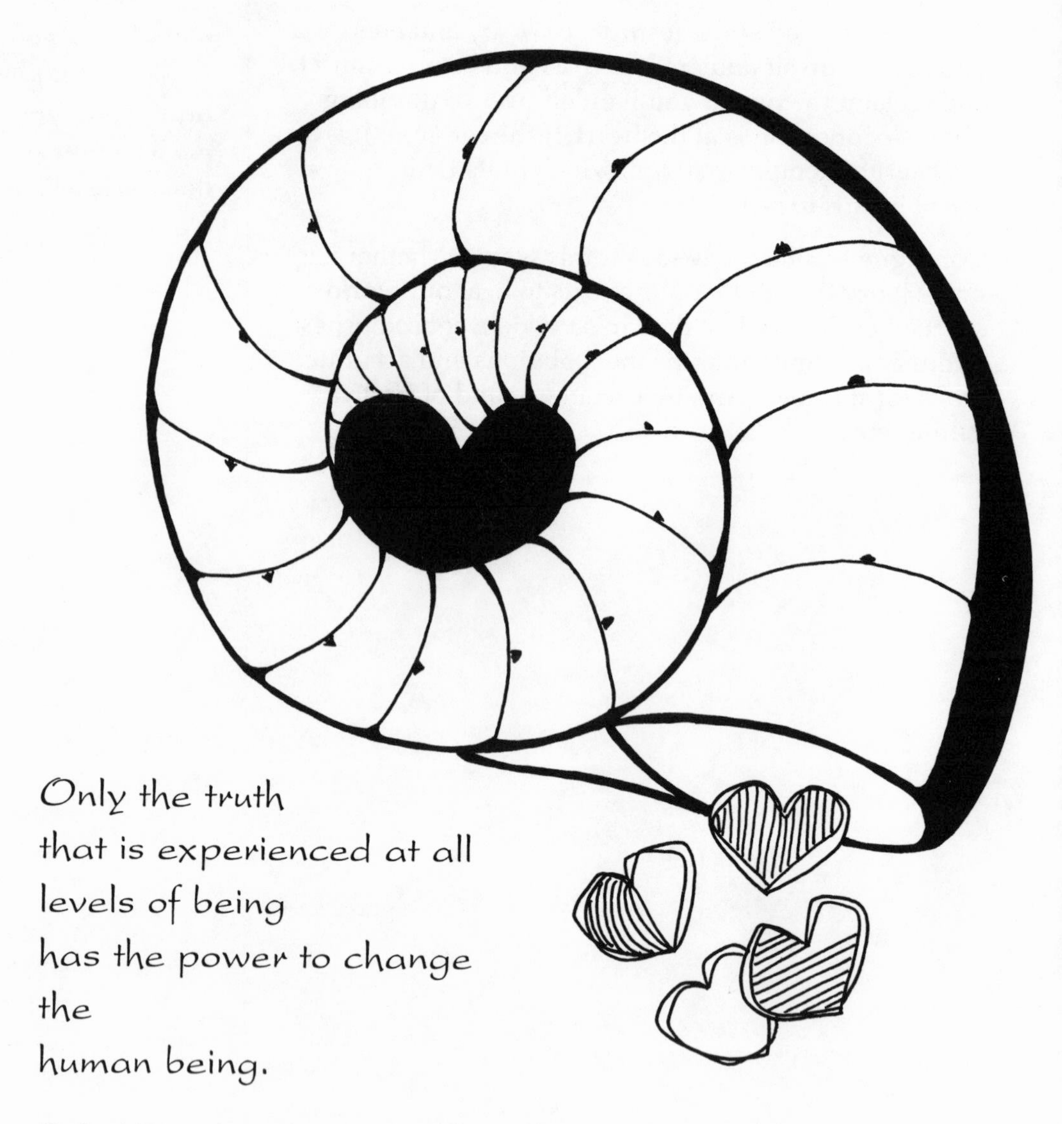

Only the truth
that is experienced at all
levels of being
has the power to change
the
human being.

Rollo May

The beliefs catalogued below are the foundation of the seminar. The pages that follow provide the overview of the seminar's many elements.

We believe

- that the lived experience of each person builds toward the insights that make for global justice, peace, and understanding.
- that our wounds are wise: recalling and recounting our own experience of injustice exposes the roots of all injustice, nurtures our life and its meaning, links us to the suffering of others. "All things are connected, like the blood which unites one family"—*Chief Seattle.*
- that the medium is the message: the design of global education events demands a careful balance of process and content. In fact, process models right-relationship—the definition of justice.
- that the content of global education is at root the dilemma and pain, beauty and delight, diversity and conflict, fact and myth, preoccupation and prognosis of the fragile planet earth.
- that our perspective (theological, sociological, economic, political) mediates and shapes our response. To wit, how we conceive the world shapes the action we birth in the world.
- that movement toward truth, through and away from denial, is heart work. A work of courage.
- that body, mind, and spirit are indeed one. Learning must engage every level.
- that right as well as left brain must be engaged for learning to take place. Affective, artistic, experiential approaches are priorities.
- that though participants are citizens of the more privileged North, "We begin with their considerable pain, promise, and puzzlement—building learning, theology, worship, growth, empathy, celebration, and action from there, thus enabling true empowerment.
- that the mending of the planet is one with the mending of ourselves. There is no more us and them, only we.
- that the unfinished business we have with the shadow side of ourselves, as individuals and nations, is the stuff of our enemy-making. "We" project our

(R)eal criticism begins in the capacity to grieve because that is the most visceral announcement that things are not right. Only in the empire are we pressed and urged and invited to pretend that things are all right either in the dean's office or in our marriage or in the hospital room. And as long as the empire can keep the pretense alive that things are all right, there will be no real grieving and no serious criticism.

Walter Brueggemann

demons on "them." "Those out of touch with themselves have no alternative but to prepare for war" (McMahon & Campbell, *Bio-Spirituality,* Loyola University Press, 1985).

- that wherever we are denying truth, we are in opposition to life.
- that the crucified Christ teaches with his body the redemptive face of vulnerability.
- that we are held, even when we do not tightly hold. Faithfulness does not mean that we must solve or fix it all.
- that a global spirituality sees justice as love in action.
- that breakthroughs in physics and biology affirm the wisdom of vulnerability. The neuron, a basic building-block of all life, *survives only by connecting,* by being thoroughly open to the flow of life energy.

The challenge to both men and women is to invent new myths. People are changed, not by intellectual convictions or ethical urgings, but by transformed imaginations.

Madonna Kolbenschlag

Foundation in place, we invite you into the creation of a household. Welcome.

We sketch here the major elements and themes of *Tales* to assist your orientation to the whole. We begin with a brief look at the origins of this effort. After a discussion of the storytelling method we employ, each section of the seminar is then briefly reviewed. A sample agenda suggests how the pieces may be stitched together. Finally, a brief pep-talk on the importance of tending the hearth around which the stories unfold.

Origins

Tales began as a leadership training project. Over a four-year period the staff of the Office on Global Education (OGE) designed, led, evaluated, and revised a seminar on global awareness for church leadership. In all, twelve seminars were organized and field-tested. Over the same period, we responded to dozens of invitations for shorter presentations of the material, soon titled "the *Tales* workshop." You hold the harvest of those labors.

It is the supreme art of the teacher to awaken joy in creative expression and knowledge.

Albert Einstein

As an Office, we have our history, inspiration, and roots in the Church World Service and Witness Unit of the National Council of Churches in the USA. This unit enjoys partnerships in over seventy nations around the world, enabling and nurturing the "abundant life for all" that Jesus' ministry sought through development, refugee-resettlement, and emergency-response activity.

Since no seminar could usefully confront all the issues touched by our global ministry, a theme was chosen for each seminar, following a case study method. An expert witness highlighted the area chosen, drawing linkages to other issues and geographic regions.

The seminars addressed feelings as well as facts. We found that attending to the wounds of the world demanded prior attention to how those wounds lived in us. "What's it like for us living and loving in a world-at-risk?" Inviting expression of our affective side became one of the most distinctive features of the seminar.

Each seminar enjoyed its own flavor thanks to the diversity of participants, co-sponsors, and case studies. Common to all were five goals:

1. To discover the meaning of a global perspective in our lives, exercising ourselves in making a difference. **Empowerment**.
2. To water the theological and scriptural roots of our peace and justice work, energizing flagging spirits. **Renewal**.
3. To spark networking, ecumenical action, and inner journeying. **Personal/political integration.**
4. To enhance global education skills, with intentional focus on our affective, feeling side. **Training**.
5. To sing and bless our treasured diversity. **Celebration**.

> I believe that our world is on the verge of self-destruction and death because the society as a whole has so deeply neglected that which is most human and most valuable and the most basic of all the works of love—the work of human communication, of caring and nurturance, of tending the personal bonds of community.
>
> Beverly Wildung Harrison

Our audience included leaders (clergy and lay) involved in religious education, women's programs, outdoor and campus ministries, mission activities, Church World Service/CROP regions, community outreach and social concerns groups, and others who chose to explore the appropriateness of a global perspective for themselves and their ministry.

What is the heart of the seminar?

Stories. Our method centers on storytelling. On the conviction that in the recounting of our lives we reaffirm self-worth, uncover new insight, reveal fresh levels of connection with one another, and move closer to our own healing. The seminar rests on three cycles of storytelling:

- **Participant to Participant—**"Recall for a moment the first time you witnessed/experienced injustice either as victim or as observer. How did you feel at that moment? What did you think? What did you do? What does that experience mean to you now?" Participants recall such moments and share them in small groups. Some are very painful to relate. Some hilarious. All are pivotal moments, breakthroughs to a different vision of self and world.
- **Witnesses—**These persons embody the global issues of the seminar case studies. They testify to the reality of structural oppression, detailing its consequences in their own lives. "Issues" gain a human face. "Their"

fears and hopes resonate as our own. The "other" becomes one of "us" and "we" one of "them."

- **Worship**—Worship centers each seminar, placing our lives and struggles within the context of the story of God's unfolding creation. Well-crafted liturgical vessels, music, bell, lamp, incense, and silence help to define the time and space, reminding us of its sacredness and our own. While some elements may be unfamiliar, participants, in our experience, respond to the tone and content of the worship with enthusiasm and gratitude.

The Overview of the Seminar's Elements

Each of the teaching sections is described below with approximate time indicated. See the section itself for suggestions on length alterations.

Building Community: A collection of favorite community-building exercises. Some lend themselves to beginnings, others as closure. We also outline a few tips for small-group facilitators. The length of the exercises varies.

Coming to Our Senses in a Global Age: An introduction to global education, this module uses humor and cartoons as a vehicle to heighten our awareness of how our worldview is formed and functions, for better and worse (2 hours).

Theologos—The Theological Basis for Justice-Seeking: Christ calls us to emulate his vulnerability. The self-opening to the world which he modeled echoes in the discoveries occurring in science (i.e. the radical interconnectedness of the material universe). Opening to the world begins as we name and own our feelings about threats to life and health on earth, wherever they occur. Through story, film, and discussion participants enter this healing practice of openness (3 hours).

Images of the Enemy: An exploration of the ways we distort our perceptions of others named "enemy." The habit of enemy-making occurs at the individual and corporate levels when we project our worst fears onto the "stranger." The nature of this process and its consequences for us are explored through stories, poems, and propaganda art (3 hours).

Exploring Our Worldview: An imaginative look at the hopes/visions cherished by the participants for a more

Nothing could be worse than the fear that one had given up too soon and left one unexpended effort which might have saved the world.

Jane Addams

There is no such thing as my bread. All bread is ours and is given to me. To others through me and to me through others.

Meister Eckhart

equitable and peaceful world. Uses guided imagery, discussion, and mime to tap the creative potential of those present. The concluding small-group presentations provide hilarious and moving moments (4 hours).

Worship: Worship teaches. This collection draws together various traditions and peoples, mirroring the global family at prayer. Here we celebrate the breadth of life, grieve its wounding, and commit ourselves to do our part toward its healing.

Organizing a Seminar: Details step-by-step instructions for planning and leading a global education seminar. For example in the *Program Subcommittee* found on page 000 we include guidance on the creation of another module called a "Case Study." We recommend that each seminar contain a Case Study developed by local planners featuring a witness who speaks to a global issue from her/his own life experience, providing a personal encounter with a (sometimes) quite different perspective.

Think of the Case Study as a session you tailor to your own needs and interests on a particular global issue. Hunger, South Africa, Nicaragua, the Philippines, homeless children are some possible issues.

Resources: Suggests leads to speakers, films, and other resources.

Once again, note that cross-references to other sections of the book appear in **Bold**.

A Sample Agenda

Time and experience will determine which of the above elements make the most sense for your event. We include here a sample 2 1/2 day design—the most commonly used during the field-testing of the seminar model. See **Organizing:** *Program Subcommittee* for longer and shorter designs.

You may want to add elements not provided in the book. Skill-building or issue workshops are examples. In the design below the local planning group included such workshops, led by local community activists, to good result.

The sections in *italics* below refer to specific sections or exercises described in this book.

Agenda

DAY I:

5:00 PM	Registration
5:30	Dinner
6:30	Opening Introduction/*Cameo* *Line of Least Acquaintance*
7:30	**Worship**: *Prayer to Humankind*
8:00	*Exploring Our World View*
9:00	*Fest* (see **Organizing:** *Logistics Subcommittee*)

DAY II:

7:00 AM	Breakfast
8:00	*Temperature Check*
8:15	*Worldview: Reports from Evening Groups*
9:30	Break
9:45	***Theologos: The Theological Basis for Justice-Seeking***
12:00 NOON	Lunch
1:00 PM	Case Study: "Rochester in the World"
5:00	Break
6:00	Dinner
7:00	*Caucus Groups*
8:15	***Coming to Our Senses in a Global Age***
9:00	*Fest*

DAY III:

9:00 AM	Breakfast
9:30	Worship: *Sabbath and Hope*
10:00	Workshops -Discerning the Media -Dealing with Conflict -Educational Design -Legislative Advocacy
12:00 NOON	Lunch
12:30 PM	*Caucus Groups: Next Steps*
1:30	*Evaluation* (see **Organizing:** *Program Subcommittee*)
2:00	**Worship**
3:00	Adjourn

The most beautiful music of all is the music of what happens.

Irish proverb

Tending the Hearth

The graphic design for a large seminar banner, created by Medical Mission Sister Eunice Cudzewicz, is at left. This 5'x 8' "global statement," brilliant silk-on-weaving, traveled to every seminar. A separate report could be written on the innovative modes of suspension devised for it in conference sites around the country!

Focal point for our seminar circle of learners, the banner spoke to participants in powerful and unpredictable ways. Often at the concluding worship persons would speak of the banner's accompaniment, sharing what they'd seen and appreciated there. Their response revealed a longing for healing both within and without. The banner became something of a Rorschach test on compassion.

The banner's purpose?

To help create an environment that reflects in some small way the world we hope for—beautiful, just, peaceful. The banner expressed our concern for hospitality, reflected as well in attention to seating arrangements, lighting, the layout of exhibits, and our commitment to meet and interact with each participant. The care, healing, beauty, and inclusiveness of the medium IS the message. Around such a carefully tended hearth, the tales of the heart can be safely told and warmly welcomed.

We reveal here certain preoccupations which you will encounter frequently in this volume: attention to the beauty of the educational environment, appreciation for the embodied wisdom of each person, and affirmation of feelings as well as facts as a mode of global understanding. Beauty entices, welcomes, builds trust. On the pragmatic side, attention to hearth-tending usually insures smooth flow and optimum use of precious time. Some specific suggestions:

- **Chair Arrangement:**
  Arrange the chairs in a circle or semicircle. In some rooms this will take some imagination, perhaps a degree in engineering! Breaking out of the old theater-style seating (rows facing forward) into a circle indicates that all persons and points of view are welcome and heard here. If the circle has to be en-

larged for latecomers, this can provide a reflection on our ever-widening circle of relationships.

While you're engaged in this applied geometry exercise don't forget to create "lanes" for folks to get in and out, and clearance for audiovisual equipment. It's a tricky and time consuming mix. Worth every moment! Here's one possibility. . .

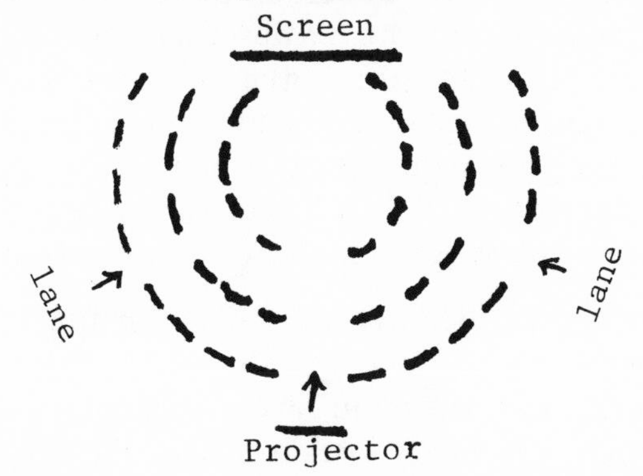

- **Lighting:**
Avoid overhead fluorescence if you can. Natural or incandescent light provides a more inviting, informal ambience. Play with what is available to see which combination of lights is most pleasing, and still bright enough for the activity at hand. For more reflective sessions (worship, conversation after films, guided imagery, or small-group work), table lamps at the room's periphery might be sufficient. Make sure you know how to turn lights off for audiovisual presentations.

- **Beauty:**
Beyond arrangement of chairs and lighting, consider adding international artifacts to beautify the space: batiks to cover display tables, banners, posters, and maps attractively displayed on the walls. Be particularly mindful of these concerns as you plan worship. A low, round table at the center of the circle can provide a focus, displaying the Scriptures, a special candle, gifts from nature, incense.

- **Music:**
Give attention to sound as well. Music sets a tone effectively and subtly. Instrumental, classical, or folk music can be employed. We often play a tape a few minutes prior to the beginning of each session. This alerts participants that we're about to begin and centers us all for what follows. (For groups number-

We have grasped the mystery of the atom and rejected the Sermon on the Mount. Ours is a world of nuclear giants and ethical infants. We know more about war than we know about peace, more about killing than we know about living.

General Omar Bradley

We cannot discover new oceans unless we have the courage to lose sight of the shore.

Anonymous

ing over thirty, a microphone is often necessary. In intergenerational groups, sensitivity to the hearing-impaired can again be a metaphor for the caring, inclusive world we are working toward.)

- **Inclusiveness:**
  Another opportunity to practice what we preach. Educating about the global family requires that the family be represented. This applies to the organizing of the event (see **Organizing**) and the event itself. Attention to the balance of leadership by gender, race and ethnic group, the use of inclusive language, and care for the needs of the physically challenged all fall under this rubric. The medium is the message.

> All the arts we practice are apprenticeship. The big art is life.
>
> M.C. Richards

Close, loving attention to the details of seating or lighting enhances the quality of an educational event. The time and energy invested in caring for the "tidbits," even though only subtly visible, infuses the space with a spirit of hospitality, enabling participants to be in touch with themselves, candid with each other, and ready to risk being architects of a world that works for all.

Community Building

There is a tendency for
living things
to join up,
establish linkages,
live inside
each other,
return to earlier
arrangements,
get along wherever
possible.

It is the way of
the world.

Lewis Thomas

"We are, each of us, parables. Theological exploration of biography is congruent with the definitive New Testament insight and instruction: the Incarnation. Listening is a rare happening among human beings. It is a primitive act of love, in which a person gives him or herself to another's word, becoming accessible and vulnerable to that word."

—*William Stringfellow*

> "Like Jesus we are called to a radical activity of love. To a way of being in the world which deepens relation, embodies and extends community, passes on the gift of life."
>
> —*Beverly Wildung Harrison*

> ". . . listen with unqualified personal regard, attending with the sense that you're hearing what is important, at this moment, for this person to say. A helpful listener doesn't have to believe or do anything about it. What's crucial is to hear it."
>
> —*Carl Rogers*

Speaking first to be heard is power over. Hearing to bring forth speech is empowering.

Nelle Morton

Storytelling permeates the seminar.

Our sagas are our wisdom texts: key to the self, gift to the neighbor.

The activities that follow ask and engender trust. They introduce and query us, they pick our brains, and wonder at our labels. They open and connect us, prelude to the discipline of a wider solidarity.

Across age, gender, class, race, ethnicity—uniqueness dawns, likenesses emerge. Our common ground reveals itself.

One sample. We spend a heritage evening together, reflecting on an artifact of our ancestry. Whence have we come? What surprises awaited us in our research? What have we to learn from our forebears? How does that feel in us now? How might it alter our view of those different from us (the "other," the "foreigner")?

Savoring the varieties of our own roots and routes, can we embrace diversity more wholeheartedly? Imagine a truly global community? While ethnic violence rips the fabric of our shared humanity?

Yes, we can imagine. In the seminar you set out to dream, leaven, and nurture such a community. Believing with Brazilian Rubem Alves "... that the overwhelming brutality of facts is not the last word." Sharing history, hopes, fears, hunches, laughter, and meals builds bridges and creates safe harbor for navigating stubborn issues ... in plentiful supply. The process is medium for the seminar message: "*There is no more us and them, only we.*"

The overwhelming brutality of facts is not the last word.

Rubem Alves

The modes of storytelling and reflection that follow are divided into three parts reflecting where they would most likely be used in the seminar: **Beginning, In the Midst, Closing.**

In addition, since small-group work forms an important part of building community, we list at the end of the section some tips for group facilitators.

"Learning is meeting."

Walter Brueggemann

You will not use all thse activities. Choose the ones that speak to you. Your instincts are the best measure of what will work. Feel free to adapt them or invent new ones.

BEGINNING

Line of Least Acquaintance

Time: 20-25 minutes

Objective: To help people get to know one another. It is a simple device for introducing a relatively large group of 20-80 people or more. This is also one way to create the small groups that will be used throughout the seminar. If you employ the exercise for this latter purpose, the starters (persons who initiate each circle) should be your facilitators.

Materials/Preparation: The aim is to end up with groups of 5 or 6 people in a standing/ sitting circle. Therefore, divide the total number by 5 or 6 to determine how many starters you need. (e.g., with a group of 40 you might start with 8 persons, resulting in 8 groups of 5 each.)

Our lives are like islands in the sea, or like trees in the forest, which comingle their roots in the darkness underground.

William Jones

Recruit participants to act as starters, ideally before the seminar begins. Do not use as starters persons who are likely to know everyone in the group. Be sure to review the steps of the process a couple of times so they are clear about their role.

Write the small-group questions (see below) on newsprint. Suspend it with the questions hidden until you are ready to begin.

Method:

1. Introduce the exercise, and the starters. Review the process of creating the groups (steps 2 & 3).
2. The starters now approach someone they don't know or know very little.
3. When the starter has picked one person, that person then chooses someone else of least acquaintance and brings him/her to the starter. Then the newly chosen person picks another, and so on, until there are five or six persons in each group.
4. Once the group has formed, either standing in place or sitting, the facilitator asks participants to answer these questions in turn (pause for a moment so all can collect their thoughts):

   a) tell me who you are by name
   b) tell me who you are by your work
   c) what's the most important thing to know about you right now?

5. Once all have answered, each person in turn says briefly what his/her hopes are for this meeting. (These can be recorded by the starter for feedback to the whole group or simply to inform the planning team.)
6. All return to the plenary.

You cannot truly listen to anyone and do anything else at the same time.

M. Scott Peck

Demographics

Time: 5 - 10 min.

Objectives: A useful exercise to develop a profile of the group as well as adding some movement and humor at the beginning of an event. The questions suggested below are illustrative. Depending on the nature of the event and the locale, other questions may come to mind. It is also fun to allow the group to develop a few of their own questions at the end.

Method: "Please raise your hand if you . . .":

- have lived outside the United States?
- have traveled outside the United States?
- traveled more than ______(either measures of time or distance) to get to the seminar?
- read the paper daily?
- believe all the news you read?
- floss your teeth daily?

- exercise regularly?
- find ways to take special care of yourself?
- have children? grandchildren? great-grandchildren?
- have ever lived on a farm?
- have ever been poor?
- are able to forgive yourself?
- feel overextended?
- are ______________ (review various denominations)

If time allows, turn this process over to the participants: "What are some things you would like to know about this group?"

Our lives extend beyond our skins, in radical interdependence with the rest of the world.

Joanna Rogers Macy

Art Gallery

Time: 20-30 minutes

Objective: Participants describe what they hope to *get* and what they hope to *give* in the workshop.

Materials/Preparation:
1. Magic Markers/felt-tip pens (enough for each participant)
2. Newsprint cut in half
3. Masking tape

Method:
1. Give each person a 1/2 sheet of newsprint.
2. On newsprint, each person writes:
   a. Name, address, telephone;
   b. Why they have come;
   c. What they want to know;
   d. What they intend to do with what they learn;
   e. Resources they bring;
   f. Something about them they'd like others to know.
3. Post the newsprint on the walls.
4. Encourage participants to browse, read, and to note down the people they would want to meet.
5. After folks have had enough time to look over the newsprint, ask each person to introduce him or herself, and mention one thing they want others to remember about them.

To teach is to create a space in which obedience to truth is practiced.

Abba Felix
Desert Father

I Introduce Me

Time: 5 minutes

Objective: A summary statement distilling central themes, concerns, and passions in the life of one or more of the seminar leaders. Our statements have evolved over time. You might consider it a meditation on the threads and pattern of your life.

This is an exercise in self-revelation, a series of statements, a "telegram" on who you are, what you care about, and how you arrived at the "who" and the "what."

We developed this activity as a way to break down the "expert" halo that is often bestowed on the person giving leadership. By taking the risk to reveal something of who we are apart from our role as "leaders" we become more real, more human, and encourage others to do likewise. These simple statements embody the view that our most precious gift to one another is our own story.

Materials/Preparation: Some suggestions on writing your statement:

- Find a quiet place to write.
- Relax and prepare to enjoy the process.
- Spend some silent, focused time.
- Begin a list on paper (not worrying about style, order, spelling). What are my defining traits, concerns, influences? Where do I find delight, energy, hope? Where have I come from? Where am I going? Let it flow easily. There are no right or wrong answers here. Enjoy the exploration.
- Come back to the statement after a few minutes. Notice what you've said and not said. You may wish to begin again or edit what you've done. Or you may feel satisfied with it as it is!

Method: Present yours at the beginning of the seminar, modeling self-reflection and self-disclosure, giving the participants an early sense of who you are, and what has brought you to this work. An example follows:

I Introduce Me

I am a tiller of the soil.

I was raised a dairy farmer in Indiana.

I spent some time in later youth in urban places in Northern Indiana and West Germany. I was not comfortable. I found myself walking in the middle of the street to get away from the houses, excited by the smell of an approaching storm, and together with a lot of Germans hiking through the hills.

I spent five years in Vietnam in my mid-twenties. Many of those days were passed with farmers. I was in the rice paddies with my feet in the mud. I experimented with mechanical tillage equipment and assisted in the upgrading of irrigation structures.

I spent two years as a graduate student at Indiana University in my early thirties. We lived in a three-room apartment on the eighth floor. I rented a garden plot through the Student Association. I carried bean poles, a hoe, and seeds in the trunk of our car and drove out of town on weekends to put my feet in the soil and get my bearing in the world again.

I have lived in Central Illinois for 11 years now. I work out of an office in Springfield; but we live on .62 of an acre in Chatham, in southern Sangamon County. I have a garden, about 3,000 sq. ft., in which I grow asparagus, eggplant, okra, peppers both hot and not so hot, and other things whose English names sound rather strange. I am in the process of putting some bulbs under a flowering pear tree. I am layering them in. Hopefully the arrangement will produce continuing, changing color over several months. I have set out mountain ash, dogwood, and redbud trees in the yard.

To rise into love you must descend into your wounds.

Robert Bly

Tilling the soil is an important theological experience. It puts us in our proper place in the created order: important actors, but not ultimate arbitrators.

I am a member of the Church of the Brethren.

This German, Anabaptist group with its emphasis on modeling the life of the suffering servant and its teaching of pacifism molded my life. I grew up in the social activism of the 1960s. My parents marched on Washington for Jobs and Freedom. I marched on Washington to End the War in Vietnam. This background led me to volunteer for service in Vietnam with CWS in 1968. During much of my time in Vietnam a numbness enabled me to function and function well in the midst of incredible violence. However, this compartmentalization of life can be highly disempowering. In the time since leaving Vietnam in 1974, I have come, slowly at first and then with increasing energy, to deal with the pain of that experience. My ties with the Church of the Brethren have been renewed during this time. Today I see action for global citizenship as witnessing to the coming Kingdom of God. God will bring it to fruition; we are called to herald its coming.

I live today with one foot in the Vietnamese culture.

My spouse is Vietnamese. Our children are Amerasian, though they do not consider themselves as such. We eat rice at our evening meal. We are in contact with the Vietnamese community in Springfield. I have in-laws in St. Louis. We occasionally receive mail from relatives in Vietnam. Life in these circles reminds me regularly of the interconnectedness of life in this world.

Dennis E. Metzger
Director, Downstate Illinois
Church World Service Office

First Experience of Injustice

Time: 30 minutes - 1 hour

Objective: To share and reflect upon a moment when participants' worldview was shaken, reshaped. To give each other the gift of unqualified presence as the story is told.

Materials/Preparation: None required. One added dimension to the procedure below asks the participants to draw a picture of the memory shared. If this appeals to you, then you will need paper and drawing materials for all present.

Note: This activity also appears in **Theologos**. It works well however, in its own right, or in conjunction with the exercise *Line of Least Acquaintance* above.

Method:

1. In plenary session ask participants to sit comfortably. Tell them you are going to ask them to engage in an exercise in remembering. After a pause for participants to settle themselves, invite them to recall the first time they experienced injustice, either as a victim or as a witness (Alternative phrasing: The first time you realized the social order of your world was

Healing occurs as we express ourselves genuinely, by saying in some way what the past has been. In expressing how it was and is, we make ourselves the witness—one who sees rather than one who has merely been tossed about by passing events.

Arthur Egendorf

flawed; first realization of resistance to an unfair world). Allow them time to re-enter this memory.

It may be helpful to encourage participants not to be scrupulous about "the very first" memory - an early memory is fine. Leave pauses between the questions below.

2. Ask them to identify their thoughts/feelings/behaviors at that moment. What meaning has the experience for them today?
3. Send the group into small groups of 4-5 persons (assigned or created by *Line of Least Acquaintance*). Ask them to share their stories briefly, 3-5 minutes each.
4. Call the whole group back together. Reflection on this experience can be very rich. Your time will determine how deeply you can mine this exercise. The questions below are illustrative of the directions you can take:

   - What reflections do you have on the stories you've heard? Any common themes, issues, patterns?
   - Was there much feeling still connected with your memories? Why?
   - How many of your memories had to do with race? school? economic class?
   - Where, if anywhere, did you find support, assistance in making sense of this experience at the time?
   - Were you able to see links between this experience and your present interests/concerns?
   - What happened to us in these moments?
   - What do these experiences have to teach us in terms of trying to teach global issues? About the resistance we encounter to our peace and justice education?

Feeling is the basic bodily ingredient that mediates our connectedness to the world. When we cannot feel, literally, we lose our connection to the world.

All power, including intellectual power, is rooted in feeling. If feeling is damaged or cut off, our power to image the world and act into it is destroyed and our rationality is impaired. But it is not merely the power to conceive the world that is lost. Our power to value the world gives way as well.

If we are not perceptive in discerning our feelings, or if we do not know what we feel, we cannot be effective moral agents.

Beverly Wildung Harrison

IN THE MIDST

Cameo *(a brief story about one's recent life)*

Time: 3-5 minutes

Objective: To build community and trust by telling/hearing one particular story from a few participants. Well-crafted stories not only allow us a deeper sense of the storyteller, they also reveal our common struggles, hopes, and fears.

Materials/Preparation: *Recruit persons for* Cameos *prior to the seminar itself.* Give them the instructions below. Encourage them to prepare carefully. Let them know when their *Cameo* appears in the seminar.

Leaven the seminar with *Cameos* throughout, usually at the beginning of a session, during worship, or before or after meals. (See the suggested design in **Seminar Elements** for examples.)

Note: The first *Cameo* in an event is a good opportunity to define a *Cameo* and mention its purpose briefly. Refer to the Stringfellow quote at the beginning of this section. This interpretation reinforces underlying messages of the seminar. Everyone's experience is valuable and significant. Storytelling is a thread to our oneness. Later in the event, you'll simply need to indicate it is time for another *Cameo.*

Method: In a *Cameo*, you are asked to:

1. *Tell a single brief story* recounting a high or low moment from your life/work over the last year (no more than five minutes in length, please). Your story may be related to family, or the larger social concerns that bring you to a gathering such as this. You will have *five minutes.*
2. Remember, this is not a speech, lecture, or advertisement. Try to be brief, clear. It is tempting to tell more than one story. Resist!
3. Practice telling the story to a friend at least once prior to the seminar to time your story and get feedback on pacing, etc.
4. You may wish to write down some notes for yourself.

Temperature Checks

Time: 10 minutes

Objective: *Temperature Checks* (TC) were developed by Virginia Satir, a pioneer in family therapy, for use in her six-week intensive workshops on systems. A *Temperature Check,* as the name suggests, attempts to determine the present state of the group. It is a vehicle for ongoing evaluation, information-sharing, and community-building. Simple in design, it can lead over time to a powerful bonding among participants. (Our thanks go to George Otero at Las Palomas de Taos, a global education center in New Mexico, who introduced us to this exercise.)

Materials/Preparation: Newsprint
Easel
Magic Marker

We travel together, passengers on a fragile spaceship, dependent on its vulnerable reserves of air and soil—all committed for our safety to its security and peace; preserved from annihilation only by the care, the work, and I will say, the love, we give our fragile craft.

Adlai Stevenson

Method: In each category below, the leader shares along with the rest of the group. The category headings should always be visible on newsprint when engaged in a *TC*. *Over time, TCs can take longer to conclude, particularly when appreciations increase.*

- *Appreciations*—Highlight people and actions for whom an individual is grateful.
- *New Information*—May be a modification of agenda, or new ideas, materials from the group. Information ideally should either be presented or captured on newsprint.
- *Problems/Solutions*—A time to surface frustrations, but with the expectation that **a suggested remedy will accompany the identified problem.** For example, "no free time," must be accompanied by "how about an hour break tomorrow"?
- *Puzzles*—Here is the time to ask questions, raise concerns about logistics, content, process, etc.
- *Hopes/Fears*—The two most important occasions to address these are at the beginning and the end of the event. At the beginning, initial hopes and fears regarding the event should be captured on newsprint and saved. During the last *TC*, return to these as a way of group evaluation.

We cannot live only for ourselves. A thousand fibers connect us with our fellow men [sic]; and among those fibers, as sympathetic threads, our actions run as causes, and they come back to us as effects.

Herman Melville

Temperature Checks need to be led with a light touch and fairly briskly. If there are no responses to a particular category, simply move on. Use of some humor during these can be a plus in defusing anxiety and building trust.

Discussion Process *for use with films, posters, and poetry*

Time: Varies according to length of audio-visual and group size. Allow a minimum of 30 minutes for the discussion itself.

Objective: To stimulate a discussion of a film, poem, poster, or other stimulus and to keep an *open record* of participant's contributions.

Method: This brainstorming technique generates a lively discussion. *All opinions and reactions of the participants are written down* by the facilitator, whether there is agreement or disagreement with the opinion expressed. The newsprint is arranged in columns according to the chart below. As participants register their reactions in the four categories, record them on newsprint.

Note: It is helpful to have someone else do the recording so the facilitator can focus on the group.

Note: The discussion focuses on the participants own perceptions and reactions. Thus the leader need not be an "expert" on the subject of the audio-visual.

The *facilitator asks a series of questions* about what's been seen. The questions are pursued in order moving from left to right on the chart below. Stay with one image and its attendant feelings, thoughts, and actions across the chart. As you move from one to the other ask if others had the same reaction. When one image has been explored, move to another.

The following are some starter questions for the facilitators.

SEE?/HEAR?	FEEL?	THINK?	DO?
• What did you *see*? • What are some of the lingering *images*? • What *scenes* will you remember most about this *image*? • What did you *hear*? (KEEP THINGS CONCRETE. IF SOMEONE SAYS "I SAW VIOLENCE", ASK THEM "WHERE DID YOU SEE VIOLENCE?")	• What were you personally feeling as you were seeing, hearing, these things in the first column? • What were your emotions? (Be prepared for an entire spectrum of emotions; from hope to despair; from shame to pride in our country for being strong. WRITE IT ALL DOWN! (Don't ask why here; simply list the feelings.)	• What do you think about all this? • To get more discussion of the things that begin to appear in this column, ask WHY. > Why do you say that? > Why do you think that? • Ask HOW things in this column relate to things written down in the first two columns?	• Is there anything that ordinary people can do about this situation? • What might U.S. Christians do about this situation? • What are some of the things that are being done?

(Our thanks to Joe Moran of the Church World Service Carolinas Office who developed this technique.)

Home is not where you live but where they understand you.

Christian Morgenstern

Heritage Evening

Time: 1-2 hours

Objective: To honor our roots by sharing the richness of our family/ethnic background through one story, related to an "heirloom." As the stories unfold we celebrate both our diversity and our underlying connectedness. A superb time for experiencing the web of life!

Materials/Preparation: In a mailing prior to the seminar invite those attending to bring an item that captures some part of their family heritage, and be prepared to tell the group about its importance to them. The artifacts should be easily portable and probably not too valuable or fragile. Past participants have brought photos, button collections, vegetables, diplomas, fishing reels, songs.

Be sure to let participants know that a time is set aside to share these items and the stories they embody.

Method: We often hold our heritage evenings in conjunction with one of our evening fests. The informality and refreshments create a welcoming atmosphere for stories.

These are unstructured events. Invite persons to share as they wish. And, of course, there is no pressure to do so. The leadership of the seminar should bring their own treasures too. Encourage everyone to be fairly brief in their stories. Expect exchange, questions, and "that reminds me of. . . ." It is all part of the sharing. Be sure that all who wish to tell their tale get a chance.

At the very end close with a brief prayer or song.

Tales on the Journey

Time: 30 minutes - 1 hour

Objective: Acting on our concern for global peace and justice can be enriching and rewarding. It can also be frustrating, exhausting, and disheartening. We rarely take time, or give ourselves permission, to acknowledge these feelings. Our silence robs us of the opportunity to learn from and support each other. This session extends an invitation to connect with both the joy and sorrow we carry as we act on behalf of a wounded world.

Method: This session can take place in small groups or in plenary. We have found the later format very rich, if the group is not too large.

1. Begin by reading this quote: "How does listening help? When people have something they very much want others to hear, they carry it around until they feel they've gotten it across. Much of the psychic pain that weighs on people comes from their having resigned themselves to the idea that they either can't say what matters, or if they did, nobody would take it in." (Arthur Egendorf, *Healing from the War: Trauma and Transformation after Vietnam).*
2. Ask if this experience sounds familiar. Review the purpose of the conversation. Ask the group: How is it for you (joys and sorrows) as you seek to promote a more just, peaceful world? Allow a minute of silence to consider the question.
3. Invite someone to share a story that illustrates their joy or sorrow (or you may wish to begin with one of your own).
4. Ask if others have had similar experiences. Solicit one or two examples. What do these experiences teach us?
5. Stay with the theme (joy or sorrow) begun by the first story. Ask if there are other stories illustrating a different aspect of this human experience? Repeat the process in #4.
6. Now switch to the other pole (joy or sorrow). Repeat the process in #4-5 What lessons do these stories teach us?
7. Close with a prayer or reading. See the quotes in the opening section of this chapter, or consult the *Readings* and *Prayers* found in **Worship**. "The Last Story," found in *Readings*, could work well here.

OPTION: Prior to the discussion view a film about others committed to the struggle for a more equitable planet. See **Resources: AVs** for description and ordering information.

Maybe "journey" is not so much a journey ahead, or a journey into space, but a journey into presence. The farthest place on earth is the journey into the presence of the nearest person to you.

Nelle Morton

CLOSING

Caucus Groups

Time: 30-45 minutes

Objective: To allow individuals in the group to convene meetings around particular opportunities for thoughtful action.

Materials/Preparation: Alert participants early on that there will be designated time for them to caucus around special interests.

You may wish to "salt" the process by recruiting two or three interested folks to initiate the newsprint sign-up sheets.

Earlier seminars have seen caucus groups on: divestment bills before the state legislature, promoting global education in the local school system, identifying possible collaborators for a future CROP walk, brainstorming plans for World Food Day observances, planning local environmental action.

Method: Ask those interested in convening a caucus group to list the topic and their name on a sheet of newsprint. Later invite participants to sign their name next to the one that interests them (this helps in deciding where to assign groups).

Prior to the caucus group time announce where they will be meeting and the time limit.

Alternatives:
- Hold caucus groups during lunch at designated tables
- Convene groups by region, town, or neighborhood to discuss ways to take next steps on their learnings from the seminar.

I don't want my children coming up to me and saying, now what did you do, and me saying I didn't know.

Dorothee Sölle

Individual Next Steps

Goal: To choose realistic next steps for promoting peace and justice.

Time: 20 minutes

Materials: Pencil and paper for each person.

Method:

1. Ask participants to divide into pairs.
2. Review the task: choosing realistic next steps for yourself.
3. Generation of options
   a. Brainstorm aloud to your partner possible next steps based on learnings from the seminar.
   b. Options are recorded by partner on paper.
   c. When finished reverse roles. Records should be on separate pieces of paper for each person to work with and keep.

4. Selection of first action
   a. Realizing that we rarely can do everything we think we can, select the one item from the list that seems most interesting and possible. Each person should make this choice.
   b. Circle this option for your partner.

5. Identification of obstacles and resources
   a. Identify the obstacles that may get in the way of accomplishing your identified action.
   b. Identify the resources available to you in enabling you to realize your action.
   c. Both a. and b. should be recorded by your partner.
   d. The partner then reads to the other, "You have chosen ___________ to do. While _______ may get in your way, you have several resources available to you to realize your goal including _______."
   e. The roles are then reversed.

Following the reading of what has been dictated, the paper containing the above material is returned to the person.

People say, what is the sense of our small effort. They cannot see that we must lay one brick at a time, take one step at a time.

Dorothy Day

Options

1. Partners promise to check in with each other in a month to see how it is going.
2. Role-play one of the obstacles identified and plan how to overcome it. Best done in triads with the third person being an observer. This could also be done as the next step in processing what had been generated (allow 30-45 minutes).
3. Create an attractive printed sheet(include graphic/ great quote) prior to the seminar with four questions:
   - To what healing are you called?
   - What obstacles stand in your way?
   - What resources are available to you?
   - What changes may your mending demand of you?

   Distribute the sheet near the end of the seminar. Allow 10-15 minutes of quiet reflection to fill out the sheet. You may wish to invite individuals to share some part of what they have written in plenary or break the group into twos or threes for the same purpose. We have also used these *Covenant Statements* as a part of closing worship. See *Ritual Actions* in **Worship** for suggestions.

I speak truth not so much as I would, but as much as I dare, and I dare a little more as I grow older.

Montaigne

A WORD ON SMALL-GROUP FACILITATORS

Small-group work is a critical dimension of the seminar modules. In participants' face-to-face interaction community is built, connections made, information appropriated, feelings shared. An interesting alternative title is "home groups." These are precious gatherings.

The facilitator will be the leader that interacts most personally with participants, therefore choose these individuals thoughtfully.

Facilitators don't need to be superhuman. They should be comfortable with humanity, theirs and others. Some characteristics of a good facilitator:

- able to listen in a non-judgmental manner
- able to empathize with another's pain
- a good sense of humor
- a genuine interest in the subject of the seminar
- free of a need to be right, in control
- in touch with their own thoughts and feelings
- alert to the flow of the whole group.

Recruit facilitators in advance of the seminar. They should be well-briefed on the design of the seminar and the particular activities they will be responsible for leading. In addition, we have found it useful to meet with the facilitators once or twice *during* the seminar to hear their impressions of how the event is going, and to see if they are encountering any difficulties.

Below are a few tips for facilitators. You may wish to review these when you meet with them.

Tips on Facilitating

- **Be sure everyone knows each other's name.** This may mean that you do your introductions more than once. Be sure you learn all participants' names. Noting them on paper may help.
- **Encourage sharing by all participants.** Be alert to who is speaking, who is trying to speak, who hasn't said a word. Prevent domination of the conversation by any one person. Respect and support the contribution of each person.
- **Take time to reflect on feelings as well as ideas.** Feelings indicate where our values are; they are the source of our power.

- **Clearly explain the task for each session and the time allotted.**
- **Assist group to stay on task.** Clarify the conversation if it becomes confused or wanders off the task too far.
- **Listen carefully to each person.** Try to understand what they are saying from their perspective. If necessary ask clarifying questions to make sure the point is understood by the group.
- **Be human.** You are not expected to have all the answers. Express your own thoughts and feelings using "I" language. Your openness will encourage a similar response in the participants.
- **Allow the group to do the work.** Your job is to assist them in their work, not do it for them.
- **Notice the nature of the group.** Age, race, gender, nationality, special needs.
- **Attend to your meeting place.** Be sure your group meeting area is attractive and comfortable. Check to be sure you've sufficient chairs for all, arranged neatly, affording eye contact with everyone in the group.
- **Use open-ended questions.** "How?" "What?" Questions encourage the person to enlarge their point. "Can you say a bit more about that?"
- **Be open to suggestions from the group.**
- **Attend to time.** You will need to be time keeper (or you may wish to designate someone in the group for that role). Since the small-group work occurs in the context of other plenary activities it is important to keep to the time limits set by the agenda.
- **Trust your intuition.** Your "gut" sense of what's taking place in the group is important information. Pay attention to it.

Relax and enjoy this brief expression of concerned community.

Respect for the vulnerability of human beings is a necessary part of telling the truth, because no truth will be wrested from a callous vision or callous handling.

Anais Nin

Coming to Our Senses In a Global Age

If by some miracle
and all our struggle,
the earth is spared,
only justice to every living thing
(and everything is alive),
will save humankind

Alice Walker

"The present condition and future prospects of our world engender natural, normal and widespread feelings of distress. Yet, because of fear of pain and social taboos against expressions of despair . . . these feelings are largely repressed.

The repression tends to paralyze; it builds a sense of isolation and powerlessness. Furthermore, it fosters resistance to painful, but essential information.

It is, therefore, not sufficient to discuss the present crisis on the informational level alone, or seek to arouse the public to action by delivering ever more terrifying facts and figures. Information by itself can increase resistance, deepening the sense of apathy and powerlessness.

We need to help each other process this information on an affective level, if we are to digest it on the cognitive level" *(Joanna Macy,* Despair and Personal Power in the Nuclear Age. *Philadelphia, PA: New Society, 1983).*

This segment of the seminar resembles a vision quest, an inquiry into a widened way of being. Some painful recognitions, passages, transformations of our worldview may be required.

Questing, inquiring, widening. Truth words. Search words. The antithesis of denial, of ". . . resistance to painful but essential information." A first and natural reflex in *homo sapiens,* denial helps us feel better by feeling less.

Denying the truth of our (good and) flawed selves, or the inequitable nature of world systems is addictive behavior: weakening, impairing, dis-easing the whole.

Repressing or ignoring the truth about the global community, and the feelings that truth engenders, consumes a great deal of creative energy—rendering the energy inaccessible, leaving us isolated, powerless to change or to participate in change. Undealt-with fear or grief is a barrier to learning and healthy living, for to numb one feeling demands deadening our capacity to feel any-

If everybody in the world says that they want peace how can we still have nuclear bombs? Somebody in the world must be lying.

Joan G.
Brooklyn
Age 10

thing. It makes us (as Macy states above) resistant to new information, deepening a sense of apathy, reducing our capacity to delight and to grieve.

Two stories:

- The most common fear identified at the beginning of the seminars has been, "Am I going to feel worse about the world, more helpless, hopeless than I already feel now?" Notice the fear is not about the information itself, but rather about the feeling the information elicits. Does the fear sound familiar?
- My cousin Chester, a member of the Denver Symphony, engages in a daily ritual with his *Rocky Mountain News.* First, he takes the national and international news and throws it in the trash, unread. The sports and business sections quickly follow. The entertainment section remains, which he carefully reads. When I asked him about this routine he said, "I can't do anything about the state of the world. It just overwhelms me. I don't understand it and I don't have time to figure it out. The world of entertainment is my world, here I know what's going on. I can make a difference."

In both instances, notice the inclination to "feel better" by feeling and knowing less. This is denial.

Anne Wilson Schaef's work on addiction deals with the same tendencies, not only in individuals, but in our whole culture.

> "As a society, we are responding (to global dysfunction) not with action, but with a widespread malaise. The market for antidepressants has never been better. Apathy and depression have become synonymous with adjustment. Rather than looking for ways to change, to save ourselves, we are becoming more conservative, more complacent, more defensive of the status quo. . . .
>
> "To say that the society is an addictive system is not to condemn the society, just as an intervention with an alcoholic does not condemn the alcoholic. The most caring thing to do is not to embrace the denial but to confront the disease." (When Society Becomes an Addict. *San Francisco, CA: Harper & Row, 1986.)*

A review of addictive characteristics hints at the syndrome in our national life: self-centeredness, the illusion of control, fear, negativism, dishonesty, defensiveness, confusion, blaming, denial, tunnel vision, frozen feelings, forgetfulness, ethical deterioration.

Recovery is possible. In oblique and humorous ways **Coming to Our Senses** asks that we recognize the potentially addictive nature of our worldview. Once named, it is owned. Change becomes possible. The personal power we formerly relinquished can be reclaimed. We begin to recover spiritually, relationally, nationally, globally. We *feel* better.

You are destined to fly, but that cocoon has to go.

Nelle Morton

A series of cartoons season this session illustrating the need for and characteristics of a global perspective. Laughter is a great teacher. Humor awakens us to the fluid character of "reality" enabling us to shift our point of view for a moment. Laughter also heals by engaging our whole body in the activity. Finally having fun together builds community.

The session concludes with a conversation on what can be done close to home to support local global education efforts.

Outline *(Time required: 2 hours)*

- *Introduction of Idea and Need for Global Perspective,* items 1-10 (25 minutes)
- *Five Characteristics of a Global Perspective,* items 11-16 (50 minutes)
- *Break,* item 17 (10 minutes)
- *Thinking about Next Steps,* item 18 (30 minutes)
- *Closing,* item 19 (5 minutes)

Leader Preparation

From birth we build a set of assumptions about how the world works. Over time this worldview changes, becoming a guide we increasingly rely on to interpret our daily life. *A worldview is always and only an interpretation.* When we confuse our interpretation of the world with reality itself, our responses to the world can become brittle and defensive. We experience life as fixed, empty, boring. Challenges to our perspective become threats instead of opportunities for new learning. To maintain a flexible, adaptable worldview requires humility and humor. If we take ourselves and our interpretation too seriously we may miss important new information.

Humor is, in fact, a prelude to faith; and laughter is the beginning of prayer.

Reinhold Neibuhr

Before looking over the session outline (which has numerous "pieces"), consider experiences that have formed your worldview. You will be asked to draw on these memories as you lead the module.

For example: Recall the first time you understood that some part of your daily life depended upon another part of the world. What happened? How did you feel? What did you think? What did you do? How did your worldview change?

Or recall a time when you encountered someone with a worldview different from yours (culturally, ethically, politically). How did you feel? What did you think? What did you do? How did this encounter influence your worldview?

Or recall the moment when you felt most in harmony with the earth. Where were you? How did you feel? What did you think? What did you do? How did this experience influence your view of the earth?

Or recall a time when you made a mistake in another culture (this event could be hilarious, disastrous, or both). What happened? How did you feel about yourself? Those around you? The country/culture you were visiting? What did you learn by this experience?

While such experiences awaken us to our limits in making sense of the world they can also enlarge our horizons, if we let them. You will be inviting participants to share similar stories with one another in order to recall and repeat such awakenings.

The universe is too great a mystery for there to be only one single approach to it.
Symmachus

Session Preparation

- Consult the *Materials Needed* list at the end of the session outline.
- Be sure to review the *Leader's Guide* (page 215).
- Carefully review the session outline. Instructions to the leader appear in **[Bold]**.
- Practice using the overhead projector. If possible place the projector on a table large enough to accommodate your notes and transparencies.
- Before the session, recruit someone to read the poem by Thich Nhat Hanh, "Please Call Me by My True Names" found on page 49. Encourage the person to read the poem slowly, clearly, with feeling. You'll cue the reader when, while the cartoon of the planet is on the overhead (# 11).
- Invite participants to read the cartoon captions aloud. It brings the cartoons to life, helps those who may have trouble reading the print, and increases participation in the presentation.

When men (sic) dream, each has his own world. When they are awake, they have a common world.

Heraclitus

- If you are using the Mercator Map and Peters Projection map, hang them on a wall or blackboard. (See **Resources**.)

Coming to Our Senses: Session Begins

Introduction of the Idea and Need for a Global Perspective *(20 minutes)*

1. **[Begin by reading this quote from Jane Wagner's one-woman play, performed by Lily Tomlin, *The Search for Signs of Intelligent Life in the Universe.*]** The central figure in the play is Trudy, a former creative consultant to multinational corporations, now a bag lady who's friendly with visiting space aliens. Early in the play Trudy reflects:

   "I refuse to be intimidated by
   reality anymore.
   After all, what is reality anyway? Nothin' but a
   collective hunch. My space chums think reality
   was once a
   primitive method of
   crowd control that got out of hand.
   In my view, it's absurdity dressed up
   in a three-piece business suit.

   I made some studies, and
   reality is the leading cause of stress amongst those
   in touch with it. I can take it in small doses, but as
   a lifestyle
   I found it too confining.
   It was just too needful;
   it expected me to be there for it all the time,
   and with all
   I have to do—
   I had to let something go."

   Jane Wagner
   The Search for Signs of Intelligent Life in the Universe
   New York, Harper & Row, 1985.

2. Global education, like Trudy, asks us to question our understanding of "reality." What are our givens, our assumptions about the world? How capable are we of stepping outside our familiar frame of reference to consider an alternative perspective?
3. The struggle to make sense of our global links often demands a shift in our worldview, i.e., the assump-

tions we make about how the world works. For example, **[Insert here one of your stories from the "What's your worldview?" exercise above. The story should be brief, told with energy.]**

4. Everyone's worldview is false in some way, because it is composed of concepts. The world is not a concept. In other words, a worldview can be handy but shouldn't be taken too seriously. If you confuse the map for the place itself, you may miss some of the most interesting sights.
5. When we confuse the map for the place we also diminish our ability to adapt to new information or environments. That can be dangerous.

[Overhead #1, Dinosaurs]

6. [OPTIONAL] Now it's your turn to tell stories. Recall the first time you understood that some part of your daily life depended on another part of the world. What happened? How did you feel? What did you learn? How did that experience influence your actions?

[You may wish to substitute one of the other questions from the "Leader Preparation" section above.]

- Now let's take ten minutes to share these stories in groups of the three people nearest you.

  - **After the groups are finished]**

  What did you notice about the stories you shared?
  What kinds of events did you describe?
  What feelings?
  What do these stories tell us about our connectedness.

7. The field of global education emerged out of the realization (which our stories have just illustrated) that we have come to a point in human history where our lives are truly linked to the life of every other person on the planet. In such a world we must cultivate a global perspective to understand accurately what's happening.
8. Awakening to a global perspective may mean giving up some cherished assumptions

[Overhead #2, Hardhat]

[NOTE: If you have already done the *First Experience of Injustice* exercise, refer to it here as an ex-

Everyone takes the limit of his own vision for the limits of the world.

Arthur Schopenhauer

ample in their own lives of how difficult it is to give up assumptions.]

. . . as a woman, I have no country. As a woman I want no country. As a woman, my country is the whole world. . . .

Virginia Woolf

9. Or it may mean reclaiming in a deeper sense our own religious tradition. As William Sloane Coffin suggests:

   "The new survival unit is no longer the individual nation; it's the entire human race and its environment. This new-found oneness is only a rediscovery of an ancient religious truth. Unity is not something we are called to create; it's something we are called to recognize." ("Faces of the Enemy" in the *Tarrytown Newsletter*. Tarrytown, NY: April 1983.)

10. Awakening to a global perspective, means at the very least, beginning to pay attention to what the rest of the world is saying to us.

Five Characteristics of a Global Perspective *(50 minutes, about 10 minutes per characteristic)*

11. How are we to make sense of life in a global age? There are at least five characteristics of a worldwise worldview **[List these on newsprint]:**

    - To See Modestly
    - To Listen Carefully
    - To Think Globally
    - To Feel Fully
    - To Act Responsibly

    Simple to say, hard to realize. These characteristics are not facts to master, but a way of life to embody in the world. They are hallmarks of a global spirituality. We will now examine each of the attributes in more detail.

12. ***To See Modestly*** means to recognize that we never see the whole picture and that what we do see is conditioned and limited by our culture, our beliefs, where we stand or sit. **[Overhead # 3]** Two examples:

    - We never see the whole picture. "Two eyes are better than one," says the proverb.

    [Overhead #4, Woman's profile] What do you see here?

[Most participants will see either an old or a young woman. Ask participants to identify which they see. Allow them time to explain to each other where the "other woman" is before moving on. Invite one participant to come forward to demonstrate. This can become quite lively. Stop when most can see both images.]

This exercise demonstrates our habit of organizing what we see into sensible, familiar patterns. The same sight can be organized in different ways with different meanings depending upon our culture and life experience. Our worldview shapes what we see in the world.

- Recall how you felt when you only saw one of the two images.
- How did you feel about those who saw another image?
- Are there persons who still only see one image? How do you feel? When have you felt like that before?

• What we see is conditioned by our culture. We learn our worldview from our culture. Becoming aware of how our vision of the world has been shaped by the culture is fundamental to global education.

[Overhead #5, Maps] Here is an example.

- Notice the two maps on the screen. *The Mercator Map,* was developed in 1569 to aid in navigation. With its perspective centered on Northern Europe, it tends to increase the size of areas north of the Equator, and diminish those south of the Equator. *The Peters Projection Map,* developed in 1974 to accurately represent the size of all land masses is centered at the Equator. Neither map is a perfect model of the world. All two-dimensional maps fail in some way to represent the globe.
- What strikes you about these two models of the world?
- The Mercator Map remains one of the maps most commonly used in classrooms. How might these different views of the world influence student's perception of the value and relationships of the Northern and Southern parts of the world?

To see the Earth
as it truly is
small and blue and
beautiful
in that eternal silence
where it floats
is to see ourselves
as riders on the Earth
altogether.

Archibald MacLeish

- The limited and conditioned character of our seeing points out our urgent need to listen to one another, the next characteristic of a global perspective.

13. ***To Listen Carefully*** means admitting that people who view the world from a different perspective or who have been shaped by another culture may have something valuable to teach us. More fundamentally, listening to the other demands going beyond "us" and "them" categories.

Not only a new speech but a new hearing. Not just cleaning out the ears, as Fred Paddock used to say, but having new ears. Hearing from a new center—the whole body.

Nelle Morton

[Overhead # 6]

- A development worker tells this story. A young woman had recently arrived in Senegal, West Africa. One morning she accompanied a group of village women to the well—a walk of some two miles. As they collected the water the village women laughed and shared stories. As they prepared to return to the village, the American woman described how in her country each home had its own water supply inside the house. She expected them to be impressed with such convenience. To her surprise they said, "How lonely for you."
  - What do you think the African women meant?
  - Would you agree that our modern conveniences may also deprive us?
- It is especially difficult to listen carefully, if you don't speak the language. **[Hand out the "Global Illiteracy: USA" fact sheet. You may wish to highlight one or two examples from "What Did You Say?" The items under "Ignorance Is Bliss?" are particularly useful for pointing out the amusing and disturbing consequences of our ignorance.]**
- When you consider the fact that by the year 2000, one out of every three Americans will be a person of color, and that the U.S. population will cover a broader socio-economic range than ever before, the need for careful listening and cultural flexibility becomes even clearer.

  [You might want to insert here another of your own life stories illustrating the challenge of listening or encountering other world views.]

- Our ability to listen carefully is further inhibited if the "other" is portrayed as the enemy, creating an "us" whose worldview and values are good and a "them" whose worldview and values are perverse, if not demonic.

[Overhead # 7, cartoon. If participants have done or will do the *Images of the Enemy* module, refer to it here.]

- Who do people in our country perceive as enemy?
- The basic question here is simply, "How large is your community?" How do you answer that question? Did you answer 5.4 billion (the current population of the world)? To be worldwise we must think in global terms, the next characteristic of a global perspective.

14. ***To think globally*** means to consider the world as a series of interconnected systems. We live and work within systems that have become global in scope. **[Option: You may wish to substitute *Big Island* or *No More Separate Futures* to illustrate thinking globally. If you choose to show one of these audio-visuals, after viewing it discuss the global systems mentioned. How do they touch our lives? What are the implications for the way we think about our place in the world? Following this conversation proceed to #15.]**

- Consider for a moment an issue that transcends national boundaries. What are some of the ones you thought of? These issues exemplify some of these global systems at work.
- Let's look at two of these systems.
  - *The global economic system.* **[Overhead # 8, cartoon]** Our credit cards and mortgages tie us into an international financial system. The interest rate on our credit accounts is influenced by, among other things: the debt of third world countries, U.S. balance of trade with other nations, U.S. participation in the world arms race.

    [Note some of the other expressions of our participation in the global economy in the "How in the World" section of the fact sheet found at the end of the session.]

It isn't important in which sea or lake you observe a slick of pollution, or in the forests of which country a fire breaks out, or on which continent a hurricane arises. You are standing guard over the whole of our Earth.

Yuri Artyukhin
USSR Cosmonaut

It is impossible to care for each other more or differently than we care for the earth. . . . there is an uncanny resemblance between our behavior toward each other and our behavior toward the earth.

Wendell Berry

- *The environmental system.* **[Overhead #9, cartoon]** The environmental system is the cradle of all life on this planet, though we are only now beginning to appreciate its complexity and fragility. Our understanding of the environmental system has grown largely as a result of discovering the negative impact of modern human life on earth's dynamic balance. **[Highlight one of the following examples]:**

  The Greenhouse Effect. A century of fossil fuel consumption combined with deforestation in the tropics is leading to an ever increasing level of carbon dioxide in the atmosphere. Each year, fossil fuel consumption releases *5 billion tons* of carbon into the atmosphere (about one ton for every person on the planet). Many scientists think that one result is a gradual warming trend or greenhouse effect, leading to dramatic shifts in the climate of the globe.

  DDT. Though in use for only forty years, and now banned in many countries, DDT continues to interfere with the formation of normal eggshells in peregrine falcons, poisons penguins in the arctic, and appears in the blood and fat of most Americans. A decade after being banned in the US, DDT was still found in carrots and spinach sold in San Francisco in 1988.

  Ozone Depletion. Chlorofluorocarbons (CFC's) manufactured as refrigerants and aerosol propellants have accumulated in the upper atmosphere, depleting the ozone layer that protects the earth's surface from ultraviolet radiation. The potential consequences: an increase in skin cancer, impairment of the human immune system and retarded crop growth. A recent international agreement has begun to address this issue.

- Each of these environmental issues has forced us to realize that our actions echo and return to us in unanticipated ways. We are not separate from our environment, we are one earth system.

- A 1986 report from the Earth Systems Science Committee of the U.S. National Aeronautics and Space Administration begins: "We, the peoples of the world, face a new responsibility for our global future. Through our economic and technological activity we are now contributing to significant global changes on the earth within the span of a few human generations. We have become a part of the Earth system and one of the forces for Earth change."

- Were we ever separate from the Earth system? No. But we in the West operated out of a worldview that thought we were. We might be much better off today if we had listened to the insight from a "primitive" native American over a century ago: **[Overhead # 10, Chief Seattle Quote]**
- **[You might want to share here a brief story of your own about sensing the connectedness Chief Seattle speaks about]**
- Chief Seattle's words are filled with feeling. Our hearts have long known what our minds are now discovering, we are one. Allowing our hearts to speak their wisdom is the next characteristic of a global perspective.

15. ***To Feel Fully*** means becoming vulnerable to the world, allowing the beauty and pain of our fragile planet into our heart. In a very real sense, a global perspective demands a change of heart.

- **[Overhead # 11, Cartoon of Planet]**
- As we've already seen, to think globally leads to some very unpleasant information. We live, love, laugh in a world at risk:
  - Hunger-related disease kills as many people every two days as the Hiroshima atomic bomb.
  - The nuclear bomb inventories of the two superpowers are already sufficient to destroy all life on earth many times over.
- Charlie Brown speaks for all of us.

[Read Peanuts cartoon out loud]

- It is not easy to stay open-hearted, vulnerable in the face of such information. Confronted with such fierce prospects, our response may be to grow numb to feelings of fear and dread, according to psychiatrist Robert J. Lifton. Or we may begin to

We need to help each other process this information on an affective level, if we are to disgest it on the cognitive level.

Joanna Macy

In the face of suffering, one has no right to turn away, not to see. In the face of injustice, one may not look the other way. When someone suffers, and it is not you, he (sic) comes first. His (sic) very suffering gives him priority. . . . To watch over a man (sic) who grieves is a more urgent duty than to think of God.

Elie Wiesel

fear that there is something wrong with us, as Cecilia does in T. S. Eliot's play, *The Cocktail Party*. **[Read her quote from the overhead aloud]**

- Denying our feelings robs us of important information and energy. Without feelings, we cannot grow in knowledge of ourselves or the world. Our worldview becomes a bulwark against unwelcome facts and the feelings they elicit. Could the ignorance of Americans about the rest of the world be a symptom of our denial? Having robbed ourselves of feelings and facts, it's no surprise we sense ourselves helpless to act.
- Opening our hearts to a global perspective does mean inviting in the pain of the world. And the world holds so much pain. But accompanying the sorrow is the joy of a rich and wondrous world. Vietnamese Poet Thich Nhat Hanh expresses this perspective with great power **[invite the person you've recruited to stand and read the poem on page 49 now]:**

16. ***To Act Responsibly***, the fifth characteristic of a global perspective, means acknowledging that our choices matter. How we act individually and corporately in the world has consequences for every other person on the home planet. **[Overhead #12, cartoon]** What kind of actions?

    - Cultivating a limber worldview. **[Overhead # 13, cartoon]** How we conceive the world determines the action we give birth to in the world.
        - Make a practice of noticing what your worldview is. **[Overhead # 14, cartoon]** Attend particularly to your feelings. Who do you fear? Where do you see danger? Of whom are you suspicious? What gives you joy?
        - Explore alternative perspectives. **[Overhead #15, cartoon]** Read alternative news sources. Listen to the songs, read the literature of other cultures, especially those whose people are por-trayed as our enemies. Meet with those from other economic and political "worlds," people who are of a different age or race or sex than yours.
    - Recognize and claim your power. **[Overhead # 16, cartoon]** You are intrinsically valuable. As a "royal person" created in the image of God, you are a gift

I may be arrested. I may be tried and thrown into jail, but I will never be silent.

Emma Goldman

to the world. No one else has your particular experiences, gifts, insight to offer. You matter. The psychologist Arthur Egendorf tells us:

"For most of us the greatest power we exert on the course of humanity is in how we choose to live our lives. That is the one vote that nobody can take from us and that registers unmistakably wherever we go and whatever we do. To live our everyday lives out of a vision of human possibility . . . requires a widened way of being, a presence in which the possibilities we envisage are embodied in whatever we say and do—not someday in the future, but here, now." (*Healing from the War: Trauma and Transformation after Vietnam.* Boston: Shambhala, 1986.)

- Find the global in the local. **[Overhead # 17, cartoon]** Global issues don't happen somewhere else. The quality of education in your schools, the development strategy of your city council, the practices of your local corporations, not to mention the policies and practices of your state and federal government all have global effects. How can you in your local situation, alone or with others, be an effective global citizen? Swim against the stream.
- Take personal responsibility for the future. **[Overhead # 18, cartoon/quote.]** The choices we make now affect not only those alive at this time but future generations as well. "We have not inherited the earth from our parents. We are borrowing it from our children," notes environmentalist Lester Brown.
- Appreciate and celebrate the world. **[Overhead # 19]** Savoring the world's beauty restores us and reminds us of our own beauty.

17. Break (10 minutes)
Let's take a five minute stretch break and then return.

18. Thinking about Next Steps (30 minutes)

Coming to our senses in a global age, as we've seen, is a process of individual and corporate recovery: recovering our sense of connectedness to the rest of life on this planet. What are your reactions to what you have heard?

To those who have hunger, give bread. To those who have bread, give a hunger for justice.

Latin American table prayer

At first I thought I was fighting to save rubber trees, then I thought I was fighting to save the Amazon rain forest. Now I realize I am fighting for humanity.

Chico Mendez

- For these last few minutes consider your own local setting:
  - Where do you see the lack of such a global perspective at work?
  - Where do you see efforts to promote such a perspective?
  - What can you do to fill the lack and encourage the efforts?
- **[After a few silent moments to consider these questions, ask the group to return to their clusters of three persons, if they have not already done so. Otherwise, divide them into threes, to share their ideas. Allow ten minutes for this discussion. At the end of that time invite the participants back to the large group.]**
- What were the areas you identified for possible future action? **[Collect the ideas on newsprint. Be clear with the group that this is a time to share ideas, not generate strategies; that will come during caucus time. Post the newsprint on a wall for the remainder of the seminar to prompt thinking about ideas and plans they might like to develop during the caucus. After you have collected their ideas, thank them for their work, applauding the positive energy generated.]**

Hope means more than just hanging on. It is the conscious decision to see the world in a different way than most others see it. To hope is to look . . . to a future not determined by the oppressive circumstances of the present.

Jim Wallis

19. Closing

As we end this section I invite you to stand and join hands in a circle.

- See the faces gathered around the circle, each with its own fragment of truth to share.
- Hear a closing reflection by Trudy, our companion in reality testing:

"On the way to the play, we stopped to look at the stars.
And as usual,
I felt in awe.
And then I felt even deeper awe at this capacity we have to be in awe about something.

Then I became even more awestruck
at the thought that I was,
in some small way,
a part of that
which I was in awe about.

And this feeling went on
and on
and on. . . .
My space chums got a word for it:
'awe infinitum.'

Because at the point you can comprehend how
incomprehensible it all is,
you're about as smart as you need to be.

Suddenly I burst into song:
'Awe,
sweet mystery of life,
at last I've found thee.'

And I felt so good inside
and my heart felt so full,
I decided I would set time aside each day to do
awe-robics.

Because at the moment you are most in awe of
all there is
about life that you don't understand,
you are closer to understanding it all
than at any other time."

Jane Wagner
The Search for Signs of Intelligent Life in the Universe
New York: Harper & Row, 1985.

Because at the moment you are most in awe of all there is about life that you don't understand, you are closer to understanding it all than at any other time.

Jane Wagner

- Think of the various ways even this small group connects to the rest of the world. **[If you have been able to learn something of the lives of the participants already, you might want to cite one or two examples of these connections.]**
- Feel the weight and warmth, pulse and life of the hands joined to yours.
- Let us act together by **[choose one of these options or make up your own]:**
  - Reciting "A Litany of the Circle". **[Overhead #20]**
  - Singing together. **[This will require either copying sheets for each person or making a transparency. Select a song from the Worship section of this book or from a source of your own choosing.]**
  - Praying about whatever is in our hearts at this time. **[After you sense closure, invite the exchange of a sign of peace.]**

Materials Required for Session

- Overhead projector, screen.
- Transparencies (easily done on most copiers using acetate sheets) made from the cartoons for use with overhead projector.
- Handout: **"Global Illiteracy: USA" fact sheet** *for each participant* duplicated from the copy in this book. Alternative: printed copies of the fact sheet can be ordered from Office on LGlobal Education, 2115 N. Charles St., Baltimore, MD 21218.
- One copy of "Please Call Me by My True Names," follows sources list.
- Newsprint, wide felt-tip markers.

Optional

- Audio-Visuals—*The Big Island* or No *More Separate Futures* and necessary A-V equipment. See **Resources** for description and ordering information.
- Peters Projection Map (available from Friendship Press, PO Box 37844, Cincinnati, OH 45222).
- Mercator Map (available from most bookstores).
- Flashlight or lamp for leader to reference notes.
- Music for *Closing*, and musician if desired.

Sources

Boyer, Ernest L. *High School: A Report on Secondary Education in America.* The Carnegie Foundation for the Advancement of Teaching. New York: Harper & Row, 1985.

Brown, Lester, et al. *State of the World.* New York: Norton/World Watch Institute, 1987.

"Educating for a Global Future." *Breakthrough*, Volume 8, nos. 3-4. New York: Global Education Associates. Spring/Summer, 1987.

Hanvey, Robert G. *An Attainable Global Perspective.* New York: Global Perspectives in Education, Inc., 1982 (first published 1976).

Joy, Carrol. *Believing is Seeing: Attitudes and Assumptions that Affect Learning about Development.* New York: National Clearinghouse on Development Education, 1990.

Macy, Joanna Rogers. *Despair and Personal Power in the Nuclear Age.* Philadelphia, PA: New Society, 1983.

Simon, Paul. *The Tongue-Tied American.* New York: Continuum, 1980.

Study Commission on Global Education. *The United States Prepares for its Future: Global Perspectives in Education.* New York: Global Perspectives in Education, Inc., 1987.

Please Call Me by My True Names

Do not say that I'll depart tomorrow
because even today I still arrive.

Look deeply; I arrive in every second
to be a bud on a spring branch,
to be a tiny bird, with wings still fragile,
learning to sing in my new nest,
to be a caterpillar in the heart of a flower,
to be a jewel hiding itself in a stone.

I still arrive, in order to laugh and to cry,
in order to fear and to hope,
the rhythm of my heart is the birth and
death of all that are alive.

I am the mayfly metamorphosing on the
surface of the river,
and I am the bird which, when spring comes,
arrives in time to eat the mayfly.

I am a frog swimming happily in the
clear water of a pond,
and I am the grass-snake who,
approaching in silence,
feeds itself on the frog.

I am the child in Uganda, all skin and bones,
my legs as thin as bamboo sticks,
and I am the arms merchant, selling deadly
weapons to Uganda.

I am the twelve-year-old girl, refugee
on a small boat,
who throws herself into the ocean after
being raped by a sea pirate,
and I am the pirate, my heart not yet capable
of seeing and loving.

I am a member of the politburo, with
plenty of power in my hands,
and I am the man who has to pay his
"debt of blood" to my people,
dying slowly in a forced labor camp.

My joy is like spring, so warm it makes
flowers bloom in all walks of life.
My pain is like a river of tears, so full it
fills all four oceans.

Please call me by my true names,
so I can hear all my cries and laughs
at once,
so I can see that my joy and pain are one.

Please call me by my true names,
so I can wake up,
and so the door of my heart can be left open,
the door of compassion.

Thich Nhat Hanh

(Poem is from the book *Being Peace,*
published by Parallax Press.)

GLOBAL ILLITERACY USA

. . .with all the talk about getting foreigners to buy more American products, how can we sell to them if we don't speak their language or even know where they are?

John Chancellor, NBC News

Where in the World?

- Almost 50% of high school seniors in Baltimore, Maryland could not locate the United States on a world map.
- 95% of American college freshmen tested could not locate Vietnam on a world map.
- 75% of Americans responding to a nationwide survey could not locate El Salvador on a map.
- 63% of Americans could not name the 2 nations involved in SALT (Strategic Arms Limitation Talks).

Joint Resolution

- Television station WNEV in Boston surveyed high school seniors in 8 cities in 1987 to see what they knew about the U.S. and the world. This is what they found:
  - 39% of Boston seniors could not name the 6 New England States
  - 63% of Minneapolis seniors could not name all seven continents
  - 25% of Dallas seniors could not identify the country that borders the U.S. on the south
  - 58% of Dallas seniors were unable to name Vietnam as the Southeast Asia country from which the U.S. withdrew in 1975.

Geography Education Update

How in the World?

No major event occurs anywhere around the globe that does not personally touch some group of families in the United States, whether it is an earthquake in Mexico, a famine in East Africa, a nuclear accident in the USSR, or a revolution in Iran.

The U.S. Prepares for Its Future

- The economic well-being of the U.S. is inextricably linked to the world economy. Our 13 largest banks derive almost half of their total earnings from overseas credits.
- Approximately 1/3 of all U.S. corporate profits come from international activities.
- 20% of our total national industrial production is for export.
- 4 out of 5 new jobs in the U.S. are generated as a direct result of foreign trade.

America's Crisis in International Competence

- One out of every three acres of U.S. cropland is devoted to export production; roughly 40% of our total grain production is exported.

Bread for the World

What Did You Say?

- Only 15% of U.S. high school students in 1979 studied a foreign language and fewer than 3% of all high school graduates achieve a "meaningful competence" in a foreign language.
- Almost 10 million Soviets study English; only 28 thousand Americans study Russian. There are more teachers of English in the Soviet Union than there are students of Russian in the United States.
- The U.S. State Department needs qualified linguists to fill important posts; only 2/3 of these jobs are adequately filled now.
- At the height of the Iranian Crisis, only one Western reporter could speak Farsi, the language of the country — and he represented the BBC.

America's Crisis in International Competence

Ignorance Is Bliss?

- The advertising campaign in Taiwan, "Come Alive With Pepsi," was translated as "Pepsi brings your ancestors back from the grave."
- The Parker Pen Company meant to advertise abroad that unwanted leaks could be avoided. What its copywriters said was that its products could help prevent unwanted pregnancies.

America's Crisis in International Competence

- Over half of the students in a recent study of American education believed that foreign governments and their ideas are dangerous to American government.

A Place Called School

Where Are Our Priorities?

Before you finish eating breakfast this morning, you've depended on more than half the world. This is the way our universe is structured . . . We aren't going to have peace on earth until we recognize this basic fact of the interrelated structure of all reality.

Martin Luther King, Jr.

France and the Federal Republic of Germany commit 1% of their national budgets to (international) educational, cultural and information activities; the U.S. Government less than .1% . . . Soviet information/cultural expenditures are estimated to total 4 times the U.S. investment in this area overall.

There is an ever-decreasing commitment of funds to education in the U.S. Federal funds for education have declined in real dollars by 50%, and private and corporate funding for international education represents less than 2% of all gifts and grants.

Internationalizing Your School

Americans tend to exaggerate their generosity and benevolence toward the Third World. The U.S. ranks 15th out of 17 Western industrialized nations in contributions to the Third World. While most countries' contributions are rising, ours is slipping: Our average per person contribution fell from $7.58 in 1970 to $5.63 in 1983.

Seeds

U.S. Foreign Aid Compared to Personal Consumption Expenditures, 1986 ($ billions)

U.S. foreign aid, particularly the part aimed at furthering development in low-income countries, is relatively small in comparison to a variety of U.S. personal consumption expenditures.

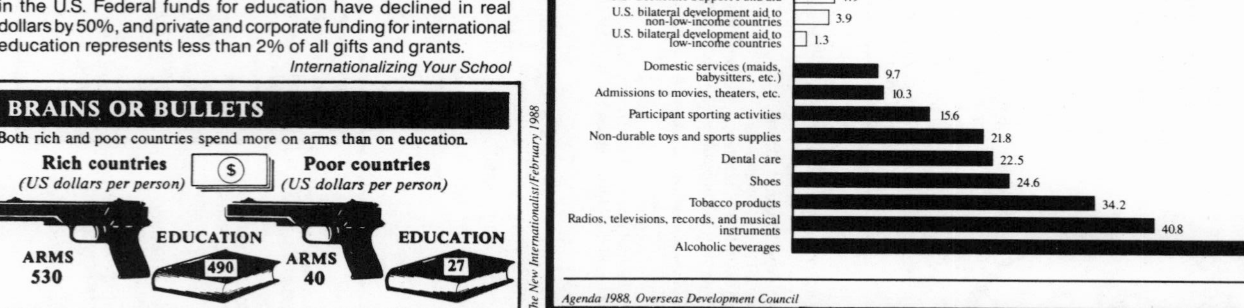

Agenda 1988, Overseas Development Council

The New Internationalist/February 1988

SOURCES

America's Crisis in International Competence, 1987, American Institute for Foreign Study, 102 Greenwich Avenue, Greenwich, CT 06830.

Bread for the World, 802 Rhode Island Avenue NE, Washington, DC 20012.

Geography Education Update, Spring 1987, National Geographic Society, Educational Media Division, Washington, DC 20036.

Global Pages, September/October 1986, Immaculate Heart College Center, 10951 West Pico Boulevard, Suite 1021, Los Angeles, CA 90064.

Getting Started in Global Education: A Primer for Principals and Teachers, 1982, National Association of Elementary School Principals, 1920 Association Drive, Reston, VA 22091.

A Place Called School, Goodlad, John I., 1984, McGraw-Hill Company, New York, NY.

Guidelines for Geographic Education, 1984, Joint Committee on Geographic Education of the National Council for Geographic Education and the Association of American Geographers, 1710 16th Street NW, Washington, DC 20009.

Internationalizing Your School, 1983, National Council on Foreign Language and International Studies, 605 Third Avenue, 17th Floor, New York, NY 10158.

Joint Resolution of the One Hundredth Congress of the United States of America, 6 January, 1987, to designate Geography Awareness Week, National Geographic Society, Washington, DC 20036.

The New Internationalist, No. 180, February 1988, 175 Carlton St., Toronto, Ontario M5A 2K3, for subscription enquiries, P.O. Box 255, Lewiston, NY 14092.

Seeds, June 1987, "Christians Concerned About Hunger," 222 East Lake Drive, Decatur, GA 30030.

Growth, Exports, and Jobs in a Changing World Economy: Agenda 1988, edited by John W. Sewell and Stuart K. Tucker, Transaction Books, New Brunswick, NJ, in cooperation with the Overseas Development Council, 1717 Massachusetts Ave., NW, Washington, DC 20036.

The United States Prepares for Its Future, 1987, Global Perspectives in Education, Inc., 45 John Street, Suite 1200, New York, NY 10038.

This FACT sheet is one of a series, each covering a facet of Global Education. All graphics used with permission. Title graphic: Sr. Eunice Cudzewicz, Medical Mission Sisters.

Office on Global Education, National Council of Churches, 2115 N. Charles St., Baltimore, MD 21218-5755 • A program of the Divisions of Education and Ministry, and Church World Service

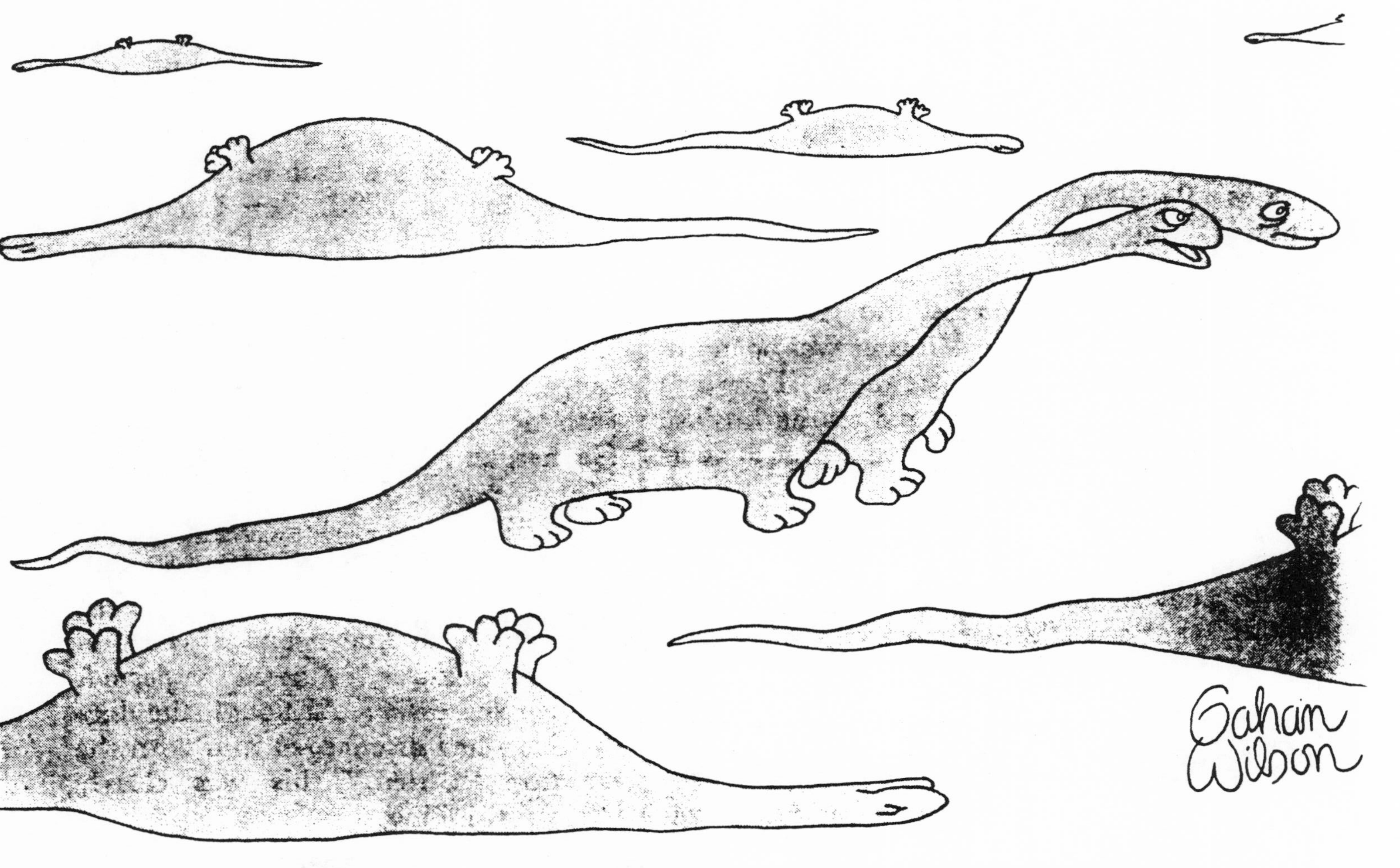

"Frankly, I don't like the way things are going."

1

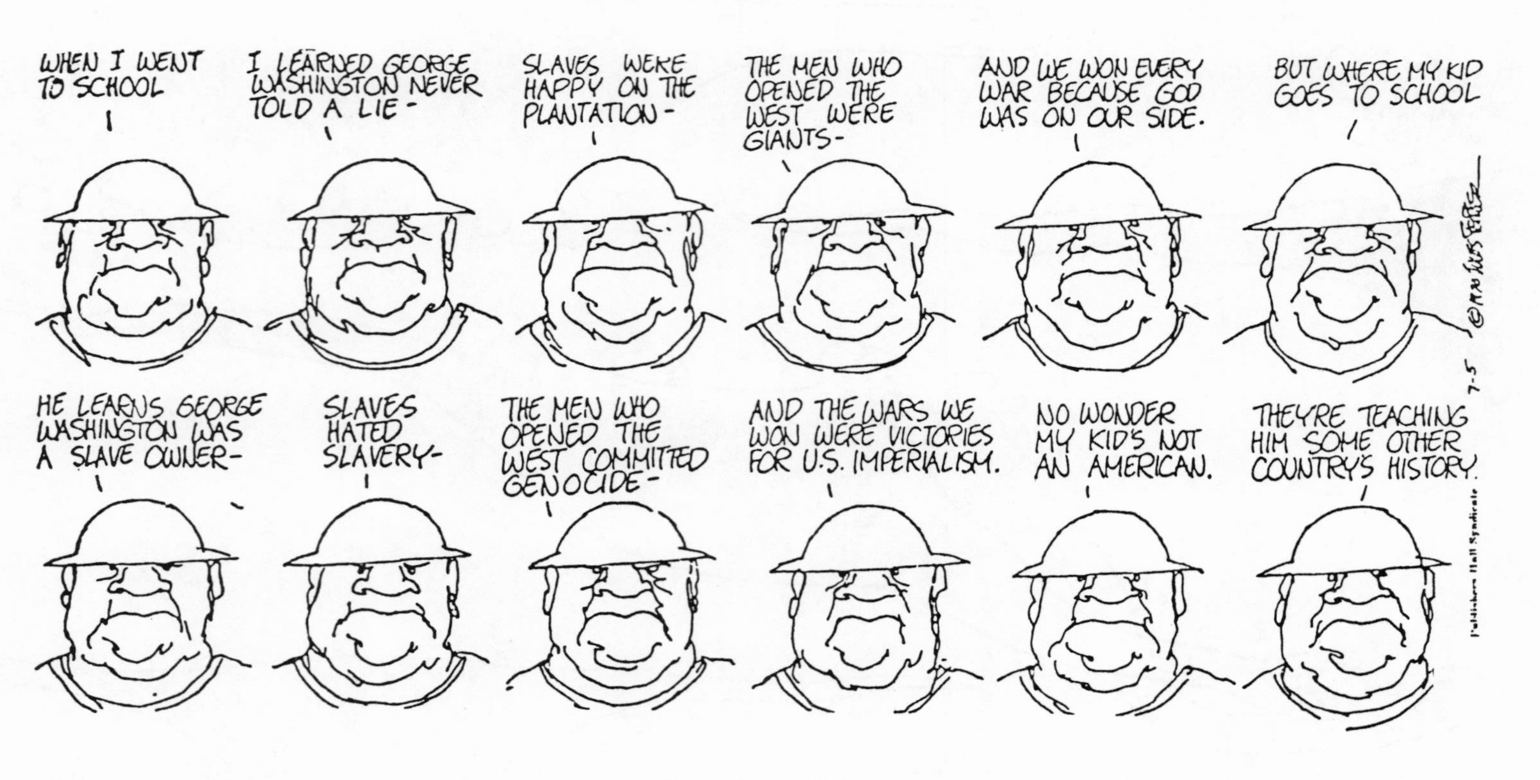
WHEN I WENT TO SCHOOL
I LEARNED GEORGE WASHINGTON NEVER TOLD A LIE-
SLAVES WERE HAPPY ON THE PLANTATION-
THE MEN WHO OPENED THE WEST WERE GIANTS-
AND WE WON EVERY WAR BECAUSE GOD WAS ON OUR SIDE.
BUT WHERE MY KID GOES TO SCHOOL
HE LEARNS GEORGE WASHINGTON WAS A SLAVE OWNER-
SLAVES HATED SLAVERY-
THE MEN WHO OPENED THE WEST COMMITTED GENOCIDE-
AND THE WARS WE WON WERE VICTORIES FOR U.S. IMPERIALISM.
NO WONDER MY KID'S NOT AN AMERICAN.
THEY'RE TEACHING HIM SOME OTHER COUNTRY'S HISTORY.
7-5
Publishers Hall Syndicate

2

"There is a perfect example of what is wrong with this country today."

"There is a perfect example of what is wrong with this country today."

3 ____

4 ____

5

WORLD MAP—PETERS PROJECTION

Europe

South America

WORLD MAP—MERCATOR PROJECTION

Europe

South America

6

"Because you've done it successfully your way for generations, it doesn't mean it works."

"That's an excellent suggestion, Miss Triggs. Perhaps one of the men here would like to make it."

Duncan/Punch/London

YES! God said "Love your enemies—" But He did NOT mean the enemies of the American people!!

"Before we demand that Parliament protect our industry against cheap foreign imports manufactured at slave-labor wages, I'd like to remind you, sir, that we own 67 percent of those foreign factories!"

8 ______________________________

Liebermann/Süddeutsche Zeitung/Munich

9 ______________________________

"This we know, the earth does not belong to us, we belong to the earth. This we know, all things are connected, like the blood which unites one family. All things are connected. Whatever befalls the earth, befalls the children of the earth. We did not weave the web of life, we are merely a strand in it. Whatever we do to the web, we do to ourselves."

—*Chief Seattle (1854)*

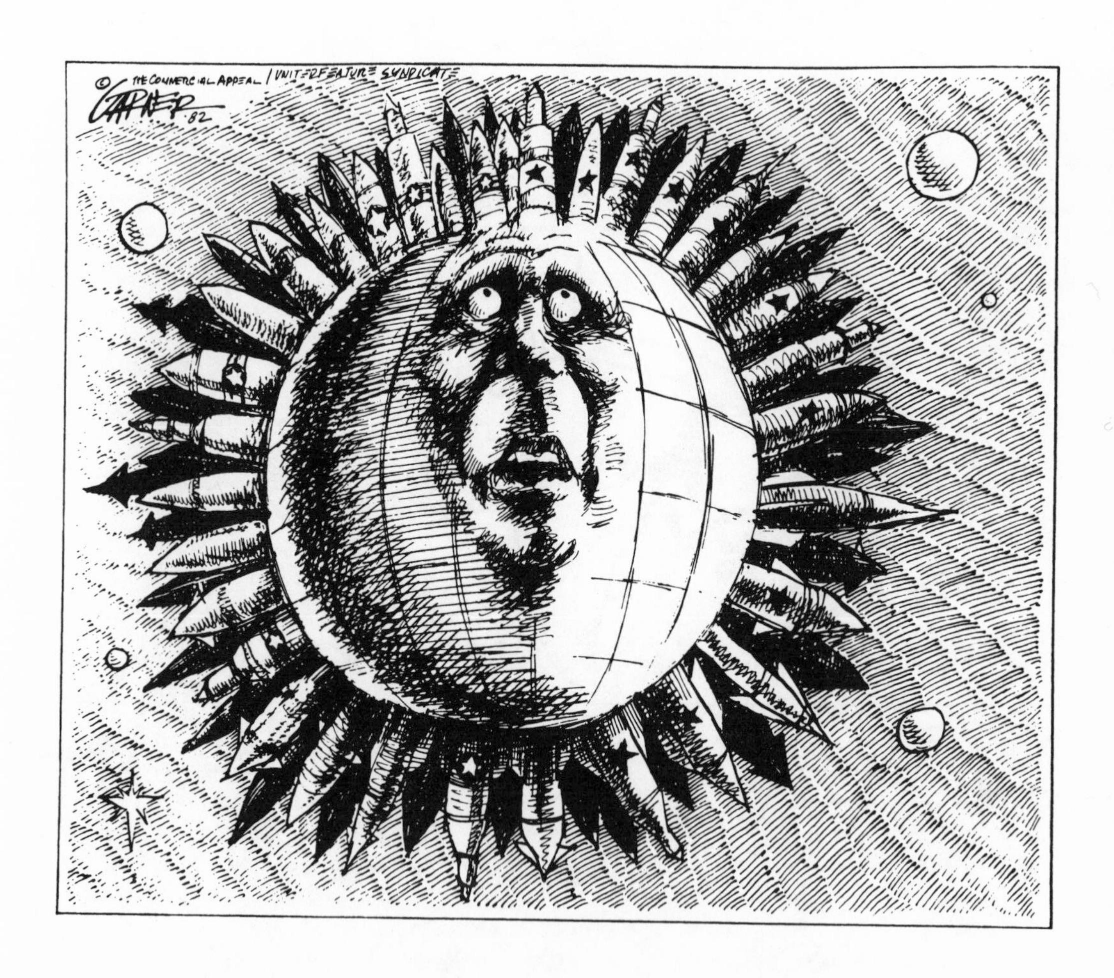

"I hope there's something wrong with me, because if there isn't, then there's something wrong with the world itself and that's much more frightening."

The Cocktail Party, T.S. Eliot

PEANUTS

WHAT CAN ONE WOMAN DO?
WHAT CAN ONE WOMAN DO?
WHAT CAN ONE MAN DO?
WHAT CAN ONE MAN DO?
WHAT CAN ONE WOMAN DO?
WHAT CAN ONE MAN DO?
WHAT CAN ONE MAN DO?
WHAT CAN ONE MAN DO?
WHAT CAN ONE MAN DO?
WHAT CAN ONE WOMAN DO?
WHAT CAN ONE WOMAN DO?
WHAT CAN ONE MAN DO?
WHAT CAN ONE MAN DO?
WHAT CAN ONE MAN DO?
WHAT CAN ONE WOMAN DO?
WHAT CAN ONE MAN DO?

"You wanna have good eyesight
if you go abroad, don't you?"

13 ______________________________

"I see creeping socialism, chiselers on relief and the erosion of fiscal integrity in government!"

14 ______________________________

15

"Just tell him one of 'the governed' is here to see him!"

Drawing by Dana Fradon; © 1979 The New Yorker Magazine, Inc.

16

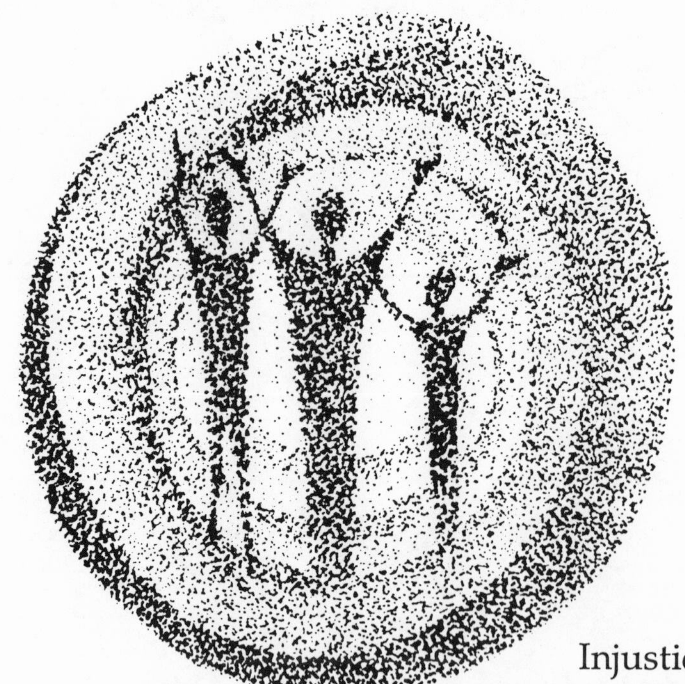

Injustice anywhere is a
threat to justice everywhere.
We are caught in an inescapable network of
mutuality, tied in a single garment of destiny.

M.L. King, Jr.

Artwork by Miriam Therese MacGillis, O.P.
From the Whole Earth Papers, printed with permission of
Global Education Associates, East Orange, NJ.

"The undecideds have it."

18

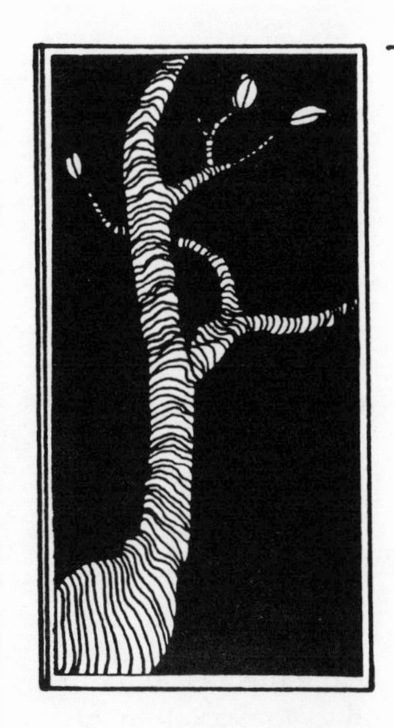

"We have only begun to know
the Power that is in us if we would join
our Solitudes in the Communion of struggle.

So much is unfolding that must
complete its gesture.

So much is in bud."

Denise Levertov

19

A Litany of the Circle

LEADER:	Every part of this earth is sacred.
ALL:	**every shining pine needle, every sandy shore,**
LEADER:	every mist in the dark woods,
ALL:	**every clearing and humming insect is holy.**
LEADER:	The rocky crest, the juices of the meadow, the beasts and all the people,
ALL:	**all belong to the same family.**
LEADER:	Teach your children that the earth is our mother.
ALL:	**Whatever befalls the earth befalls the children of the earth.**
LEADER:	The water's murmur is the voice of our father's father.
ALL:	**We are part of the earth, and the earth is part of us.**
LEADER:	The rivers are our brothers; they quench our thirst.
ALL:	**The perfumed flowers are our sisters.**
LEADER:	The air is precious,
ALL:	**for all of us share the same breath.**
LEADER:	The wind that gave our grandparents breath also receives their last sign.
ALL:	**The wind gave our children the spirit of life.**
LEADER:	This we know, the earth does not belong to us;
ALL:	**we belong to the earth.**
LEADER:	This we know, all things are connected,
ALL:	**like the blood which unites one family.**
LEADER:	All things are connected.
ALL:	**Our God is the same God, whose compassion is equal for all.**
LEADER:	For we did not weave the web of life;
ALL:	**we are merely a strand in it.**
LEADER:	Whatever we do to the web
ALL:	**we do to ourselves.**
LEADER:	Let us give thanks for the web and the circle that connects us.
ALL:	**Thanks be to God, the God of all.**

Chief Seattle

This litany was drawn from the writings of Chief Seattle (1854). He wrote this in a letter to the President of the United States at the time his people were removed to a reservation. It reflects wisdom that transcends time and cultures and speaks to us anew today.

Theologos: The Theological Basis for Justice-Seeking

All who are broken shall be whole

Miriam Therese Winter

This volume, and the healing it sets out to enable, has its foundations in the Christian ethic. "Change of heart" and the arduous passage that implies describes the pilgrimage . . . a global spirituality.

The guide and forebear on the road is one Jesus of Nazareth.

His Way and Word,
formative in many of us from childhood,
schools us
in our God's embodiment
in our humanity as eminently worthy
in self-emptying compassion
in vulnerability as power
in the handing over of life in love
in the promise of abundant life for all

in life reborn from death
in irrepressible hope

in a central teaching of LOVE
of self, (again)
of self,
of neighbor,
of enemy, (and again)
of enemy,
of one who is "other"

in a teaching focused
not so much on what we should DO
as on who we should BECOME:

wayfarers toward self-knowledge
and right-relationship.

Sojourners within and without.

The Christ as Way.

A heart tuned to such a teaching, seeking for global peace and justice, evolves the spirituality addressed in the next seminar experience.

We set out now on a varied, reflective, three-hour journey, probing our faith tradition in a fresh light. *En route* we examine three contemporary sources of God's Word (theo-logos): scripture, ethics, science as they teach about justice or "right relationship."

Spending some "exercise time" with our own pain at witnessing injustice, we'll notice that pain as revelation of an embodied and vulnerable God-with-us. A ritual of hope, of letting go into the God of Sabbath will close the time—seen throughout as having a sacred and prayerful character.

Outline

(Session total time: about three hours and 10 minutes)

I Introduction to Seminar Theology and Spirituality (30 minutes)

Three-Minute Standup Break

II Video: *Women for America . . . for the World* (30 minutes)

III Meditation; and description of small group task (15 minutes)

Twenty-Minute Break

IV Small-Group Task: *First Experience of Injustice* (40 Minutes)

V Plenary (20 minutes)

VI Worship: *Sabbath and Hope* (30 minutes)

Leader Preparation

Enjoy reading through this module and making it your own. God's Word lives in you . . . in your intuitions, concerns, involvements, insights. Trust that, and see this

Like Jesus, we are called to a radical activity of love, to a way of being in the world that deepens relation, embodies and extends community, passes on the gift of life. Like Jesus, we must live out this calling in a place and time where the distortions of loveless power stand in conflict with the power of love.

Beverly Wildung Harrison

morning as a rich exchange of wisdom in the group. No need to feel burdened by it all weighing on you. The Spirit hovers.

You can hold back from the suffering of the world, you have free permission to do so, and it is in accordance with your nature, but perhaps this very holding back is the one suffering you could have avoided.

Franz Kafka

Session Preparation

- Carefully review the session outline. Note that instructions to the leader appear in [**Bold**].
- Review *Leader's Guide* (page 215).
- Audio-visual equipment set up (see space comments in **Seminar Elements**).
- Copy the Fiorenza and Harrison readings handouts (see **Worship: *Readings***), find and orient opening readers, as well as worship readers, cueing them to leave at least thirty seconds of silence between the readings.
- Work with your "resident musician" (even if that's you!) on the teaching of "Hosea" at the beginning of the morning, and its use and placement during the end-of-morning worship. Decide whether to do "How I Have Longed" as a solo for worship.
- Prepare whatever notes on newsprint you will find helpful. We usually have a "great quote" visible right from the outset, and tend to cover up other newsprinted material, until ready to use it. It can distract from "being in the present."
- Thoroughly familiarize yourself with "Illustrated Mini-Lecture on Power" by Joanna Macy. Notes and sketches on newsprint can be very helpful to teacher and learner alike.
- To broaden your background in *First Experience of Injustice* (Small-Group Task, pp. 74, 75), check alternate style in **Community Building.**
- Place music copies on each chair. (Hold the Worship handout until just before the ritual.)

Theologos: Session Begins

I. Introduction to the Theology and Spirituality of the Seminar

First, a moment with these two familiar words.

- **Theo-logos** = God-word. **[chapter opening (page 68) reflects on Jesus as Word. Read aloud, or paraphrase perhaps, as part of your introduction.]** With that portrait of our discipleship, we now examine numerous other sources, aware that the doing of theology is not a professional discipline only, but a faith-filled quest for all.

- **Spirituality** = "the tuning of the heart." The contemporary world is alive with new frequencies, new wave lengths, so to speak. Hints of these are examined below. A global spirituality asks that we adjust ourselves to resonate with these signs of our times.

Toward that end, these next few hours will see us exploring matters of life and death, conflict and community, relationship and vulnerability. Each distills insights of our Christian tradition. We set out to be blessed again by God's Word in each, as we examine them through the wide lens of the whole earth community. We set out to notice how this fresh look may alter our Christian practice, how it may define a global spirituality.

Again, the morning has a quality of praise and prayer. We begin by learning a sung text (to be used later in worship) from the First (or Old) Testament. Here, as elsewhere through the morning, we listen for God's Word, we inquire what practice it calls us to.

Song learning: "Hosea" by Benedictine Brother Gregory of Weston Priory.

Next we listen to two readings. First, a New Testament commentary, next, a perspective from Christian Ethics on who we are, who we are called to be in the earth community. May we be open to God's Word.

First Reading: From *In Memory of Her* by New Testament scholar Elisabeth Schüssler Fiorenza

Second Reading: From *Making the Connections* by Beverly Harrison, Ethicist/Union Theological Seminary

Prayer: God of Mystery
Hold us in the heart of love.

Disarm and open us
as we re-member
the nature of right relationship,
the nature of justice,
the nature of hope.
Be with us
in this blessed Sabbath time
set apart for study,
reflection,
care for our good selves.

Speak to and among us
as we tune heart and hearth,
journeying within, welcoming without,
at one with our beloved, wounded
earth community.

In Jesus' name,
in the vulnerability of the Cross
we pray.

We gather from those two readings that **we are to companion each other** (com-pane = "break bread with"), **and pass on the gift of life.** God's Word to us on what we must be and do. **[Allow for some group discussion here on the ideas and readings so far. Encourge responses, reflections.]**

Science without religion is lame and religion without science is blind.

Albert Einstein

We move now to the perspective of new exploration in science. Seeking what it may say to theology as the 20th century closes.

Changed views of the basic building blocks of life imply change in cell, psyche, and solidarity. As we move through these breakthroughs, there is no need to take notes. A handout will be available at the end of the session.

[You now walk through your notes and sketches on newsprint, from "Illustrated Mini-Lecture on Power" by Joanna Macy (pg. 78). Convey it deliberately. It's a great deal to take in. You'll enjoy watching it "connect" for your audience.

Spend a few moments at the end with participants' questions. A brief discussion can help reinforce the material, assuring listeners that they "have it." Ask if Macy's distinctions are clear, reiterating points where necessary. Possible questions to the group: what strikes you about the linkage between "vulnerability as power," and a crucified God? Urge your audience to focus on that point as the morning progresses.]

Now if the first woman God ever made was strong enough to turn the world upside down, these women together ought to be able to turn it back and get it rightside up again. . . .

Sojourner Truth

Three-Minute Standup Break

II. Video: *Women for America . . . for the World* (28 minutes)

[Before the showing, mention that this is an Academy Award-winning film made by Vivian Verdon-Roe. Though (happily) dated by recent weapons reduction agreements, it remains eloquent on topics of enemy-

making, patriotism, national priorities, human emotion and more. Urge viewers to notice whatever feelings arise, owning and allowing them. There will be time at the end to process felt responses to the film, via a brief guided meditation.

Allow the film to run through the credits to the dedication beyond. Leave the room in darkness and lead the group through the following guided meditation: (You may need a flashlight.)]

III. Breathing Through (guided meditation)

[Relax, get comfortable and enter into this yourself, as you read it slowly. Pause at each period.]

This simple process called *Breathing Through* helps us deal with painful information, without erecting defenses and blocking it out. It is adapted from an ancient meditation for the development of compassion. I invite you to enter into it with me.

Relax. Close your eyes. Put your feet flat on the floor. Your back fairly straight against the chair. Notice your breathing . . . visualize your breath as a stream flowing up through your nose, down through windpipe and lungs. Take it down through your lungs. Picture an opening in the bottom of your heart, allowing the breath-stream to pass through your heart and out, reconnecting you with the larger web of life around you. Let the breath-stream, as it passes through *you*, appear as one loop within that vast web, connecting you with it. As you breathe . . . keep connecting.

Now open the door of your body's awareness to the suffering that is present in the world. Open to your knowledge of that suffering and how you carry it in your body. Attend to the images that come to you . . . let it come as concretely as you can . . . concrete images of your fellow beings in pain and need, in fear and isolation.

No need to strain for these images, they are present to you by virtue of our inter-existence. Relax and just let them surface. Breathe them in . . . the vast and countless hardships of these persons and of our animal companions as well, as they swim the seas and fly the air of this ailing planet.

Breathe in that pain like a dark stream up through your nose down through your trachea, lungs, and heart, and out again into the world net.

Something inside of me has reached to the place where the world is breathing.

Kabir

You are asked to *do* nothing for now. No need for thinking, or fixing. Let all suffering pass through your heart. As you breathe, keep connecting . . . be sure that stream flows *through* and out again, do not hang on to the pain, *surrender* it for now to the healing resources of life's vast web. Keep breathing . . . keep connecting . . .

With a Hindu saint we can say, "let all sorrows ripen in me." We help them ripen by passing them through our hearts . . . making good, rich compost out of all that grief . . . so we can learn from it, enhancing our larger, collective knowing . . .

While we are still relaxed and focused—a comment on this exercise: In daily life "breathing through" the bad news, rather than bracing ourselves against it, or denying it, strengthens our sense of belonging in the larger web of being. It helps us remain alert and open, whether reading the newspaper, receiving criticism, or simply being present to a person who suffers.

We should not pretend to understand the world only by the intellect; we apprehend it just as much by feeling. Therefore the judgment of the intellect is, at best, only the half of truth, and must, if it be honest, also come to an understanding of its inadequacy.

Carl Jung

For activists working for peace and justice, and those dealing most directly with the grief of our time, the practice provides protection from burnout. Reminding us of the collective nature of both our problems and our power, it offers a healing measure of humility. It can save us from self-righteousness.

For when we can take in our world's pain, accepting it as the price of our caring, we can let it inform our acts without needing to inflict it as a punishment on others who might be, at the moment, less involved.

That ends the meditation, which exercises a way of being, of allowing our pain, of connecting. A way of vulnerability.

Adapted from Joanna Rogers Macy.
Despair and Personal Power in the Nuclear Age
Santa Cruz, CA: New Society Publishers, 1983.

* * *

We'll move to our small groups in a few minutes, but while we're still centered, let's take a first step in what will be our task.

[Here you give the small group task: *First Experience of Injustice.]*

[Slowly] Gently switch channels, and recall the first time you discovered that the world was not fair. Recall the first time that you experienced injustice, as a witness, a victim or a perpetrator. What was your earliest experience of injustice? **[Pause]**

Don't spend a lot of time struggling back to the very first. But attend to the memory that emerges first, or most powerfully. **[Pause]**

Notice the emotion that is around it. Remember the outlines of the story. What happened?

- What did you think?
- How did you feel?
- What did you do?
- What impact did that incident have on who you are?

Let's be with that for a few minutes. **[Repeat the questions slowly, then a 3-minute pause.]**

Now, bring that reflection gradually to a close. Take your time. When you're ready open your eyes. Next, we'll take a 20-minute break, then spend 45 minutes in our small groups sharing these stories with some facilitator guidance. We'll regroup here to process our learnings from this exercise, and from the morning in general.

[Mention where break is set up, if necessary, and specify a time when all should be in their small groups. Outline the site for each small group, if this hasn't been done before. It's usually good to check for any lingering questions on timing or process at this juncture. Questions of substance can be referred to the coming plenary. Handouts for the "Illustrated Mini-Lecture on Power" can be offered at this time to those interested.]

Twenty-Minute Break

IV. Forty-Five Minutes in Small Groups: *First Experience of Injustice*

Remember this: all suffering comes to an end. And whatever you suffer authentically, God has suffered from it first.

Meister Eckhart

[This would be a good time to touch base with the worship leader, offering support.]

[Someone needs to alert facilitators when they're five minutes from session's end, leaving time for people-movement back to the plenary. You'll need to be firm and persistent . . . once storytelling begins, the human race seems highly reluctant to cease!]

V. Plenary

Let's spend the next while on two things. First, some debriefing of the exercise around your first experience of injustice, and then conversation on the morning as a whole, including the film.

[Take the questions below one at a time.]

. . . Between grief and nothing I will take grief.

William Faulkner

What struck you about the exercise? What was it like as the memory surfaced? Did something emerge from very early in your life? Was this the first time you'd recalled it? How did you feel as you told it? Were there emotions present? How strong? What was it like to be the listener?

Were there commonalties in the stories in your group? Were there current impacts in persons' lives? Related life directions or commitments?

[These are some of the seminar insights that can be braided together in this exchange:]

- This first experience of injustice forever altered our view of the world. A profound perception shift, it needs to be worked with, told, heard, marked as sacred revelation for us. The "take-off" point the stories have become in our work, attitudes, child-rearing, pastoring or teaching needs to be acknowledged, celebrated. Its emotional content needs to be invited, welcomed, embraced, and assessed for the engine that it is in our present . . . for good or for ill.
- Working with our stories in this way, "hearing ourselves and others into speech" (feminist foremother Nelle Morton) allows a coming home to ourselves and to our truth. It can engender precious understanding of the angle of approach of "the other."
- Such storytelling offers a first healing step as we struggle against our penchant for enemy-making. Whether the story reveals a child's first sense of powerlessness, a young person's disorientation at betrayal by parents, a student's disillusionment at unjust accusation and punishment . . . revisiting and embracing that vulnerability is at the very heart of Christian and global spirituality. We are thus disarmed, can abandon war, can heal, be whole (". . . as our God is whole") and be epiphany, sacrament of wholeness in our broken world.
- The pain of this passing-over (and its accompanying truth) is the paradox we invite others into as we entice them into change. Ah, is that why the human race so effectively flees the mere idea of change? Is

that why our numbing and denying skills are so well honed?

[After about twenty minutes of exploration of as many insights from the group as are forthcoming, perhaps woven through with the above, indicate that the closing period of the morning will be spent in worship. Hand out a copy of the worship outline (found in its entirety in Worship).]

Two-Minute Standup Break

The worship theme is *Sabbath and Hope.* It underlines our ability to "rest in God," recognizing the paradox that the work of peace and justice is ultimately not one of control, but of letting go and letting God.

Our search for God's Word this morning reveals our task: opening to our own truth, becoming vulnerable to the other, recognizing the embrace of our pain as our power, accompanying one another, as the opening readings suggested
in the breaking of bread
in passing on the gift of life.

A life agenda that we now celebrate.

VI. Worship: *Sabbath and Hope* **[This closes the morning. Let us pray.]**

* * *

Materials Required for Session

- video; a VCR and monitor
- newsprint/markers/tape (if you want to create some notes for your presentation)
- copies of worship and music handouts for each person (see **Worship** for originals)
- copies of "Illustrated Mini-Lecture on Power" (see end of module)
- flashlight (for reading guided meditations in dim light)

Let my hidden weeping arise and blossom.

Rainer Maria Rilke

Illustrated Mini-lecture on Power (15 Minutes)

The connection between power and vulnerability is spelled out in a short "Chalk-talk" I like to offer. It is the most standard means I personally employ for the turning. Here is an abbreviated version of it, with diagrams I sketch out on a large sheet of newsprint or chalkboard as I talk.

Let's look at our notions of what "power" is. Those notions in any culture derive from that culture's worldview. In the dominant Western worldview over the last two millenia, reality has been seen as consisting of separate and discrete entities or substances. Atoms, molecules, plants, people, rocks . . . these separate entities, like so many billiard balls, are seen as what is real. Whether you're classifying them like Aristotle or studying their motions like Newton, they make up the real world.

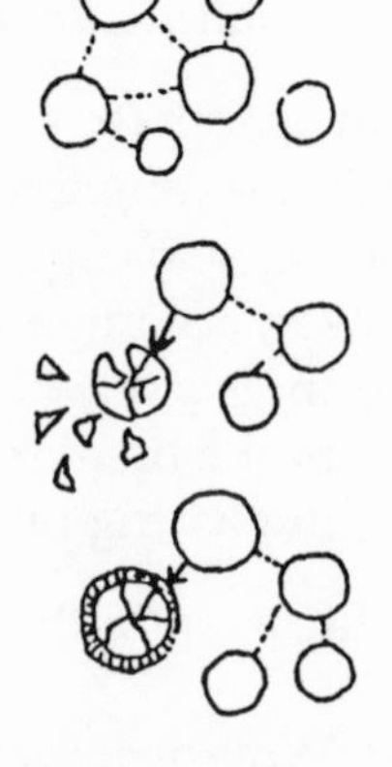

What happens between these entities, that is their actions, communications, relationships, has been considered less real, because it cannot be seen or measured. It's hard to weigh or measure messages or energy exchanges, love or hate. Of course, in these interactions one entity can shove another around. That seems the most obvious measure of its power: power gets defined as domination. If the impact is forceful enough, one entity can damage or shatter another.

If I am one of these entities, then, I certainly want to protect myself, so I won't be wiped out; I want to ensure that I'll continue to exist. I build defenses — whether as a personality or as a nation-state. Defenses can take many forms: nuclear arms, numbness, belligerence, even the need to please. So, as you can see, power has become equated with invulnerability. To be powerful is to have strong defenses.

Let's note, too, that if power is seen in terms of the capacity to have your own way, to dominate others, it is a zero-sum game. The more someone else has, the less you have — and vice-versa. Power-over presupposes and creates a win-lose situation. You have got to win over if you are not to lose out.

Now in our century the old view of reality, as being composed of separate, self-existent entities, has changed radically. Scientists have discovered that life phenomena are created and sustained by deep interconnections. They have turned the lens through which we can see the world, so that instead of beholding separate substances, we see flows and currents of energy, matter and information. Substances turn to process. What had appeared before as separate entities dissolve into flows, and are seen to be patterns in these flows — patterns that sustain each other by means of their relationships and exchanges. Atoms, cells, plants, people, societies . . . all are dynamic patterns, or open systems within systems. They influence each other so deeply that it is hard to decide where one leaves off and the other begins, indeed all boundaries are essentially arbitrary distinctions in this dynamic, flowing web.

A frequent image that systems scientists use, to convey the nature of this interconnectedness, is that of a nerve cell or neuron in a neural net.

That is how our brains and bodies work. It is also how an ecosystem works, or a family or a society. We are each like a neuron within the neural net of an organ that in turn is a subsystem within a larger body.

Now what does this say about the nature of power? Of what does the power of a neuron consist? If power is equated with invulnerability, and I as a neuron build defenses around me, what happens to me? Yes, I become dysfunctional, I atrophy and weaken the larger system of which I am a part and on which I depend.

The power of a neuron lies in its capacity to open to the charge, open to the messages travelling through the larger body. From that capacity arise ever more intricate and appropriate responses. That is how we learn and how society learns; that is how intelligence flowers.

So now we see power in a new light. It is not invulnerability, but openness. It is not a zero-sum game (you win/I lose), but a win/win or lose/lose game. It is not power-over, but power-with — this is what systems scientists call synergy.

In a way we have known this all along. We know it because that is the direction of evolution: life forms as they evolve become ever more vulnerable to their environment, the better to connect and respond. And we know it because we experience synergy in our own lives. When we fall in love or raise a child or even play frisbee, we experience the personal sense of enhancement that comes from enhancing the potential of others. We also know it because our spiritual traditions attest to this kind of growth and potency. But having been conditioned by the old patriarchal paradigm of power, we are not accustomed to viewing and naming this capacity as power. It is important that we do so now, because our survival depends on our moving beyond the primitive, competitive, win/lose notions of power. And as we do, we can see how our very capacity to feel pain for the world can empower us to connect with it, and act to heal it.

Joanna Macy
Despair and Personal Power in the Nuclear Age

Sources

Balasuriya, Tissa. *Planetary Theology.* Maryknoll, NY: Orbis Books, 1984.

Brueggemann, Walter. *The Prophetic Imagination.* Philadelphia, PA: Fortress Press, 1978.

de Chardin, Teilhard. *Hymn of the Universe.* New York: Harper & Row, 1961.

Fiorenza, Elizabeth Schüssler. *In Memory of Her: A Feminist Theological Reconstruction of Christian Origins.* New York: Crossroad, 1984.

Fischer, Kathleen. *Reclaiming the Connections.* Kansas City, MO: Sheed & Ward, 1990.

Harrison, Beverly Wildung. "The Power of Anger in the Work of Love" in *Making the Connections.* Boston, MA: Beacon Press, 1985.

Lifton, Robert J. *The Broken Connection.* New York: Simon and Schuster, 1979.

Macy, Joanna. *Despair and Personal Power in the Nuclear Age.* Philadelphia, PA: New Society Publishers, 1983.

"Psychosocial Aspects of Nuclear Development," *American Psychiatric Association Task Force Report,* No. 20, 1982.

Schaef, Ann Wilson. *When Society Becomes an Addict.* San Francisco, CA: Harper & Row, 1986.

Images of the Enemy

There is, in fact, no other way
to God for our time
but through the enemy . . .

Walter Wink

"Those out of touch with themselves have no alternative but to prepare for war."
Edwin McMahon and Peter Campbell

This next seminar experience has to do with one angle on *where to begin to make a difference.* It may seem an odd first step. Please risk entering, nonetheless. It is a vital, early doorway on the path of peacemaking.

The doorway is our own heart. We begin with locating, naming, owning our own hungers. Our own impoverishment, brokenness. This hidden self within, often disowned, can become our armament, our moat, our weapon, our wall. We protect and distance with this (we think) less worthy self. In so doing, we put all our relating at risk. We foil our own attempts at world-healing.

We forget that our wounds are wise.

Befriending our woundedness (a considerable labor) fine tunes our capacity for healthy empathy, understanding, effective action. Empowered, we arrive at the threshold of a truly global perspective.

We grasp, perhaps for the first time, "no more us and them, only we." We recognize our inclusion in "the poor." Alert to the work to be done on the home (heart) front, we awaken to "here IS there, them IS us." The reality of unity comes home.

Instead of hating the people you think are warmakers, hate the appetites and the disorder in your own soul, which are the causes of war.

Thomas Merton

Just as we global citizens need to map the conflicted areas of Central America: the oppressors' tactics, the refugee dilemmas, the peace initiatives, the low-intensity conflict, the war of attrition, the call to advocacy by North American Christians—*so too, do we need to map the oppressor, the refugee, the peacemaker, the combatant, the advocate in our inner landscape.* We meet our many selves—a work of peace.

Personal healing and "disarmament" follow. Peace becomes possible.

A global spirituality asks this new asceticism. Our process toward wholeness mirrors (indeed effects) the unity toward which we labor in the earth community. One is sign and sacrament of the other. As we own and work with our own wounds, we become available as healing agents.

Conversely, to the degree we disown, resist and deny those shattered parts of self, we project them on others —as "enemy," as that which evokes our attempts at control, at elimination. Enter labeling, blaming, stereotyping, scapegoating. Prime ingredients in the invective of racism and sexism, these behaviors characterize our dis-eased society.

So we gather, apprentice ourselves, and plan for change. What follows leads us through some fascinating learning. You'll likely find yourself on or between every line.

The mind creates the abyss; the heart crosses it.

Stephen Levine

This session explores how we create and picture enemies. As the 20th century closes we see extraordinary opportunities to create a more humane world. Unfortunately those openings are threatened by an upsurge in ethnic, racial, and religious violence globally. Once again our desires for peace seem shackled to a set of simplistic stereotypical images of other nations or groups. The "enemy" image is the most dangerous expression of this mindset, significantly contributing to international conflict.

All of us participate in the enemy-making habit to some extent, and therefore each has a story to share. The session circles from political to interpersonal to intrapersonal stories and back again, reflecting our belief that enemy-making is a psycho-social pattern that can be discerned as clearly in the world as in our own hearts. Stories elicited during the module will illustrate this pattern.

If we could read the secret history of our enemies, we would find in each man's [sic] life a sorrow and a suffering enough to disarm all hostility.

Henry Wadsworth Longfellow

Outline: Total time required for the entire session is 3 hours 20 minutes. You may shorten the session by selecting from among the several elements (marked by ******* in the outline). Mix and match to suit your needs. Time estimates for each element appear below along with a few suggested combinations:

- *Introduction* – 5 minutes
- *Profile of Enemy-making* – 1 hour
- *Break* – 10 minutes
- *Film/Discussion* – 45 minutes
- *Reflection* – 20 minutes
- *Break* – 10 minutes
- *Signs of Hope* – 20 minutes
- *Worship* – 30 minutes

Options for a 50-Minute to 1-Hour Module.

A	B	C
Film/Discussion	Introduction Reflection Worship	Profile

Options for a 1 Hour 30 Minute to 2 Hour Module

A	B
Introduction	Introduction
Film	Profile
Signs	Signs
Worship	Worship

Pain and suffering are a kind of false currency passed from hand to hand until they reach someone who receives them but does not pass them on.

Simone Weil

Leader Preparation

Examine your own life for experiences of "enemy-making." Who are your enemies? Who are the people that distress, frighten you? Make you suspicious? When have you been perceived as an enemy? How did you feel? Did that experience make a difference in shaping your worldview? You may wish to draw on such experiences as you lead the session.

Session Preparation

As the outline above indicates, this session can be tailored to suit a variety of time segments. You and the Program Subcommittee need to decide what schedule is realistic in light of the design of the whole seminar.

- Be sure to review the *Leader's Guide* (page 215) as you prepare.
- Consult the *Materials Needed* list at the end of the session outline.
- Carefully review the session outline. Note instructions to the leader appear in [**Bold**].
- You may wish to substitute a local resource for one of these segments. Some ideas:
    - a testimony by someone who has been treated as the enemy (refugees, victims of racial, ethnic or gender discrimination)
    - a story of one person's own experience at overcoming enemy images (a veteran who discovered the humanity of his or her opponent, a person who has begun to overcome their racism, sexism, ageism)
    - Consult "The Enemy Images Project" of Psychologists for Social Responsibility, 1841 Columbia Road, N.W., Suite 207, Washington, D.C. 20009, (202) 745-7084. They have organized a nationwide speakers bureau on this issue.

A human being is a part of the whole, called by us the "universe," a part limited in time and space. He [sic] experiences himself, his [sic] thoughts and feelings, as something separated from the rest—a kind of optical delusion of his [sic] consciousness.

This delusion is a kind of prison for us, restricting us to our personal desires and to affection for a few persons nearest to us.

Our task must be to free ourselves from this prison by widening our circle of compassion to embrace all living creatures and the whole of nature in its beauty.

Albert Einstein

Images of the Enemy: Session Begins

************Introduction************

(* * indicates optional components of the session)*

1. We begin with a quote **[Write on newsprint prior to beginning this section. Read it aloud to participants]:**

   "There is, in fact, no other way to God for our time but through the enemy, for loving the enemy has become the key to both human survival in the nuclear age and to personal transformation. Either we find the God who causes the sun to rise on the evil and the good, or we may have no more sunrises." (Walter Wink, "We Have Met the Enemy," *Sojourners.)*

2. During this period **[indicate length]** we will study the face of the enemy. We will focus on how we picture the enemy and how that image in turn shapes our view of the world. We will speak of "enemy-*making*" because these images are *constructed for a purpose.* We will see that our images of the enemy reveal at least as much about us as they do about the one portrayed. Finally, you will notice that we approach the pattern of enemy-making at three levels: the social-political, the interpersonal, and the individual. We do so out of a belief that the roots of enemy-making lie within our own divided hearts.

   Until we are able to enter there and meet the stranger that lives within, we will continue to manufacture enemies and be vulnerable to the enemy images manufactured for us. The face of the enemy is our own.

3. Through stories and images, a profile of enemy-making will emerge in *four elements* **[Write these on newsprint in advance and refer to them here]**—dualism, fear, projection, domination. They narrow and harden our worldview, inhibiting our ability to perceive our connection to one another and the world as a whole. To relinquish these images requires *acknowledging the enemy within us* (individually and corporately), letting go of our need to be perfect, pure. We will attend to:

   - What enemy-making is;
   - How it works;

- What it costs; and
- What we can do to "kick the habit."

4. Enemy is a strong word. What images, feelings, words, associations come to your mind when you hear that word? Who are your enemies? **[Solicit a few responses to this question]**

5. What do we mean by enemy-making? *Enemy-making means the practice of turning a person or persons into something less than human.* We can then dismiss, ignore, kill them without blame.

6. It's important to remember that *we are talking about our perceptions of another, not the other's intentions toward us.* Others may indeed wish us ill. The issue is how we think about others and the way that thinking may actually contribute to conflict and war. To refrain from enemy-making does not equal being naive, but rather becoming truly realistic, *seeing those who are before us in their splendor, weakness, selfishness.*

Believing ourselves to be possessors of absolute truth degrades us: we regard every person whose way of thinking is different from ours as a monster and a threat and by so doing turn our own selves into monsters and threats to our fellows.

Octavio Paz

*** * * * * * * * * A Profile of Enemy-Making * * * * * * * ***

7. *How does enemy-making happen?* Theologian Sam Keen, among many thoughtful persons, has studied this habit extensively. He outlines four elements of enemy-making that link our psychological, social and political lives. Each element tends to bias our perception and expectations of the other. Taken together these elements outline the steps of an ancient dance whose rhythms set the pace for many of our current conflicts. **[Return to newsprint, outlining these four *or* you may wish to write separate pieces of newsprint for each element and include the brief definitions listed below.]**

   - *Dualism*—The identification of some part of ourselves or someone else as "other," not like "us."
   - *Fear*—Perception, based on reality or not, that the "other" is a threat.
   - *Projection*—Attributing to the other characteristics of ourselves that we don't like or even admit to.
   - *Domination*—Discounting, ignoring, subduing, destroying the other to protect "us" from the demonic "them."

   We will look at each of these elements in turn.

8. **Dualism** means perceiving ourselves as a member of an "in" group opposed to some other "out" group. We can see this practice at work in children's secret clubs, adolescent gangs, our suspicion of immigrants. In his comedy routine, "The 2,000-Year-Old-Man," Mel Brooks displays this spirit as he recites the caveman national anthem: "Let them all go to hell except Cave 17."

   - Take a moment to remember a time in your own life when you may have felt yourself in an "out" group. **[Pause briefly]** What group was it? Who was the "in" group? How did you feel? Think? Act? What does that memory mean to you now? **[Pause again]**

   - **[Invite one or two persons to share their experience, or you may wish to share your own story.]**

9. When dualism builds a house just for "us," **fear** comes to live in it. Those not like us appear strange, threatening. A different race, ethnic group, political philosophy, gender cannot be trusted. We fill in what we don't know or understand with simplified, stereotypic depictions. White people are thoughtless oppressors and consumers; Russians are cold and calculating; Afro-Americans are lazy and aggressive; peace activists are simpleminded dupes. Such "consensual paranoia," to use a phrase of Keen's, is a characteristic of the human condition in virtually all cultures. The result—a viewpoint that divides the world into:

   - "us" versus "them";
   - good versus evil;
   - sacred versus profane.

   Where do you see this practice happening today? What other divisions do you see?

   A U.S. president vividly articulates this vision.

   [Write this quote on newsprint in advance, and then read it aloud.]

   "It may seem melodramatic to treat the twin poles of human experience represented by the United States and the Soviet Union as the equivalent of Good and Evil, Light and Darkness, God and the Devil; yet if we allow ourselves to think of them in that way, even hypothetically, it can

> Though I am different from you, we were born involved in one another.
>
> T'ao Chien

help clarify our perspective on the world struggle."(Richard Nixon, *In a Dark Time.)*

- How might such an attitude influence the approach to arms negotiations?
- How many of us have demonized Richard Nixon as he has demonized the Soviet Union?
- How has your image of the Soviet Union changed in recent years? Why?

Stereotypes not only explain behavior, they shape what we expect and remember. Enemy images frame our vision of the other so that we notice and remember negative qualities while we discount or do not notice positive qualities. Thus the image becomes self-sustaining. Let's take some time with two illustrations:

- "In a study conducted in southern India, where there is extensive conflict between Hindus and Moslems, Hindu office clerks read short descriptions of either a Moslem or a Hindu behaving in friendly or unfriendly ways. The clerks then chose the major reason that the person in the description behaved as he or she did. The Hindu clerks ascribed the friendly behaviors of the Hindu story to their personalities and the unfriendly behaviors to external circumstance (e.g., someone had been rude to the clerk earlier). In contrast, the clerks attributed the negative Moslem behaviors to negative personalities (e.g., they were unfriendly persons), and they ascribed friendly Moslem behaviors to external circumstances. Thus they made positive attributions about the Hindus and explained away their negative behaviors, but they make negative attributions about the Moslems, ascribing their negative behaviors to unpleasant, hostile personalities." ("Rethinking Enmity: An Introduction to the Psychology of Enemy Images." Washington, D.C.: Psychologists for Social Responsibility, 1990.)

- How do stereotypes shape the perceptions of the Hindu clerks?

- Do you see any parallels in your life, our society?

"ERA Story" **[Note: ask someone else to read this story, found at the end of this section.]**

- What almost happened in this encounter? What got in the way?

Now let me suggest . . . that if we are to have peace on earth, our loyalties must become ecumenical rather than sectional. Our loyalties must transcend our race, our tribe, our class, and our nation, and this means we must develop a world perspective. No individual can live alone; no nation can live alone, and as long as we try, the more we are going to have war in this world. Now the judgment of God is upon us and we must learn to live together as brothers or we are all going to perish together as fools.

Martin Luther King, Jr.

World peace starts right here. I will not raise my child to kill your child.

Barbara Choo

- Have you had a similar experience? Recall a time when you struggled to communicate with someone different from you in some significant way (nationality, values, physical ability, race, sex, etc.). How did you feel? What happened? What did you learn? **[Invite participants to share these stories in pairs.]**
- Is there anything from your stories that you'd like to share with the whole group?

10. The third element in enemy-making is **projection,** "the process of throwing out onto some other person ideas or impulses that belong to and are denied by oneself." What we don't like about ourselves we attribute to the enemy. For example recall the way motives are attributed in the media to the PLO, or before "perestroika" to the Soviet Union, in contrast to U.S. motives. We are honest, fair, striving for peace. "They" are tricky, unreliable, dishonest, etc. This double standard obstructs our ability to determine the actual motives of the other, or ourselves.

    Keen found vivid evidence of this habit in his extensive study of propaganda art. Regardless of historical period, political belief or culture, certain images or themes kept reappearing. Here are a few examples. Let's spend a moment looking at these images of the enemy. **[Hand out the "Images of the Enemy" Sheet.]**

    - What do you notice about these images? Which ones strike you most powerfully?
    - How is the enemy portrayed? What attributes are being ascribed to the enemy?
    - Do you see similarities in the ways enemies portray each other? What does that suggest?
    - What common human fears are employed to give these images power?
    - What is accomplished by portraying the enemy in this manner?

    [Allow about 15 minutes for this conversation. Conclude with the Sam Keen poem, page 98.]

    After looking at thousands of such images, Sam Keen summarized his observations in a poem. **[Ask the person you've chosen to stand and read at this time.]**

11. As Keen's poem makes clear, the fourth element of enemy-making is **domination** or destruction of the enemy. The manufactured image of the enemy serves both a political and a psychological purpose as it justifies controlling or extinguishing that enemy.

   - *Politically*, the image of the enemy is a propaganda tool supporting, legitimizing a government's policy of aggression, or the preparation for aggression (e.g., burgeoning arms sales). The enemy serves to bond a group together against their common "foe." An enemy can also be a convenient distraction from domestic problems. What other political purposes might an "enemy" serve? For example, insuring the nation's moral superiority, reinforcing the need to maintain present leadership in the government, etc.

   - *Psychologically*, the dehumanized image reduces the hesitation and guilt connected with harming or killing another human being. They simply aren't really human. They're "gooks," "japs," "wogs," "krauts," "gringos," etc. Furthermore, the destruction of the "enemy" temporarily redeems us from those nasty habits of our own we attributed to "them."

12. While these advantages serve a certain end, the costs are severe. What costs do you see? **[Note these on newsprint. If they have not been mentioned add to the list the following.]**

   - Becomes a self-fulfilling prophecy, perpetuating conflict.
   - Restricts communication, understanding.
   - Reduces our ability to see real areas of common interest.
   - Diminishes our ability to know and heal ourselves.

13. Letting go of the images we have of the enemy leads to a rediscovery of our connectedness.

   Sometimes this can occur in most unpredictable ways. Listen to the following story, perhaps familiar to you. **[Ask the person you've recruited, to stand and read the handout, "Christmas 1914," page 99.]**

   - What happened here?
   - What is your reaction to this reading? Do you see any lessons here for us?
   - How might we begin to awaken from the "spell" of

Once a nation bases its security on an absolute weapon, such as the atom bomb, it becomes psyschologically necessary to believe in an absolute enemy.

Patrick Blackett (President of the Royal Society), 1956

I destroy my enemy by making him my friend.

Abraham Lincoln

enemy- making? **[Take a few moments to allow for ideas to surface.]**

14. **BREAK** - 10 minutes

* * * * * * * * * *Film* * * * * * * * * *

15. **FILM**

- **[Introduce the film you have selected. Indicate that it illustrates one facet of our enemy-making habit.]**
- **[After the film invite participants to attend silently to the feelings elicited by the film.]** Let the feelings or mood called forth by the film continue. **[Pause]** Is there a word, phase or image from the film that particularly touched you? **[The purpose here is to gather feelings/impressions, not to discuss the film. So, encourage brief comments without responses or rebuttals.]**
- **[For a longer consideration of the film, use the discussion process outlined in *Community Building*. Frame your questions to address the ways in which enemy images play a role in the subject of the film.]**
- How can we begin to cultivate empathy for those who are different from us? Empathy for ourselves?

* * * * * * * * * *Reflection* * * * * * * * * *

Who is a holy person? The one who is aware of others' suffering.

Kabir

16. **REFLECTION**: "Forgiveness Meditation" **[The text for this meditation is found toward the end of the module.]**

- Our enemy images obstruct our view. In our fear we cling to those images to protect ourselves, closing our heart and preserving the distance between "us" and "them." We do this too when we discount our feelings or other aspects of our inner richness. To forgive the enemy within or in the world requires us to let go of that clutched image in order to broaden our vision both of our enemy and ourselves. Before we can let go, however, we must notice how we cling to our fear, anger, resentment. What is the clinging about?
- This meditation on forgiveness invites just such awareness. Place your feet on the floor. Put down

pens, pencils. Close your eyes. Relax. Notice your breathing.

[Now go to text of meditation. Read slowly. At the conclusion remain silent for a few moments. Gentle music in the background can help people enter a reflective attitude.]

- Take a few moments now to write down, for yourself, anything from this meditation you want to be sure to remember.

17. **BREAK** 10 minutes

18. What was your experience during the meditation? Were you able to allow yourself to forgive? How did that feel? Did you sense a shift within? **[Allow a few minutes for people to describe their experience if they choose. Be sure to mention the source of the meditation—Stephen Levine's *Who Dies: A Guide to Conscious Living and Conscious Dying.*]**

*** * * * * * * * * *Signs of Hope* * * * * * * * * ***

19. Throughout the world people are venturing beyond enemy categories. This sheet documents some of the hopeful efforts being made to befriend the enemy, and ourselves. **[Hand out sheet. Allow a few moments for people to read it.]**

- Which efforts do you find most interesting, exciting?
- Clearly, what we have explored today is only a beginning. What might be next steps for you? **[Invite people to keep the sheets for later reflection and possible action. Remind them that the caucus time will provide an opportunity for planning next steps, if they wish.]**

*** * * * * * * * * *Worship* * * * * * * * * ***

Introduction [Distribute the music]: Jesus became the enemy, the despised one, for us. If we want to follow Jesus words, "Love your enemy," and his example, we will find ourselves called to befriend the enemy within, as well as the enemy without. Befriending the enemy means crucifixion. Crucifixion of our pride, our desire for control, our ego. Befriending the enemy means entering into the life and death of Jesus, emptying ourselves of the illusion of our separateness and superiority.

To find the way to make peace with ourselves and to offer it to others, both spiritually and politically, is the most important kind of learning. To accept our abilities and limitations, and the differences of others; this is the contentment that gives life its highest value. It frees us to grow without restraint and to settle without pressure.

Wendy C. Schwartz

Those who say, "I love God," and hate their brothers and sisters, are liars; for those who do not love a brother or sister whom they have seen, cannot love God whom they have not seen.

1 John 4:20

Song: "Were You There When They Crucified My Lord?" **[Sing verse one, slowly, seated]**

Reflection [To be read aloud, as a guided meditation]:

Close your eyes.
Place yourself at the foot of the cross. You are a witness to the crucifixion of Jesus. As you stand there how do you feel? What are your thoughts? What do you want to do?

Keep that image before you as I read a passage from Isaiah,

> "Like a sapling he grew up before us,
> like a root in arid ground.
> He had no form or charm to attract us,
> no beauty to win our hearts;
> he was despised, the lowest of men,
> a man of sorrows, familiar with suffering,
> one from whom, as it were, we averted our gaze,
> despised, for whom we had no regard."
>
> Is. 53:2–3

Song: "Were You There," verse two.

Close your eyes. Return to the cross, only now imagine that the person on the cross is you.
Place yourself there: helpless, afflicted, alone, dying.
Listen to the taunts of the people. They call out your weaknesses and failings. You know those voices well.
Listen to how they despise you. What are they saying?

[Note: we give two suggestions here for expressing those inner voices: writing or speaking. Speaking may feel more risky. There is no right choice here. Choose the one that feels most comfortable to you and seems to fit with what you have done up to now in the seminar.]

Option A. Take a moment and write down on the back of your music what these voices are saying to you. This is for your eyes only.

Option B. Give voice here to the voices you are hearing. No need to be polite and wait for each other—after all this is a mob. Say aloud with as much feeling as you can the taunts of your own inner crucifiers. **[Allow time for response. Be patient. It may take a minute or two for persons to feel courageous enough to speak. When it feels like those who wish to speak have done so, proceed.]**

Slowly, the taunts of the crowd fade. You are dying on the cross. Let yourself die, overwhelmed by the enmity of the crowd who despises you.

Song: "Were You There," verse three.

Close your eyes. Take your own body off the cross. There at the foot of the cross cradle your own disowned, despised self. Assume a posture that feels right and cradle your self. Notice how you feel now.

As you hold your own crucified self, listen to the compassionate words of psychologist Carl Jung:

> "The acceptance of oneself is the essence of the moral problem and the epitome of a whole outlook upon life. That I feed the hungry, that I forgive an insult, that I love my enemy in the name of Christ—all these are undoubtedly great virtues. What I do unto the least of my brethren, that I do unto Christ.
>
> But what if I should discover that the least amongst them all, the poorest of all the beggars, the most impudent of all the offenders, the very enemy himself—that these are within me, and that I myself stand in need of the alms of my own kindness—that I myself am the enemy who must be loved—what then?
>
> As a rule, the Christian's attitude is then reversed; there is no longer any question of love or long-suffering; we say to the brother within us "Raca," and condemn and rage against ourselves. We hide it from the world; we refuse to admit ever having met this least among the lowly in ourselves. Had it been God himself who drew near to us in this despicable form, we would have denied him a thousand times before a single cock had crowed." (C.G. Jung, *Modern Man in Search of a Soul,* New York: Harcourt, Brace and World, 1933.)

Song: "Were You There," verse one.

Jesus, the crucified, was an enemy, but not an enemy-maker. The prayer he taught us invites us to forgive our enemies, ourselves included. Let us stand and pray, "Our Father . . ."

Jesus crucified and risen, told his disciples, "Peace is my gift to you." Let us offer a sign of this same peace in the hope of our own healing and rising.

Scripture scholar Walter Wink tells us, "It cannot be stressed too much that love of enemies has, for our time, become the litmus test of authentic Christian faith." I invite you in this circle of prayer to pray for your enemies, for that which you dislike, fear, suspect, despise, both within and without.

[When the group is finished, offer your own spontaneous prayer to conclude.]

Song: "In Christ There Is No East or West"

Materials Required for Session: Varies according to which elements of the session you use. Materials for duplication appear on following pages.

If you are doing Profile of Enemy-Making

- Newsprint, magic markers
- One copy each for the readers of
  - ERA Story
  - Poem
  - "Christmas 1914"
- Copies for each participant of "Images of the Enemy" sheet.

If you are using the film

- Select and order film. Suggestions: *Children of Apartheid, Cry of Reason, Women—for America, for the World* (Note: This film is also suggested for use in **Theologos**. Beware of duplication.) See **Resources** for description and instructions on ordering.
- 1/2-inch VCR player and monitor—the larger the screen the better.

If you are using the Guided Reflection

- Cassette tape player
- Tape of instrumental music for use with the guided meditation. Tapes by Kitaro, Steve Winfield, George Winston lend themselves to this purpose.

Materials Required for Session

If you are using the "Signs of Hope" *sheet*

- Make copies for each participant

If you are using the Worship

- Copies of song (found in **Worship**) for each participant

SOURCES

Overviews

Cole, Jim. *Filtering People: Understanding and Confronting Our Prejudices.* Philadelphia, PA: New Society, 1990.

Keen, Sam. *Faces of the Enemy: Reflections of the Hostile Imagination.* San Francisco: Harper & Row, 1986.

U.S.-Soviet Rivalry

English, Robert D. and Halperin, Jonathan J. *The Other Side: How Soviets and Americans Perceive Each Other.* Washington, D.C.: Committee for National Security, 1987.

Silverstein, B. "Enemy Images: The Psychology of U.S. Attitudes and Cognitions Regarding the Soviet Union." *American Psychologist, 44,* 1989, 903-913.

White, R.K. *Fearful Warriors: A Psychological Profile of U.S.-Soviet Relations.* New York: Free Press, 1984.

Attitudes of and about Other Nations

Dower, John W. *War Without Mercy: Race and Power in the Pacific War.* New York: Pantheon, 1986.

Hess, J. Daniel. *From the Other's Point of View: Perspectives from North and South of the Rio Grande.* Scottdale, PA: Herald, 1980.

Isaacs, Harold. *Scratches on Our Minds: American Views of China and India.* New York: M.E. Sharpe, 1980.

Joy, Carrol. *Believing Is Seeing: Attitudes and Assumptions That Affect Learning about Development.* New York: National Clearinghouse on Development Education, 1990.

Said, Edward W. *Covering Islam: How the Media and the Experts Determine How We See the Rest of the World.* New York: Pantheon, 1981.

Shipler, David K. *Arab and Jew: Wounded Spirits in a Promised Land.* New York: Times Books, 1986.

Befriending the Enemy

Campbell, Peter and McMahon, Edwin. *Bio-Spirituality: Focusing as a Way to Grow.* Chicago: Loyola University Press, 1983.

Forest,Jim. *Making Friends of Enemies: Reflections on the Teachings of Jesus.* New York: Crossroad, 1987.

Swimme, Brian. "More Hot Air: Learning from Our Enemies" in *Creation,* Sept/Oct, 1985.

Vanderhaar, Gerard A. *Enemies and How to Love Them.* Mystic, CT: Twenty-third Publications, 1985.

Wink, Walter. "On Not Becoming What We Hate" series of three articles appearing in Nov. 1986, Jan. and Feb. 1987 issues of *Sojourners.*

Something we were withholding made us weak
Until we found it was ourselves.

Robert Fr

Civilization . . . is the acceptance, and the encouragement, of differences.

Mahatma Gandhi

TO CREATE AN ENEMY

Start with an empty canvas
Sketch in broad outline the forms of
men, women, and children.

Dip into the unconscious well of your own
disowned darkness
with a wide brush and
stain the strangers with a sinister hue
of the shadow.

Trace onto the face of the enemy the greed,
hatred, carelessness you dare not claim
as your own.

Obscure the sweet individuality of each face.

Erase all hints of the myriad loves, hopes,
fears that play through the kaleidoscope
of every finite heart.

Twist the smile until it forms the downward
arc of cruelty.

Strip flesh from bone until only the
abstract skeleton remains.

Exaggerate each feature until man is
metamorphosized into beast, vermin, insect.

Fill in the background with malignant
figures from ancient nightmares—devils,
demons, myrmidons of evil.

When your icon of the enemy is complete
you will be able to kill without guilt,
slaughter without shame.

The thing you destroy will have become
merely an enemy of God, an impediment
to the sacred dialect of history.

Sam Keen

(From *Faces of the Enemy: Reflections of the Hostile Imagination.* San Francisco, CA: Harper & Row, 1986.)

CHRISTMAS 1914

We have all read what happened between those two opposing armies, and how it came unexpected, undesigned, and yet willed with all the unconscious force of their natures. Not once or twice but again and again we hear of this sudden change upon the night of Christmas Eve, how there was singing upon one side answered by the other, and how the men rose and advanced to meet each other as if they had been released from a spell. Everyone who tells of it speaks also of his own wonder as if he had seen a miracle; and some say that the darkness became strange and beautiful with lights as well as music, as if the armies had been gathered together there not for war but for the Christmas Feast. Our men, as if from mere habit, began to sing "Christians Awake." And then the Christians did awake in English and in German, and they were no longer German or English to each other, but men. It was not done by an effort or with fear and suspicion and awkwardness. It happened as if it were a change of weather, the sun coming out after a storm; and when it happened it seemed more natural even than wonderful. *What was unnatural was the former state of war in which men had been to each other not men but targets: and now they had come to life for each other,* and in a moment they were friends.

A. Clutton-Brock, "Christmas 1914"
cited in *In a Dark Time: Images for Survival.*
ed. Robert Jay Lifton and Nicholas Humphrey.
Cambridge, MA: Harvard University Press, 1984.

ERA STORY

We had struggled for several years, and on the night the Equal Rights Amendment passed in our state, I saw one of the women who had opposed us at the election headquarters. We were both monitoring the count. When the result became clear, she looked at me. I wanted to reach out to her. She was just another woman—equal rights for her too. She gave me this very determined look, without anger, but you knew she wasn't all that happy.

So I tried, "Well, back to the kids for a while?" She said, "Oh yes, homework has completely deteriorated in our house." And I said, "Mine too. Equal rights for dummies." She sort of laughed. And it was nice there for a moment. Then she said, "You know it isn't over yet. We're going to win. You're not going to be able to get enough states to ratify." And that's where it got left. That thing about the homework . . . it just evaporated. She walked off; I walked off. And that took a little off the victory celebration for me.

Ram Dass and Paul Gorman
How Can I Help? New York: Alfred A. Knopf, 1986.

FORGIVENESS MEDITATION

Reflect for a moment on that quality we call forgiveness. Bring into your mind, actually into your heart, the image of someone for whom you have much resentment.

Take a moment to feel that person right there at the center of your chest in the heart center.

And in your heart say to that person, "I forgive you for anything you may have done in the past, either intentionally or unintentionally, through your thoughts, words, or actions that caused me pain. I forgive you."

Slowly allow that person to settle into your heart.

Don't judge yourself for how difficult it is.

No force, just opening slowly to them at your own pace.

Say to them, "I forgive you. I forgive you for the pain you caused me in the past, intentionally or unintentionally, by your thoughts, your deeds, your words. I forgive you."

Gently, gently open to them. If it hurts, let it hurt. Gradually open to that person. That resentment, that incredible anger, even if it burns, ever so gently though. Forgiveness.

"I forgive you."

Let your heart open just a bit more to them. Just a moment of opening, of forgiveness, letting go of resentment.

Allow them to be forgiven.

Now opening more to forgiveness, bring into your heart the image of someone from whom you wish to ask forgiveness.

Speak to them in your heart. "I ask your forgiveness for anything I may have done in the past that caused you pain, either by my thoughts or my actions or my words. Even for those things I didn't intend to cause you pain, I ask your forgiveness."

"For all those words that were said out of forgetfulness or fear. Out of my closedness, out of my confusion. I ask your forgiveness.

Don't allow any resentment you hold for yourself to block your reception of that forgiveness. Let your heart soften to it. Allow yourself to be forgiven.

Let yourself be freed.

Let that unworthiness come up, that anger at yourself - let it all fall away. Let it all go.

Open to the possibility of forgiveness.

"I ask your forgiveness for whatever I may have done in the past that caused you pain. By the way I acted or spoke or thought, I ask your forgiveness."

It is so painful to hold yourself out of your heart.

Bring yourself into your heart. Say "I forgive you." Open to that. Let it be. Make room in your heart for yourself.

"I forgive you."

All those resentments, let them fall away.

Open to the self-forgiveness. Let yourself have some space.

Let go of that bitterness, that hardness, that judgment of yourself.

Say, "I forgive you" to you.

Let some glimmering of loving-kindness be directed toward yourself. Allow your heart to open to you. Let that light, that care for yourself, grow.

Self-forgiveness.

Watch how thoughts of unworthiness and fears of being self-indulgent try to block the possibility of once and for all letting go of that hardening.

See the freedom in self-forgiveness. How can you hold to that pain even for a moment longer?

Feel that place of love and enter into it.

Allow yourself the compassion, the care, of self-forgiveness. Let yourself float gently in the open heart of understanding, of forgiveness, and peace.

Feel how hard it is for us to love ourselves. Feel the pain in the hearts of all those caught in confusion. Forgive them. Forgive yourself. Let go gently of the pain that hides the immensity of your love.

SIGNS OF HOPE: BEFRIENDING THE ENEMY

"It would appear that God has ordained that we can only enter the reign of God arm and arm with our enemies."

Walter Wink

Creative efforts at befriending the enemy abound. We offer here a sampler for your consideration and inspiration.

MEETING THE ENEMY FACE TO FACE

USA - Soviet Encounters.
In 1987 over 100,000 US citizens visited the Soviet Union. A sampler of opportunities:

- The Citizen Exchange Council, 18 East 41st St., New York, NY 10017, (212) 889-7960.
- Peace Odysseys, 5250 Patriot Lane, Columbia, MD 21045,(301) 730-8296
- Bridges for Peace, Box 710, Norwich, CT 05055, (802)649-1000.

NOTE: A detailed description of these and other tours can be found in "To Russia with Love: A Tour Guide for Citizen Diplomats," Nuclear Times, *Mar/Apr 1988.*

Third World Encounters.
While Nicaragua was portrayed almost nightly in our news as an enemy of the United States prior to the elections, many Americans have returned from that country with a different perception. Witness for Peace alone took over 3000 Americans to that country. Visits to other "foreign" areas can be equally powerful. Some opportunities:

- Witness for Peace, P.O. Box 567, Durham, NC 27702, (919) 688-5049.
- Center for Global Service and Education, Augsburg College, 731-21st Avenue South, Minneapolis, MN 55454.
- GATE (Global Awareness Through Experience), 936 Winnebago St., La Crosse, WI 54601 (608) 791-0462.
- Plowshares Institute, P.O. Box 243, Simsbury, CT 06070, (203) 651-4304.

For a listing of other opportunities for alternative tourism see "Making the Links," Seeds, Feb. 1988.

LINKING YOUR COMMUNITY TO THE WORLD

Sister Cities efforts have linked 759 American cities in 1,120 sister city relationships including 18 with cities in the Soviet Union and 38 with cities in China. Analogous efforts to link or partner churches in the US and abroad accomplish a similar goal of breaking down the "us" vs "them" perspective.

- Sister Cities International, 1625 Eye Street, NW, Washington, D.C. 20006.
- Madre, 853 Broadway, Room 301, New York, NY 10003.
- Peace Corps Partnership Program, 806 Connecticut Ave, NW, Suite M-1210, Washington, D.C. 20526.

ECUMENICAL LIFE AS WITNESS TO RECONCILIATION

Ecumenical life itself reveals our ability to overcome inherited differences and prepares us to confront more difficult barriers of race, class, nation, gender.

- Local, state and regional councils of churches have been at the forefront in struggles for economic and political justice, responding to local disasters, refugee resettlement.
- CWS/CROP events can bring diverse elements of a community in a unique way. For example Oil City, PA and Franklin, PA, historic rivals in the economically depressed Allegheny River valley, have joined together in a CROP Walk to assist local hunger as well as the hungry overseas. Church World Service, P.O. Box 968, Elkhart, IN 46515 (219)264-3102.

RECONCILIATION THROUGH THE ARTS

Artistic expression can bridge the chasms of our enmity in beautiful and playful ways.

- "Peace Child," a musical fantasy about children bringing peace to the world, has been produced and presented by local people throughout the United States and the Soviet Union. Beginning in 1986 the Peace Child Foundation initiated joint US-Soviet performances using Soviet and American children who toured both countries. Peace Child Foundation, 3977 Chain Bridge Road, Fairfax, VA 22030, (703) 385-4494.
- Third World Crafts. Alternative trade offers a way to enjoy the creativity of other cultures and support local artisans.
  - Friends of the Third World, 611 W. Wayne St., Ft. Wayne, IN 46802.
  - Jubilee, 300 W. Apsley St., Philadelphia, PA 19144.
  - Pueblo to People, 1616 Montrose Blvd., Houston, TX 77006, 1-800-843-5257.
  - SERRV Self-Help Handcrafts, 500 Main St., P.O. Box 365 New Windsor, MD 21776, (301)635-6464.

STANDING WITH THE ENEMY

Political prisoners regardless of ideological persuasion have found an ally in Amnesty International (A.I.). A.I. is a worldwide movement which works impartially for the release of prisoners of conscience: men and women detained anywhere for their beliefs, color, ethnic origin, sex, religion or language, provided they have neither used nor advocated violence. In 1977 A.I. received the Nobel Peace Prize.

During the first 10 years of their Appeals for Prisoners of Conscience, a letter writing campaign, 49 percent (178 persons) of the prisoners they spoke up for were either subsequently granted improved prison conditions or were released.

Amnesty International USA, National Office, 304 West 58th St., New York, NY 10019, (212) 582-4440.

From *Tales of the Heart*, Hampson/Whalen, Friendship Press, 1991.

LISTENING TO OURSELVES AND OTHERS

"The first duty of love is to listen" remarked Paul Tillich. We end with some examples and suggestions for active listening.

In Tokyo, Bangkok and Delphi, Fran Peavy sat on a bench in a central square with a simple sign, "American willing to listen." She was curious what ordinary folks thought about the future of their world and hers. She was not famous or an expert, yet in every case people stood in line to talk to her. See Fran Peavy, *Heart Politics*, New Society Pub., 1986.

Since 1981 the Third World Women's Project has enabled more than 200 women from the so-called developing world to have face to face meetings with citizens throughout the US and Canada.

These dialogues with women from Latin America, Asia and Africa have opened new channels for listening.

Third World Women's Project,
Institute for Policy Studies,
1901 Que St., NW, Washington, D.C. 20009
(202)234-9382.

RESOURCES ON ENEMY-MAKING

Keen, Sam. *Faces of the Enemy: Reflections of the Hostile Imagination.* San Francisco: Harper & Row, 1986.

Forest, Jim. *Making Friends of Enemies: Reflections on the Teachings of Jesus.* New York: Crossroad, 1987.

Frank, Jerome. *Sanity and Survival.* New York: Random House, 1982.

Dass, Ram and Gorman, Paul. *How Can I Help?* New York: Alfred A. Knopf, 1986.

Shipler, David K. *Arab and Jew: Wounded Spirits in a Promised Land*, New York: Times Books, 1986.

English, Robert D. and Halperin, Jonathan J. *The Other Side: How Soviets and Americans Perceive Each Other.* Washington, D.C.: Committee for National Security, 1987.

Levine, Stephen. *Who Dies? An Investigation of Conscious Living and Conscious Dying*, New York: Anchor Press/Doubleday, 1982.

Images of the Enemy

Every so often (Gallup Polls) ask their respondees to select from a list of adjectives the ten which best describe members of other nations. . . . Back in 1942, Germany and Japan were our bitter enemies, and Russia was our ally; and in 1942, among the first five adjectives chosen to characterize both the Germans and the Japanese were: "warlike," "treacherous," and "cruel." None of these appeared in the list for the Russians at that time. In 1966, when Gallup surveyed responses to mainland China, predictably, the Chinese were seen as "warlike," "treacherous," and, being Orientals, "sly." After President Nixon's visit to China, however, almost immediately these adjectives disappeared about the Chinese, and they are now characterized as "hardworking," "intelligent," "artistic," "progressive," and "practical."

Jerome D. Frank, "Prenuclear-Age Leaders and the Nuclear Arms Race," 1982

The Spanish Brute Adds Mutilation to Murder

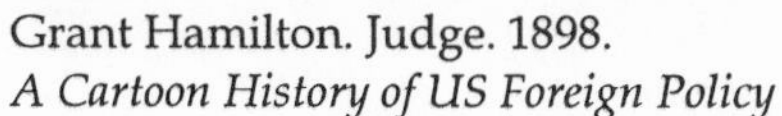
Grant Hamilton. Judge. 1898.
A Cartoon History of US Foreign Policy

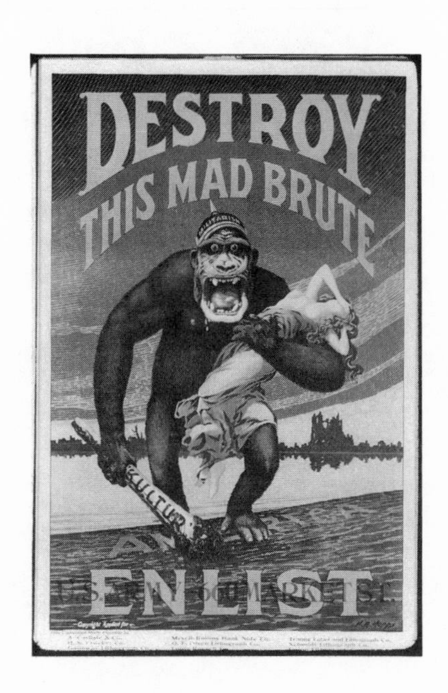

Cartoons courtesy of Sam Keen

From *Tales of the Heart*, Hampson/Whalen,
Friendship Press, 1991.

Exploring Our Worldview

An education for the
making of peace
needs to reconnect
persons with one another
and with the
mystery
of their being.

Matthew Fox

You must give birth to your images. They are the future awaiting to be born.

Rainer Maria Rilke

Reach deeper than words.

Exercise your be-longing.

Meditation quiets us, putting us in touch with our fondest hopes for ourselves, our children, and the earth. We attend to Carl Jung, ". . . the life of the individual makes history. Here alone do great transformations first take place. *The whole future ultimately springs, as a gigantic summation, from these hidden sources in individuals."*

After tending our images in meditation—enjoying the silence of that invitation to a scarcely-used side of ourselves—we have a conversation. We build a common image, and craft a non-verbal vehicle for communicating it. Performance. Pictures in action.

Picturing how things are in our earth community, integrates the "knowing" of body and spirit. According to Einstein, "I didn't get to the theory of relativity through my intellect, but through my intuition." Not through facts, but through images.

Images also tap our feelings. We practice celebration of feelings, learning to act from their power. We recognize compassion (feeling with) as the richest source of energy, the proper name for spiritual living in the global village.

As Thomas Merton noted in a talk just hours before his death, "Compassion is... the interdependence of all these living beings." Homecoming to our mutual belonging.

Welcome to "Exploring Our Worldview." Enjoy the group's absorption, the "forgetting of self," the sense of delight, of cooperation . . . a conspiracy of creativity. Note the movement from feeling powerless to powerful—a balm in our beleaguered time!

Echo of Kenneth Rexroth, "Against the ruin of the world, there is only one defense—the creative act."

In the labor toward consensus, a quality of centeredness emerges. Catalyst for our "reconnecting to our origins and the mystery of our being." Curtain up.

Reach deeper than words.

Exercise your be-longing.

This luxuriously long session falls into two generous parts: one for dreaming, discerning, discussing, designing, and the next for doing.

Involving body, mind and spirit, it first savors silence and a focusing of attention through guided meditation. Inquiring "how we are" as we contemplate earth from space, it exercises intuition and imagination, enticing us to enter these underused doors of our "knowing."

In the sharing of responses, we build consensus and community preparatory to exploring the challenge, delight and power of non-verbal communication.

The debriefing etches laughter and learning into our communal and personal memory. "Societies generate images of the possible and then draw their behavior from these images" —*Elise Boulding.*

Societies generate images of the possible and then draw their behavior from those images.

Elise Boulding

Outline

(Total Time Required—4 hours 15 minutes)

Part I (1 hour and 15 minutes)

- *Introduction* (15 minutes)
- *Guided Reflection* (15 minutes)
- *Small-Group Work* (45 minutes)

Part II (From 2-3 hours, depending on group size, and resulting number of small groups)

- *Finishing touches and rehearsal for "performance"* (1 hour)
- *Communication from each group to the plenary* (10 minutes per small group, plus an additional 5 minutes per group for set up, and some exchange on their vignette)

Leader Preparation

Some elements of this module may be fairly uncharted territory to you. The leader's instructions, and the chapter opening will assist you through it. (Remember, global education has everything to do with an unmapped place!)

As we say often in this handbook, spend the time necessary to become familiar and comfortable with the module's elements and flow. Then, relax and enjoy it. You are not required to be an expert here. It has been tested many times, and faithfully (often hilariously, always movingly) achieves its goals. The genius of this module lies in the imagination and creativity of the participants. You are simply providing the space for all that energy to emerge.

Especially in the introduction, feel free to use examples and anecdotes of your own that illustrate the points made . . . always thought through in advance, in order to remain within suggested time.

In this and other seminar sessions, you will need facilitators for the small groups. The Program Subcommittee will recruit facilitators in advance and arrange for a brief orientation for them at which you should be present. Look over the facilitator's directions for the module at the end of this outline. Copy and distribute them.

Session Preparation

- Review Session Outline. Note instructions to the leader appear in [**Bold**].
- Review *Leader's Guide* page 215.
- Recruit two persons: One to run the cassette player, another for lights, during the guided reflection. Practice at least once to establish the beginning cue. (At the "get comfortable" direction as the meditation opens: music on and gradually up, and lights down.) As you practice, also set up a good balance between the audio volume and your voice, as you speak over the music. (Remember, you may need a flashlight to read in the dark, here and elsewhere throughout the seminar.)
- List on newsprint whatever notes may be helpful to you, and the instructions to the small groups.

When you look out
he other way toward
the stars you realize
-'s an awful long way
to the next watering
hole.

Loren Acton

Exploring Our Worldview: Part I.

In this segment we will spend a few minutes setting a context, do a brief guided reflection together, and then work in small groups. In all, the time will be about an hour and fifteen minutes. The module's conclusion comes at a later time. **[Mention the time scheduled for Part II.]**

Introduction to Guided Meditation

[The following points—perhaps the *italicised* sections—can be outlined on newsprint, if doing so fits your way of teaching, offers you support as you mention the points, or in your opinion, helps your audience grasp the points more readily.]

1. *Teilhard de Chardin,* Jesuit anthropologist, theologian and mystic, spoke often of each person's, indeed each creature's *"unique lookout point on the universe."* This next part of the seminar encourages thoughtful time at our own lookout point.

2. We are going to assume for the moment that *we have enough information,* enough facts about the state of the earth community. We'll be paying attention to *"picturing" and feeling what we already know.* Simply said, we're moving from our more heavily taxed left brain, over to the right. So, this is NOT a quiz!

3. *Images work better than arguments to awaken us to consciousness.* Images unlock our deep knowing. In the recent history of the U.S., for example, the Civil Rights Movement and the Vietnam War flooded us with pictures of our national tendencies and priorities. We said, "Stop! Enough!" and significant change occurred. *Are there current examples* of pictures that awaken you? **[Ask question of the group. Spend a few moments exchanging on that.]**

4. We're about to do a guided meditation together. It will evoke some *pictures within* us, and *encourage us to simply be with them.* Noticing and allowing whatever feelings accompany them. No thinking, figuring, or fixing is called for. Just silence, relaxation, and travel in inner space. Our body, mind, and spirit are about to have a meeting. We enter our "knowing" through the rarely used door of imagination and intuition.

Looking at the Earth from afar you realize it is too small for conflict and just big enough for cooperation.

Yuri Gagarin
Cosmonaut

The Guided Reflection

[Read the following text *slowly*, being sure you can be heard by all. By practicing ahead of time (perhaps even leading a friend through the reflection, and asking for his/her feedback) you will insure your own relaxation, awareness of your own breathing, and the timing of your pauses—thus, more effectively engaging others. Each time the text breaks, it implies a pause. Feel your way into it.

The first day or so we all pointed to our countries. The third or fourth day we were pointing to our continents. By the fifth day we were aware of only one earth.

Sultan Bin Salmo al-Sau

You already have someone cued to begin and end the music in the places indicated, and to lower the lights, creating an atmosphere of quiet and focused attention.]

Text to be Read:

"With those points as our context, let's move into the relaxation of a brief guided meditation. You may want to shift your chair to allow a comfortable space around yourself. **(Music up gradually, lights down.)** To prepare, get comfortable in your chair. Put your feet flat on the floor. Close your eyes.

Become aware of your breathing. **(Music begins: softly at first, then to a previously agreed volume.)**

Focus your attention on your breathing. Be in its comforting, dependable rhythm. Rising and falling. Breathing in and breathing out. **[Pause for 10-15 seconds, breathing deeply yourself.]**

As an accompaniment, savor the music of Carl Sagan's 'Cosmos.'

[Pause to allow the music to establish itself.]

To begin, allow the great blue and green marble that is our mother earth to rise before you. Notice the sapphire of her waters, her emerald forests, her vermilion sands. Notice the swirl of her cloud cover, the shimmer of her abundant life in the pulsing void of space.

Bask for a moment in the beauty and vibrancy of this home of yours . . . hung in the deep reaches of the universe.

How are you as you sit before this beautiful and fragile earth? Let an image of how you are in the presence of the earth play within you.

Quiet your thinking and allow your feelings to be alive within you. Notice how your body feels. Patiently await an image of how you are in the presence of earth. **[Pause]**

Trust the image that's emerging. This is how *I am* in the presence of the earth. In her presence. Not doing or fixing. Just being. (What a rare treat!) Examine the image. . . . Play with it. Enjoy it. We'll spend a few minutes quietly here. **[2 minutes of silence]**

I am trying to save the knowledge that the forests and this planet are alive, to give it back to you who have lost the understanding.

Paulinho Paiakan

Move that image gently aside for the moment. We will return to it. Bring your attention back to your breathing, **[pause]** back to the pristine beauty of the home planet.

Consider how fragile is her balance, how multiple her wounds, and those of her human partners. **[Pause]**

Next, allow an image to emerge of your vision of *healing* the earth community. A list of how-to's is not needed now. Rather, what gesture will make whole, bind wounds? What awakens as your way of healing the earth? Logic need not apply. Let the image dwell before your inner eye for a while. Allow it to speak to you. Welcome and enjoy it. Give it time. We'll wait quietly. **[2 minute pause]**

Now coax your two images together: How are you in the presence of the earth's life and grandeur? By what gesture do you heal the earth's wounds?

Be confident that your images are important. Trust and enjoy them. Do they have something to say to each other?

How do your two images relate? Spend a few minutes allowing some possible interactions. **[2 minute pause]**

Slowly return your awareness back to your breathing, to your body, to this room. When you are ready, open your eyes.

[Gradually bring the music down and off.]

You'll have a chance later to comment on this exercise.

For now, let's get into our small groups and do the tasks outlined on the newsprint. **[Review the tasks for the group, making sure they're clear.]** We'll take about 45 minutes and let you know when the time is up.

[The group does not come back into plenary session. An end is called to the small groups after about 45 minutes.]

Small-Group Tasks [These should be listed on newsprint]

1) Briefly share your experience during the meditation, your images and their connections. Each person take about *3 minutes.* **[Emphasize brevity, so that all are heard.]**

A vision without a task is but a dream, a task without a vision is drudgery, a vision with a task is the hope of the world.

Church Inscription
Sussex, England, 1730

2) Building on the sharing, identify possible points of *convergence* toward a worldview held in common. Let a corporate image or feeling begin to emerge.

3) How could you communicate that worldview to the whole group NON-VERBALLY in an under TEN MINUTE vignette? **[Mention when this will happen in the schedule. Note that mime, drama, dance, comedy, charade are all possibilities for communication.]**

   There will be an additional hour **[say when]** for completing and rehearsing your presentation.

   Enjoy one another, the fruits of your reflection, and some "acting out"!

* * * * * *

Exploring Our Worldview: Part II

The moment we begin to fear the opinions of others and hesitate to tell the truth that is in us, and from motives of policy are silent when we should speak, the divine floods of lights and life flow no longer into our souls. . . .

Every truth we see is ours to give the world, not to keep ourselves alone, for in doing so we cheat humanity out of their rights and check our own development.

Elizabeth Cady Stanton

[You are in a part of the seminar schedule now where the small groups have reconvened, and are spread about doing their hour of final "rehearsal" for presentation to the plenary. The plenary time is set. Each group will have up to ten minutes to communicate its image of the earth community to the whole. It expedites things if the groups have less than a minute's "set up," and know in what order they will present. You might organize the latter now, taking group wishes into consideration, and pacing them, depending on the nature of the presentation.

The plenary room can be set up either completely "in the round" (if space is sufficient at the center for the performance) or, in a more conventional theater style with the audience facing the performing space.]

1) Performance: A series of *ten minute* (or less) wordless vignettes.
2) After each, 3 minutes of exchange: first, the audience addressing "what did you see there?" and, as final comment, the actors sharing their intent. All noticing the power of gesture, posture, and expression, in the absence of the verbal. Agreement, or insistence on "getting the point" is not a goal here. Rather, enjoyment, savoring of a range of feelings, and celebrating our creativity. (If our long experience holds, there will be MUCH to celebrate!)

[Take a break after about 40 minutes. Be very clear and vigilant (without being heavyhanded) throughout this module about attending to TIME. The activity tends to be so refreshing and engaging that it can get away from you!]

3) Conclusion: When all the performances are finished, spend about ten minutes around these questions with the whole group:

   - How did you feel when the task was first given?
   - Did anything "get in the way" of your jumping into the task?
   - What struck you most about the process?
   - What did you learn?
   - How do you feel now?

   Ask someone in the group to close with a blessing/ prayer, extending the "cry of the earth community" that you have just crafted together. Amen.

   [Alternate: check in *Worship* **for a reading or prayer that touches your experience together. Miriam Simos' "The Last Story" comes to mind. OR, end in a circle of silence, as a final witness to that powerful, underused medium.]**

Materials Required for Session:

- "The Music of Cosmos: Selections from the PBS TV Series" cassette tape. RCA, ABK1-4003. You will need to purchase or borrow this tape.
- Cassette tape recorder
- Newsprint/markers/tape
- Copies of facilitator's sheet
- A flashlight

The shared exploration of our deepest fears and longings about our Earth has in it the seeds of a profound spiritual renewal. It draws upon the riches of existing traditions, yet is solidly grounded in the fresh love and faith born of opening our deepest selves to one another. Come join us in this widening circle.

Joseph Havens

FACILITATOR SHEET
Exploring Our Worldview

You will be leading the group through four tasks: sharing images, arriving at consensus, rehearsing, performing. Your task is to enable the group's conversation, being sure that all are heard. You are not expected, nor should you attempt, to solve the riddle of how the various images converge or how that convergence should be portrayed. The group will do this, and will often surprise themselves with their imagination and creativity. Enter into the conversation, share your ideas, perform with the group, but spare yourself the burden of having to "make it work." It works, the group works, enjoy it.

Here is an outline for the whole module:

Part I (1 hour and 15 minutes)

- Introduction (15 minutes)
- Guided Reflection (15 minutes)
- Small-Group Work (45 minutes)

Part II (From 2-3 hours, depending on group size)

- Finishing touches and rehearsal for "performance" by Small Groups (1 hour)
- Communication from each group to the plenary (up to 10 minutes per small group)

The Small-Group Work mentioned above will be assigned in the plenary. The assignments:

1) Share your images with one another, each person taking about 3 minutes.
2) Building on the sharing, identify points of *convergence* toward a worldview held in common. Let a corporate image or feeling begin to emerge.
3) How will you communicate that worldview to the whole group without using words? (By now, you should know when this will happen in the schedule.) Note that mime, drama, dance, comedy, charade are all possibilities for communication. The sky's the limit!

Celebrating life
when death is the
norm
is to be a
community of
resistance.

Sojourners Community

At this stage the reader knows that *Tales of the Heart* sets out to create a fruitful space where the earth community's longing for oneness may ripen.

Worship centers and grounds the whole.

Woven through the time, it allows for ritually acting-out, affirming, celebrating the wisdom of our own and other faith-filled traditions. Reading, song, silence, and action mark these moments, enhancing their Sabbath character.

Body, mind, and spirit attend. The unique gift of each finds its place in liturgy that longs for wholeness. Here, as elsewhere in the seminar, we enlarge our capacity for mending the torn. Fabric rent (body from spirit) by our dividing culture is rejoined. Rejoice!

We connect in Word and Bread to the Body of Christ globally. Music, bell, candle, incense, silence, often define and bless the circle of praise, reminding us of its sacredness and our own.

Ritual is the primordial human way of affirming the continuity of past and future. Gesture, word, posture, clothing, action, calendar, story all combine to remember and to imagine, to memorialize and to anticipate.

The seminar gratefully marks the global vision and character of the ecumenical movement, often welcoming partners from other nations as witnesses and concelebrants. What a superb environment for prayerful concern about "the whole inhabited earth," "the household of God."

In seminar worship we practice Sabbath. We practice compassion for ourselves and for the earth community. We resist submission to the drivenness so characteristic of our time, ". . . trusting that we are held, even when we do not tightly hold."

Three worship outlines follow. They have graced dozens of *Tales* events. Two pages each, they lend themselves to duplication. Special notes on their use, and on the crafting of all worship follow on page 125.

The Worship of God is not a rule of safety, it is an adventure of the Spirit. . . .

Without the high hope of adventure, religion degenerates into a mere appendage of a comfortable life.

Alfred North Whitehead

A PRAYER TO HUMANKIND

- Song-learning
- Call to Worship
- Opening Song
- Selections from "A Prayer to Humankind" (Chief Medicine Story, Wampanoag Nation):

Reader I: Hear O Humankind, the prayer of my heart.
Are we not one?
Have we not one desire,
to heal our Mother Earth,
to bind her wounds?

Reader II: Are we not all sisters and brothers?
Are we not all grandchildren of the same mystery?
Do we not all want to love and be loved?
Do we not want to work and play, and sing,
and dance together?

Leader: May we live forever
All: May we live forever
Leader: In Jesus' name
All: In Jesus' name

Leader: As with one desire
All: As sister and brother
Leader: Together as one
All: May we live forever.

Reader I: But we live in fear
Fear that is hate
Fear that is mistrust,
and envy and greed . . .
Fear that is anger
and cruelty, loneliness
and bitterness.

Reader II: We live in fear that is love, twisted
and turned back on itself.
Love denied and love rejected.

Leader: In Jesus' name we pray: let us love forever.

All: May we love forever in Jesus' name.

Reader I: Hear my heart's prayer, O Humankind!
Life is the only treasure.
We are the custodians of it.
It is our sacred trust.
Life is wondrous, awesome, and holy.
Life is burning glory
And its price is simply this: Courage.
We must be brave enough to love.

- A visual reflection

  "Child of the Universe"
  (the repeating refrain in this sung version of "Desiderata" is:

  You are a child of the universe,
  No less than the trees and the stars:
  You have a right to be here.
  And whether or not it is clear to you,
  No doubt the universe is unfolding as it should.)

- Silent reflection

- Litany of the Earth Community

  Share aloud concerns we bring to this time and place.
  Response: "In Jesus' name we pray."

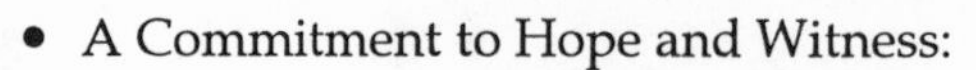

- A Commitment to Hope and Witness:

I: We, who grieve over the loss of lives
in South Africa, the Middle East, Colombia, our inner cities.
We, who are appalled by the death of children
by abuse and murder,
We, who live in the shadow of destruction,
today declare our hope in the future!

II: Sustained by the faith of our fathers and mothers,
and by the dreams of our children,
We renew our belief in the holiness of life,
and the transforming power of God.

I: We affirm that our earth's security rests
not in armaments and economic superiority, but
In the justice of adequate housing and food,
In the justice of meaningful education and work,

II: In the justice of a world order that gives everyone
a share in the earth's abundance.
In the justice of human relationship
nourished by cooperation and caring.

I: We choose struggle rather than indifference.
II: We choose to share the suffering rather than ignore the pain.
I: We choose to make peace rather than wait for war.
II: We choose to proclaim the Good News rather than sit in silence.

All: We unite with sisters and brothers the world over
to resist the powers which dehumanize and destroy people
created in the image of God.

Leader: God sets before us this day Life and Death

All: We choose life—that all may live!

- Closing Song

From *Tales of the Heart*, Hampson/Whalen, Friendship Press, 1991.

The Mountains are Calling

- Song-learning
- Call to worship

Creator God,
as spiritual beings,
we experience earth's suffering
as our own.
Earth is not apart from us.
Our skin is not a dividing membrane
but a permeable membrane,
through which earth events
and those of our inner life
flow one into the other.

Be with us as we quiet and center,
as we re-member again,
"How wholly infused
is this one big word of love
we call the world"!

May your Spirit hover, as we pray.

Song: Creation's God, We Humbly Pause (Dykes/Abbott)

Reading: A Winter's Evening (Berry/MacGillis)

Response:

From "Something Which Is Known," Gregory Norbet, O.S.B., Weston Priory, The Benedictine Foundation of the State of Vermont, Inc.

Reading: Mountains are Calling—John Muir

Response: Brief silent reflection, then brief sharing in pairs on "I mourn this loss (name one) from creation's wealth. And commit to this one small gain . . ."

Litany: Litany of the Circle—Chief Seattle (Standing in a circle)

Closing Song: God of This Great Creation—O'Driscoll/Strathdee

"The whole wilderness seems to be alive and familiar, full of humanity. The very stones seem talkative, sympathetic, sisterly. No wonder when we consider that we all have the same Father and Mother.

Nature is ever at work building and pulling down, creating and destroying, keeping everything whirling and flowing, allowing no rest but in rhythmical motion, chasing everything in endless song out of one beautiful form into another.

Isn't it wonderful how completely everything in wild nature fits into us, as if truly part and parent of us. The sun shines not on us but in us. The rivers flow not past, but through us, thrilling, tingling, vibrating every fiber and cell of the substance of our bodies, making them glide and sing. The trees wave and the flowers bloom in our bodies as well as our souls, and every bird song, wind song, and tremendous storm song of the rocks in the heart of the mountains is our song, our very own, and sings our love.

Listen to them! How wholly infused is this one big word of love we call the world! Is it any surprise that when we try to pick out anything by itself, we find it hitched to everything else in the Universe?"

Essay by Larry Windslow, using the words of nature mystic John Muir (1838-1914) who founded the Sierra Club, preserved Yosemite Park and birthed the national park system.

From *Tales of the Heart*, Hampson/Whalen, Friendship Press, 1991.

*In the dark of moon, in flying snow, in the dead of winter, war spreading, families dying, the world in danger, I walk the rocky hillside sowing clover.**

A winter's evening, fingering packages of seeds. Hard as stones. Old as the first seed. I lay seeds across the wooden table, muted tones, varied shapes, altogether understated wrappings for the universe inside. I finger seeds like prayer beads, connecting me to Mystery; connecting me to life, to hope, to the barest promise I have known, ancient as this journey round the sun.

We must "walk the rocky hillside sowing clover". . . we must. Each of us, in spite of the dark or danger, we must pocket our seeds and go out into the night. It is where we claim the significance of our lives. In spite of everything that would reduce our power, we must sow our seeds, build our families, dignify our work, enflesh our dreams and keep our promises. We must make bread, vigils, petitions, laws, friendships, treaties, babies, dances and worship. We must believe that the darkest aspects of our humanness contain the seeds of transformation. We must resist our lack of hope, our loss of fire. We must finger our very lives and times as prayer beads, sow them on the rocky hillside. The equinox holds promises for the rest. It is the faithful face of Holy Mystery. We edge toward it, eyes awake.

---

*Wendell Berry, "February 2, 1968," from *Farming: A Handbook*, 1970, Harcourt Brace Jovanovich, N.Y.

Miriam Therese MacGillis is director of Genesis Farm and a trustee of Global Education Associates.

Miriam Therese MacGillis

Sabbath and Hope . . .

a time of worship

- Song-learning
- Sung Call to Worship: How I Have Longed
- First Reading: Thomas Merton
  Sung Response: Hosea, Verse 2

  Second Reading: "Celebration and World Order" by Mary Bouchard
  Sung Response: Hosea, Verse 1

  Third Reading: Exodus, II Corinthians, Abraham Heschel
  Sung Response: Hosea, Verses 2 & 3
- Storytelling: This will be a time of silence, and shared "stories of hope and Sabbath."

  A time to remember silently & aloud the desires & dreams, the sufferings/events of our lives where hope is establishing itself & Sabbath is made real.
- Summary Prayer: Standing in a circle with hands joined.
- Closing Song: "Live Into Hope" (Truro)

". . . there is a treasure in my storehouse: Sabbath is her name."

Abraham Heschel

SABBATH READINGS

FIRST READING

There is a pervasive form of contemporary violence to which the idealist fighting for global justice and peace by non-violent methods most easily succumbs: activism and over work. the rush and pressure of modern life are a form, perhaps the most common form, of its innate violence. To allow oneself to be carried away by a multitude of conflicting concerns, to surrender to too many demands, to commit oneself to too many projects, to want to help everyone in everything is to succumb to violence. The frenzy of activists neutralizes their work for justice and peace. It destroys the fruitfulness of work, because it kills the root of inner wisdom which makes work fruitful. (Thomas Merton, *The Hidden Ground of Love: The Letters of Thomas Merton*. William Shannon, ed., Farrar, Straus, Giroux, NY, 1985.)

SECOND READING

Hope is the intuition that imagination is more real and reality less real than it looks. It is the hunch that the overwhelming brutality of facts that oppress and repress is not the last word. (Rubem Alves, *Brazil, Tomorrow's Child*. Harper & Row, NY, 1972.)

Hope is not something we happen to have when we are feeling good. Hope is something we do. This is the point of the Sabbath or holy day. Persons without hope cannot easily pause from work for celebration because those persons see human action as absolute. They feel themselves alone in the universe rather than as part of the whole picture of inter-energized beings. When the project seems beyond their own capacity (which it is) they become paralyzed and cannot act at all. (Mary Alban Bouchard. From "Celebration and World Order," *Whole Earth Papers, No. 15*. Global Education Associates, 1980.)

THIRD READING

Remember the Sabbath Day, to keep it holy. Six days you shall labor and do all your work, but the seventh day is a Sabbath unto the Lord your God. (Exodus 20:8)

When the time came for me to show you favor, I heard you. When the day arrived for me to save you, I helped you. Listen! This is the hour to receive God's favor. Today is the day to be saved. (II Cor. 67:2)

The seventh day is a time of rest: not so much to recover lost strength and so to become fit for labor, rather it is a time for the SAKE OF LIFE.

All your life is a pilgrimage to the seventh day.

Sabbath truth, is that we can afford to rest and work with eyes steadily open, trusting that we are held even when we do not tightly hold. A more sane rhythm of life then is possible, one that meshes Sabbath and ministry, rather than desperate achievement and escape. (Abraham Heschel, *The Sabbath*. Farrar, Straus, Giroux, NY, 1975.)

* *"How I Have Longed" is available in the collection* Joy Is Like the Rain, *by Miriam Therese Winter; cassette, LP or sheet music; Medical Mission Sisters, 92 Sherman St., Hartford, CT 06105. Also in Tales music section.*

From *Tales of the Heart*, Hampson/Whalen, Friendship Press, 1991.

Notes on Three Previous Rituals

You've already encountered three orders of worship that are complete in themselves. The notes on each below might be helpful to contextualize and detail them, as you set out to use them.

All good liturgy and ritual that has power to change is filled with metaphor.

Nelle Morton

I. Prayer to Humankind: We typically use this as an opening on the first seminar evening. It is fairly brief (20-30 minutes), bringing together Native American wisdom, global concerns, care for ourselves, and positive images of the human family. It touches many of the themes elaborated on as the gathering moves forward.

After the four-minute video *Child of the Universe,* (see ***Resources***: **A-V's**) leave the room in darkness, and indicate aloud to the group a short period of reflection. Say slowly aloud (in the style of a guided meditation):

> "We take a moment to notice and be present to the feelings evoked in us by the images we've just seen. We allow the feelings time, letting them file by. Acknowledge them. Welcome them. Bless them as a source of our power. We savor them in this silence."

After about two minutes of silence, move on to initiate the *Litany of the Earth Community.* Then, *A Commitment to Hope and Witness,* is read in two choirs—a simple division of the group, indicated by Roman numerals.

You'll need readers. Opening and closing music, as well as the *Call to Worship* are of your choosing.

II. Sabbath and Hope: "Hope is not something we happen to have . . . it is something we do." This worship closes the module **Theologos,** but can also be used in a variety of other settings. The heart of it is responsive reading and song, as you will see. Our experience is that it resonates deeply with those in the struggle for global justice and peace.

Decide whether you prefer the *Call to Worship* to be a solo, or a song of the whole community. The closing prayer in the circle can be spontaneous, gathering themes of what has gone before. You'll need readers. Urge them to leave generous periods of silence between the sung response and the next reading.

III. The Mountains are Calling: "How wholly infused is this one big word of love we call the world". (John Muir) A brief gem of worship (perhaps 30 minutes) to be savored both musically and textually. Delight in it!

You'll need readers. Point out to them the poetic quality of the texts, urging them to prepare and proclaim slowly and with the thoughtfulness the texts deserve. Enjoy (as we repeat below) the song-learning as a part of the ritual. A dimension of entering and welcoming the unknown. A work of peacemaking. Note particularly the lovely descant for the Alleluia. Easily learned. We work toward a harmonious world.

Craft a brief setting-of-tone for the reflection and sharing in pairs. Perhaps lead a spontaneous communal prayer to close it. You'll need to copy the *Litany of the Circle* for everyone (found in **Coming to Our Senses**, graphic #20). A wonderful gift for all to carry away.

. . . We must be loved into roundness, where apart is spelled a part and the call is to the gathering.

For God has called a People, not "them and us."

"Them and Us" are unable to gather around, for at a roundtable there are no sides. And ALL are invited to wholeness and to food. . . .

Roundtabling means no preferred seating, no first and last, no better, and no corners for "the least of these."

Roundtabling means being with, a part of, together, and one.

It means room for the spirit and gifts and disturbing profound peace for all. . . .

Chuck Lathrop.

Details: Crafting Worship's Sacred Time

- **Include song-learning** at the opening of worship, naming this time and effort part of our ritual, part of our commitment to the healing of the earth community. Underscore this openness to something new, risk-taking, harmonization and teamwork-in-praise as a metaphor for much that our activism entails. It is all one.

- **Prepare the worship space** with care before each ritual. The casting of the sacred circle, even if as simple as straightening the chairs you've been using, is a sign of specialness, a marking of time and place, a centering of expectation and attention. No matter the season, add a touch of nature, an open Scripture, a bit of color or fabric. If the latter brings a distant corner of the globe closer, so much the better. The seminar is a conscious quest for beauty and truth in the web of life.

- If using **audio-visuals**, have them cued up for smooth transitions. Persons handling the projector and lights for you will be valued partners. You'll need to spend preparation time with them. Care for detail immeasurably enhances the contemplative time you seek in worship.

- Insure **inclusivity of language and leadership.** The seminar and its rituals can model the just world we work toward. A reading or prayer in another language, perhaps with a paraphrased translation, can powerfully remind of the world's wideness.
- **Work with readers,** starting with an early recruitment. Urge them to be familiar with the reading and to proclaim it from a standing position, either at their place or from a central point. Agree to allow at least thirty seconds between one segment of the ritual and the next. Let a broad rhythm establish itself.
- **A moment of prayer** between you and the other leadership, that you be conduits of God-presence in the ritual's unfolding, will open and center you. Be thankful for the privilege of preparing, presiding at, and enabling prayer.
- **Introduce each worship** with an economy of words, stating the focus and intent of the time. Perhaps this can be done as part of the call to worship, as you place yourself and the group in God-presence, naming the particular longing/learning of that graced moment.

Below, we collect the words, songs, and actions of sisters and brothers around the world. They are clue and suggestion only. Browse freely. Choose. Mix and match. Use them for your own reflection. Weave into the sacred moments of your particular seminar these strands from other sources.

The peculiar grace of a Shaker chair is due to the fact that it was made by someone capable of believing that an angel might come and sit on it.

Thomas Merton

Calls to Worship

God of all the earth
giver of life and nurture

Entice us to full presence
in this sacred time and place.

Make of us a Sabbath people
resting in you
letting go into your wholeness
rejoicing in your Holy companionship.

Accompany now our praise and prayer
our silence and song,
our breaking of the bread of our lives,
our questing after a community of candor.

Reveal us to ourselves,
as we open our hearts to you.

May your Spirit hover
over these blessed and waiting waters.
May it be so.

* * * * *

God of all peoples
We gather here and claim your presence.

Be with us, faithful to that ancient promise.
Re-mind us, with the Buddhist poet,
that "we need in our time
to hear the sound of the earth
crying."

Help us now celebrate
the earth community
in its brokenness and brilliance
in its desolation and hope
in its pain and in its promise.

Enhance our healing power:
within and among ourselves
within and among the nations.

Enhance our capacity to see the two as one.

* * * * *

Never before has the church experienced such priority to witness to the global dimension of its life.

C. Dean Freudenberger
School of Theology at Claremont

God of passion
and com-passion
be with us as we rekindle our own.

Enter with us a time of learning
a time of listening and feeling
a time of welcoming our weariness,
promising respite to flagging energies.

Empower us anew.

From the open arms of the cross
re-mind us of power as vulnerability.

Open and re-open us.

From the perspective of death
hold forth life,
Re-seeding in us that paradox as birthright.

* * * * *

Life-giving God,
Mother and Father of all creation,

We gather in this place
to exercise ourselves
in going beyond the familiar.

We trust your accompaniment
as we risk working at our edge,
confessing our hopes, our dark despairs.
Be with us on this Way and in this Truth.

Let us deeply attend to the words we now share,
the silence we now allow,
the song to which we now give voice.

May their treasured and familiar truth
now enter us anew. Heart and mind.

Seekers, with you,
of abundant life for peoples everywhere,
we proclaim, we entrust ourselves and these labors
to God-with-us. May it be so.

Readings

What is hope? It is the insight that **imagination is more real and reality less real than it looks**. It is the hunch that the overwhelming brutality of facts that oppress and repress is not the last word.

The two, suffering and hope, live from each other. Suffering without hope produces resentment and despair. Hope without suffering creates illusions, naivete, and drunkenness.

Let us plant dates, even though those who plant them will never eat them. . . . **We must live by the love of what we will never see.** This is the secret discipline. It is a refusal to let the creative act be dissolved away in immediate sense experience, and a stubborn commitment to the future of our grandchildren.

Such disciplined love is what has given prophets, revolutionaries, and saints the courage to die for the future they envisaged. They make their own bodies the seed of their highest hope.

Rubem Alves, Brazilian,
Tomorrow's Child

Deeply spiritual persons experience the suffering in the world as their own suffering. The world is not something apart from them. Their skin is not a dividing membrane that separates them from the world but a permeable membrane, through which events of the world and events of their inner life flow into one another.

Patricia Mische,
co-founder of Global Education Associates

If the Earth were only a few feet in diameter, floating a few feet above a field somewhere, people would come from everywhere to marvel at it. People would walk around it, marveling at its big pools of water, its little pools and the water flowing between the pools. People would marvel at deep rich soil on it, and they would marvel at the very thin layer of gas surrounding it and the water suspended in the gas. The people would marvel at the creatures walking around the surface of the ball, and at the creatures in the water. The people would declare it as sacred because it was the only one and they would protect it so that it would not be hurt. The ball would be the greatest wonder known, and people would come to pray to it, to be healed, to gain knowledge, to know beauty and to wonder how it could be. People would love it, and defend it with their lives because they would somehow know that their lives, their own roundness, could be nothing without it. If the Earth were only a few feet in diameter.

Miriam Therese MacGillis,
Genesis Farm, New Jersey

The biblical vision of creation, covenant, and community, as well as the summons to discipleship, unfolds under the tension between promise and fulfillment. The whole bible is spanned by the narratives of the first creation (Gn.1-3) and the vision of a restored creation at the end of history (Rev. 21:14). Just as creation tells us that God's desire was one of wholeness and unity between God and the human family and within this family itself, the images of a new creation give hope that enmity and hatred will cease and justice and peace will reign (Is. 11:6; 25:1–8). Human life unfolds "between the times," the time of the first creation and that of a restored creation (Rom. 8:18–25). Although the ultimate realization of God's plan lies in the future, **Christians in**

union with all people of good will are summoned to shape history in the image of God's creative design, and in response to the reign of God proclaimed and embodied by Jesus.

U.S Catholic Bishops'
Pastoral on the Economy

Real criticism begins in the capacity to grieve because that is the most visceral announcement that things are not right. Only in the empire are we pressed and urged and invited to pretend that things are all right—either in the dean's office or in our marriage or in the hospital room. And as long as the empire can keep the pretense alive that things are all right, there will be no real grieving and no serious criticism.

Walter Brueggemann,
The Prophetic Imagination

I have great hope in humanity. Every day I am more respectful for what humans can do. It is a tremendous species. We have a special purpose, an incredible destiny in the universe. I would throw in my gauntlet for the human species at anytime. I will never give up. It is a magnificent adventure, probably one of the greatest in the universe and we must succeed. **I would therefore beg you to feel proud to be human,** and to do everything in your power in thousands of ways and through thousands of people you meet in life, through your letters, through what you say, to contribute your personal health, consciousness, peace and happiness to the health, peace and spiritual transcendence of the proud human race.

Robert Mueller,
Healing Ourselves and
Healing Our Planet

Like Jesus, we are called to a radical activity of love, to a way of being in the world that deepens relation, embodies and extends community, passes on the gift of life.

Like Jesus, we must live out this calling in a place and time where the distortions of loveless power stand in conflict with the power of love.

We are called to confront, as Jesus did, that which thwarts the power of human personal and communal

becoming, that which twists relationship, which denies human well-being, community, and human solidarity to so many in our world.

Beverly Harrison,
"The Power Of Anger In The Work Of Love,"
Making the Connections

The focal point of early Christian self-understanding was not a holy book or cultic rite, not mystic experience and magic invocation, but **a set of relationships:** the experience of God's presence among one another and through one another.

God's presence is found in **"the midst of us"** (Luke 17:21). Christian spirituality means eating together, sharing together, drinking together, talking with each other, receiving each other, **experiencing God's presence through each other,** and in doing so, proclaiming the gospel as God's alternative vision for everyone . . . especially for those who are poor, outcast, and battered.

Elizabeth Schüssler Fiorenza,
In Memory of Her

We shan't get anywhere with hatred. We have so much work to do on ourselves that we shouldn't be thinking of hating our so-called enemies. Every atom of hate that we add to this world makes it still more inhospitable.

Against every new outrage and every fresh horror we shall put up one more piece of love and goodness, drawing strength from within ourselves. We may suffer but we must not succumb.

That's when you said: "But that's nothing but Christianity."

And I retorted quite cooly, amused by your confusion: "Yes. Christianity. And why ever not?"

Etty Hillesum,
An Interrupted Life,
A Jewish woman from Holland,
perished at Auschwitz, November 1943.

The church's good name is not a matter of being on good terms with the powerful. The church's good name is a matter of knowing that the poor regard the church as their own, of knowing that the church's life on earth is to call on all, the rich included, to be converted and be saved alongside the poor, for they are the only ones called blessed.

Oscar A. Romero
Archbishop of El Salvador

In our African language we say "a person is a person through other persons." I would not know how to be a human being at all except I learned this from other human beings. **We are made for a delicate network of relationships,** of interdependence. We are meant to complement each other. All kinds of things go horribly wrong when we break that fundamental law of our being. Not even the most powerful nation can be completely self-sufficient.

The fulfillment of God's dream for human beings happens in the new dispensation when we are incorporated in Christ where "there is neither Jew nor Gentile, slave nor free, male nor female, but we are all one in Christ."

. . . There can be no true liberation that ignores the question raised by the movement for the liberation of women.

White South Africans are not demons. White South Africans are ordinary human beings. Most of them are very scared human beings. My flock is black, my flock is white. One has got to say to all our people, "I love you, I care for you enormously." And when I care about black liberation, it is because I care about white liberation."

Words of Desmond Tutu,
compiled by Naomi Tutu

The natural world is subject as well as object. The natural world is the maternal source of our being as earthlings and the life-giving nourishment of our physical, emotional, aesthetic, moral, and religious existence. **The natural world is the larger sacred community to which we belong.** To be alienated from this community is to become destitute in all that makes us human. To damage this community is to diminish our own existence.

Thomas Berry,
Dream of the Earth

THE LAST STORY

LEADER And so the time comes when all the people of the earth
can bring their gifts to the fire
and look into each other's faces
unafraid . . .
See us come from every direction
from the four quarters of the earth
See the lines that stretch to the horizon
the procession, the gifts borne
see us feed the fire
Feel the earth's life renewed
And the circle is complete again
and the medicine wheel is formed anew
and the knowledge within each one of us
made whole . . .

A We say we remember
a time when we were free
We say
that we are free, still, and always
And the pain we feel
is that of labor
And the cries we hear
are those of birth . . .

B Go to the stream, kneel down, drink the sweet water
As you can anywhere water runs in this world
For it runs clean; and breathe the clear air
And know that there was a time
When the waters and the very air itself
`Were poisoned and the people died

ALL We remember that time

A Look around the circle, look at our faces
Each one different, each special
And we so love the hue of our different skins
And the carved planes of our faces
And our beautiful hair, like moss, like water
But there was a time
When people feared each other
And hated what they saw in different eyes

ALL We remember that time

B And look up into the sky, see the stars, see the moon
Know that there is nothing in the sky
To threaten or harm you
But there was a time
When we were all targets
And we didn't know, from one day to the next
When the bombs might come
Whether we would have a world to leave to you

ALL We remember that time . . .

LEADER Look at the old ones
See the power in those old eyes and frail, cupped hands
Breathe it in
Know it is your own power, too
You are of them
They live in you as you in them
and you marvel at them
How did they survive?
How did they stand it?
They wait
You realize they are waiting for you
and you wonder what it is they want you to do
And you think maybe they want you to ask them
something
So you say
Tell me, old ones
How did you do it?
How did you change our world?
And they smile

Listen
Hear what they say to you

A We struggled
B We held out our hands and touched each other
A We remembered to laugh
B We went to endless meetings
A We said no
B We put our bodies on the line

A	We said yes
B	We invented, we created
A	We walked straight through our fears
B	We formed the circle
A	We danced
ALL	We spoke the truth We dared to live it

Miriam Simos, Adapted from Truth or Dare

Suggested Scriptural Passages

The church in America doesn't have to decide whether it is going to engage in subversive activity. What the church in America really has to decide is whether it's going to read the Bible.

Walter Brueggeman

Exodus 12–13:10 - the Passover
Exodus 16–17:7 - manna, meat, and water in the wilderness
Deuteronomy 8 - do not forget that Yahweh brought you out of Egypt
Deuteronomy 10:14-19 - the Lord secures justice
Deuteronomy 15:1-11 - sabbatical year
Deuteronomy 24:10-22 - doing justice
Isaiah 25:6-10 - the Kingdom as a feast
Isaiah 55:1-2 - come to the table, without paying
Isaiah 58:1-10 - the fast that is pleasing to God
Isaiah 61:1-3 - sent to bring good news to the poor (see also Lk. 4:16-22)
Isaiah 65:11-25 - a new heaven and a new earth (see also Rev. 21:1-4)
Micah 4:1-7 - they shall beat swords into plowshares (see also Is. 2:2-5)
Amos 5:21-24 - let justice roll down like waters
Matthew 5:1-10 - the beatitudes (see also Lk. 6:20-25)
Matthew 14:15-21; 15:32-39 - feeding the multitudes (see also Mk. 6:31-44; 8:1-9, Lk. 9:10-17, Jn. 6:1-14)
Matthew 25 - parables of the last judgment
Luke 1:46-55 - Mary's song
Luke 3:9-11 - preaching of John the Baptist
Luke 10:25-37 - the good Samaritan
Luke 12:13-21 - the rich fool
Luke 12:32-48 - to whom much has been given, much will be required
Luke 16:19-31 - Lazarus and the rich man
Luke 24:13-35 - Christ is recognized in the breaking of bread
Acts 2:42-47, 4:32 - sharing in the early church
1 Corinthians 11:17-33 - selfishness in the Christian assembly
2 Corinthians 8:7-15 - a question of equality
2 Corinthians 9:6-15 - he gives freely and frees us to give

James 2:14-17, 26 - faith without works is dead
1 John 3:17-18, 4:7-5:2 - loving in deeds, not just in words

Bread for the World Educational Fund

Prayers

Oh our Mother the Earth, Oh our Father the Sky,
Your children are we, and with tired backs
We bring you the gifts that you love.
Then weave for us a garment of brightness;

May the warp be the white light of morning,
May the weft be the red light of evening,
May the fringes be the falling rain,
May the border be the standing rainbow.

Thus weave for us a garment of brightness
That we may walk fittingly where birds sing,
That we may walk fittingly where the grass is green,
Oh our Mother the Earth, Oh our Father the Sky.

Translation from Songs of the Tewa
by Herbert J. Spinden.

You know, O God,
how hard it is to survive captivity without any hope of the Holy City.
Sing to us, God, the songs of the promised land.
Serve us your manna in the desert,
and give us grace to enjoy your day of rest
as an expression of our trust.

Let there be, in some place,
a community of men, women, elderly, children and new born babies
as a first fruit, as our appetizer,
and an embrace of the future. Amen.

Rubem A. Alves, Brazilian,
With All God's People (WAGP)

Bakerwoman God,
I am your living bread.
Strong, Brown, Bakerwoman God,
I am your low, soft and being-
shaped loaf.
I am your rising bread, well-kneaded
by some divine and knotty pair of
knuckles, by your warm earth-hands.
I am bread well-kneaded.

Put me in your fire, Bakerwoman God,
put me in your own bright fire.

I am warm, warm as you from fire.
I am white and gold, soft and hard,
brown and round.
I am so warm from fire.

Break me, Bakerwoman God.
I am broken under your caring Word.
Drop me in your special juice in pieces.
Drop me in your blood.
Drunken me in the great red flood.

Self-giving chalice, swallow me.
My skin shines in the divine wine.
My face is cup-covered and I drown.
I fall up in a red pool
in a gold world
where your warm sunskin hand is there
to catch and hold me.
Bakerwoman God, remake me.

Alla Renee Bozarth,
USA Womanpriest: A Personal Odyssey

Litany of Gratitude

L: Let us celebrate our friends and neighbors, men and women whose faith and wisdom have enriched the earth.
(silence)
Seek the truth.
P: Listen to the truth.
L: Love the truth.
P: Serve the truth.
L: Teach the truth.
P: Live the truth.
L: Let us remember with gratitude to God some aspects of the contribution which religions have brought to the lives of the people.

Voice 1: We remember the Jewish people, their life centered in God and God's will. We remember the common heritage of scripture which we share with them.

Voice 2: We remember the rich spiritual traditions of the Hindus; their conviction about the moral laws that rule the universe; the Hindu saints and sages who have dedicated their whole lives in the quest for truth.

Voice 3: We remember Buddhists who follow the Buddha in the path of enlightenment and seek to live a disciplined daily life.

Voice 4: We remember the followers of Confucius and Lao-Tse and their conviction that right relationships between people are the path to wisdom.

Voice 5: We remember Muslims in their total submission to God; in their zeal of devotion and strength of comradeship.

Voice 6: We remember the followers of the religions of Africa; and the Native peoples of the Americas whose religious understanding embraces the whole of life; and all whose religious traditions have enriched the earth and affirmed the sacredness of all creation.

L: We remember Sikhs, Parsis, and many other religious groups who witness to your unsearchable glory and love. Teach us to discern your presence in the midst of all your people.

Adapted from New World Liturgy,
Yohan Devananda, Sri Lanka (WAGP)

Mother God, Father God

LEADER: Mother God,
Father God,
God of our ancestors,
God of our future,

ALL: Living God,
loving God,
God of tradition,
God of surprises,

LEADER: Ebony God,
Great Spirit God,

ALL: God of all people,
God of all cultures,
hear our prayers
of petition
and praise.

Help us understand
and overcome
all attitudes of oppression,
especially within our midst.
Help us broaden
our vision
and widen our tents,
so that plurality
and diversity
determine who we are,
people called
and committed
to a world united
in justice and peace,
now and forever.
Amen.

LEADER: Spirit of power,
time and again
throughout history,
you have anointed
your servants
and sent them on mission:
to speak your word
to the poor,
to heal the sick,
to free captives—
always renewing
the face of the earth
in such a variety of ways
that creation itself
sings of your glory
and the human family
reflects your beauty
in a thousand different ways.

ALL: We pray
that through the power
of his compelling Spirit,
we might know the unity
that is ours:
sisters and brothers
of a common family,
sharing a single home
on this, our earth,
as children of one God.

LEADER: We are a people,

ALL: We are God's people
renewing the face
of the earth.

Adapted from: More Than Words
by J. Schaffran, P. Kozak

Affirmation of Peace and Justice

ALL: I believe in God, who is love and who has given the earth to all people.

I believe in Jesus Christ, who came to heal us, and to free us from all forms of oppression.

I believe in the Spirit of God, who works in and through all who are turned towards the truth.

I believe in the community of faith, which is called to be at the service of all people.

I believe in God's promise to finally destroy the power of sin in us all, and to establish the kingdom of justice and peace for all humankind.

GROUP A: I do not believe in the right of the strongest, nor the force of arms, nor the power of oppression.

GROUP B: I believe in human rights, in the solidarity of all people, in the power of non-violence.

A: I do not believe in racism, in the power that comes from wealth and privilege, or in any established order that enslaves.

B: I believe that all men and women are equally human, that order based on violence and injustice is not order.

A: I do not believe that war and hunger are inevitable and peace unattainable.

B: I believe in the beauty of simplicity, in love with open hands, in peace on earth.

ALL: I do not believe that suffering need be in vain, that death is the end, that the disfigurement of our world is what God intended.

But I dare to believe, always and in spite of everything, in God's power to transform and transfigure, fulfilling the promise of a new heaven and a new earth where justice and peace will flourish.

Adapted from a creed from Indonesia (WAGP)

Leader: O God, we are persons, each of us.

People: We stand alone in history, yet there are others, only a hand's length away, with whom we could join our spirits, to bring into being a soul-force that might spread to many and transform us all.

Leader: Make us aware, O God, of the pain of the world.

People: Help us to hear the cry of the oppressed,

Leader: The poor,

People: The prisoners.

Leader: Make us aware, O God, of the joys of life.

People: Help us to hear the beauty of the earth,

Leader: Of people,

People: Of ourselves.

Leader: O God, help us to listen.

People: For in listening, we will speak our love,

Leader: And by listening

People: We will be moved to act in faith.

Ruth Duck,
Bread for the Journey: Resources for Worship

I salute the light in you.

Hindu greeting

A Prayer for the Church

- Let us pray for deliverance of the church,
  from its own infidelities
  from those who would make the church
  captive to a cause
  from triumphs of messianic success
  from the wrath of its own righteousness
  from images of God that it has made into idols

from the dis-ease of power and privilege
from the delusions of celebrity
from sins of too quickly forgetting,
and of too long remembering.

- Lead us as a church once again into the wilderness:
Pilgrim and penitent, an insecure, wandering
rag-tag remnant,
who have only one Hope.
Tent-makers, at whose hearth
anyone may find a *home*
A people whose midwives
can dance before the altar
or lead a revolution against Pharaoh.
Orphans, who have made a Dwelling
for the Love of God,
where all flesh and creatures of earth
may touch, heal and hallow one another.
A community, where each can be all things
to each.
Ark of our covenant,
in which the dove that is released
and does not return
is a sign of Life.

- Bless this ancient, timbered Ark
wherein we shall survive
- two by two -
or perish in the threatening flood
of chaos and darkness and violence.

- Two by two, we shall live or die,
Jew and Greek, slave and freeman,
male and female,
gay and straight.
Black and white, East and West,
North and South.
Arab and Israeli, Hispanic and Anglo,
the right and the left,
the "haves" and the "have-nots,"
and most of all,
man and woman,
women and men.

- Some may seek the way of Judith,
and behead the oppressive Holofernes,
Others will seek the way of Jacob,
hoping through patience or cunning
to mollify the patriarch.

Some, like Jonah, will run away.
But we are descendants of Paul, too.
Let us meet in Jerusalem, the city of peace.
Let us confront Peter and James,
and our brothers and sisters.
Reconciliation is not some distant reincarnation.
worlds apart, aeons away,
the substance of our hope only.
It is kenosis, and resurrection, here and now,
the fruit of bittersweet, but life-giving struggle.

- Let us pray.
Let us greet each other as saints.
Let us sit down.
(It is difficult if one of us remains standing.)
Let us speak to one another.
Let us hear one another.

Amen.

Madonna Kolbenschlag

God of All People

LEADER Our Mother, our Father . . .
ALL All-merciful, Almighty . . .

LEADER who inspired our forefathers in all they achieved,
ALL who consoled our foremothers for all they were denied,

LEADER blessed is Your power among us,
ALL blessed is Your presence within.

LEADER May we freely and faithfully preach Your word,
ALL and translate that word into visible deeds,

LEADER deeds of justice,
ALL and deeds of mercy,

LEADER feeding and sheltering,
ALL witnessing to peace.

LEADER Help us to follow the right path.
ALL Shape our spirit with Your Holy Spirit,

LEADER a spirit of wisdom and compassion,
ALL an abiding hunger for truth.

LEADER Bless all ministers, clergy and lay,
ALL and our many ministries, ordained and unordained.

LEADER Hasten the day when all are equally valued,
ALL and true mutuality is a hallmark of the Church.

LEADER God of all people,
ALL of women as well as men,

LEADER as You stand by our brothers who are committed to change,
ALL as You strengthen our sisters whose vision brings hope,

LEADER we praise You,
ALL we bless You
we sing of Your glory.

M. T. Winter, Womanprayer, Womansong

Psalm 126

- When the day comes on which our victory
  will shine like a torch in the night,
  it will be like a dream.
- We will laugh and sing for joy.
  Then the other nations will say about us,
  "the Lord did great things for us";
- Indeed, God is doing great things for us;
  that is why we are happy in our suffering.

- Lord, break the chains of humiliation and death,
  just as on that glorious morning
  when you were raised.
- Let those who weep as they sow the seeds of justice and freedom,
  gather the harvest of peace and reconciliation.

- Those who weep as they go out as instruments of your love
  will come back singing with joy.
  As they will witness the disappearance of hate
  and the manifestation of your love in your world.

Paraphrased by Rev. Zephania Kameeta, Deputy Bishop of the Evangelical Lutheran Church of SWA/ Namibia, Why, O Lord? *Kameeta has been imprisoned and tortured for his courageous leadership during the long struggle for freedom in Namibia.*

O, Lord, I do not know what to ask of you. You alone know my true needs. You love me more than I myself know how to love. Help me to see my real needs which are concealed from me. I dare not ask either a cross or consolation. I can only wait on you. My heart is open to you. Visit and help me, for your great mercy's sake. Strike me and heal me, cast me down and raise me up. I worship in silence your holy will and your inscrutable ways. I offer myself as a sacrifice to you. I put all my trust in you. I have no other desire than to fulfill your will. Teach me how to pray. Pray yourself in me.

Metropolitan Philaret of Moscow (1553-1633) - (WAGP)

My Lord God,
We have no idea where we are going.
We do not see the road ahead of us.
We cannot know for certain where it will end.
Nor do we really know ourselves,
and the fact that we think that we are following your will does not mean that we are actually doing so.
But we believe that the desire to please you does in fact please you.
And we hope we have that desire in all that we are doing.
We hope that we will never do anything apart from that desire.
And we know that if we do this,
you will lead us by the right road though we may know nothing about it.
Therefore will we trust you always though we may seem to be lost and in the shadow of death.
We will not fear, for you are ever with us,
and you will never leave us to face our perils alone.

Thomas Merton, Thoughts in Solitude

The blessing of the God of Sarah and Hagar, as of Abraham,
the blessing of the Son, born of Mary,
the blessing of the Holy Spirit who broods over us
as a mother over her children,
be with you all. Amen.

Lois Wilson, Toronto (WAGP)

As the earth keeps turning, hurtling through space;
and night falls and day breaks from land to land;
Let us remember people—people waking, sleeping,
being born, and dying—of one world and of one humanity.
Let us go from here in peace. Amen.

Closing prayer, WCC Assembly, Vancouver (WAGP)

A Blessing

May the Great Spirit send His
Choicest gifts to you;
May the Sun Father and the Moon Mother
Shed their softest beams on you;
May the four winds of Heaven
Blow gently upon you and
Upon those with whom you share
Your heart and home.

Coahuila Nation

RITUAL ACTIONS

It is our experience that simple actions, related to the central message of worship, say much more—more memorably and movingly—than do hundreds of words. Congruent with the kind of learning that the seminar celebrates, an action can embody the theme: be it a learning, a concern, a source of hope or despair, a feeling, a dilemma, a question. Habituate yourselves for these few days, to heightening your symbolic sensitivities. It will widen and reframe your world.

The higher goal of spiritual living is not to amass a wealth of information, but to face sacred moments.

Rabbi Abraham Heschel

Familiar actions that bear new nuances and placement:

- **A greeting of peace:** or, of hope, "May you trust enough to let go into Mystery."; or of solidarity at the Seminar's conclusion; or, of healing of your heaviest burden.
- **A laying-on of hands:** hands on the globe for earth's mending; hands on the shoulders of those on either side of you, that the yoke of our justice task be lightly borne; hands extended in blessing and empowerment over a basket of personal covenant statements at the center of the circle; hands held around a silent circle, signaling our intention toward linking, going beyond our own boundaries, taking risks in community.

- **A eucharistic celebration:**
  - the use of breads, dress, and music from many nations
  - the offering of bread and cup, one person to another
  - a procession with offertory gifts (which might include goals at the beginning of a seminar or conclusions/covenants at the close), a fragment of local nature, a lightweight inflatable globe, an infant child whom a participant may have brought along.

The child should be presented last. The celebrant lays hands on the child's head in silent blessing then, "we offer our intention to labor toward an hospitable world for the nurture of this young life." The infant is returned to his/her place.

Odd how the creative power at once brings the whole universe to order.

Virginia Woolf

- Strike a **particularly beautiful bell** slowly a number of times at the opening and closing of each session, marking your deliberations as a sacred time. Have different participants light one candle at the outset as well. It burns until extinguished at the end of the session. Perform both solemnly-done gestures before an opening prayer/reading. Take time with these moments. Allow them to nourish the group and your work together.

- Assemble a number of **unusual candles** (you might choose to ask participants to bring a favorite of theirs), or a menorah. Design worship around light and darkness, remembering that despite our cultural biases, both light and darkness have life-giving as well as destructive character. Flames can be extinguished one by one as earth losses are mentioned, perhaps echoed with a single drum beat.

- **A Christ Candle:** Depending on what you are trying to illustrate, tapers can be lit from the central pillar, as commitments are made, newness is celebrated, life is shared, empowerment is sought. Silence in a dimly lit room with a brief personal reflection on the lit taper, in the context of the theme, followed by the extinguishing of the flame, shared reflection in and on nurturing qualities of darkness. Darkness of the nourishing womb, of the germinating seed, of the cooling shade, of the waiting dawn, of expectation, of deep sleep, of the learnings of loss, of the unknown

Life in death. As elsewhere in this seminar, push beyond what is familiar. Break through.

- **Forgiveness:** Each mentions on a fragment of paper something needing to be reconciled in them. Fold, collect in a beautiful, yet fireworthy container. At a particular moment of worship, the fragments are burned, blessed (by all), and used as a sign (cross on forehead or palm) of forgiveness and healing. **[Needs careful preparation and a practice run.]**

- **Make paper cranes,** using the story of Sadako (published in *Make a World of Difference* by the Office on Global Education, Friendship Press, 1990). After some hours of "head" activity, this can ground and center our energy. Our folding hands make concrete our commitment to inner and outer peacemaking. Can be an elective prelude to worship, with the cranes incorporated into offering, mime, communion reflection. **[Needs practice, so that you can make and teach with ease.]**

- **"Word-Verbs":** As the group is planning worship, you might spend a few moments reflecting on what you're trying to say in the worship experience and give thought together on ways to wordlessly ritualize that. (An introduction, call to worship, sermon, post-communion reflection, or benediction.)

  An interesting way to proceed, is to choose a fragment of scripture that relates to what the worship focuses on. Ask a group of three to five persons, as their contribution, to spend time considering how they could wordlessly convey that message, that insight of the Christian tradition, to the gathered community, in one to three minutes. Humor is warmly welcomed . . . engaging still another level of our being.

- Perhaps **repeating one of the vignettes** that emerged out of **Exploring Our Worldview** would reinforce one of the more moving seminar moments and learnings as call to worship, Scripture lesson, sermon, offering, creed, benediction, closure.

- Check to see if one of the participants knows **the art of signing for the deaf.** Perhaps teach the whole group the gestures of the signing for a particular song or text. The beautiful movement calls us beyond our normal "boundaries," providing another action/

After the final no
there comes a yes,
And on that yes the
future of the world
depends.

Wallace Stevens

image of reaching across differences, moving from "us" and "them," to "we."

- In the Hindu tradition, a lovely **gesture of greeting and farewell** is incorporated in *Namaste* (pronounced NA-ma-stay), with hands lifted and joined, palms flat in an attitude of prayer, head slightly inclined, so that the tips of the thumbs are at the level of, and a few inches in front of, the eyebrows. The translation of Namaste: **"I salute the light in you."** This provides closure to a worship, when done in a large circle. Each can greet the person to their left *or* right (be clear in these directions, so that no one is omitted and chaos doesn't ensue), and then again face into the whole circle, repeating the greeting. Another of many possibilities: the reader greets the Scripture in this way before commencing.

How easily we slide into thinking of our prayers as the "real" prayer—the grace we say at the table, or the meal that follows it? And if we pray at all times, as we should, our eating and drinking will be prayer. . . . Gratefulness will turn the whole meal into prayer, for after we pray our prayers, we will pray our soup, salad and dessert, and then pray another set prayer at the end as a reminder to continue to pray even after the meal. . . . It is not prayers that count, but prayerfulness.

David Steindl-Rast

In addition to the above special moments, gesture and symbol make their presence felt, as we bring consciousness to EVERY MOVE WE MAKE throughout the Seminar:

- **The arrangement of the chairs:** struggle with space, hoping always for the possibility of a circle. If the room forbids that, try two concentric circles, drawing a lesson from that, perhaps in opening remarks or prayer.

> The circle of love
> is repeatedly broken
> because of the sin
> of exclusion.
> We create separate circles:
> The inner circle
> and the outer circle, the circle of power
> and the circle of despair,
> the circle of privilege
> and the circle of deprivation.
> We carefully define our circles,
> and function,
> not always willingly,
> within their parameters.

Here, you can invite the group to further reflection on the inner and outer circle image, perhaps closing with something that resembles the following:

> As we pray, dream, and struggle
> toward one unbroken circle,

wide-open and welcoming,
let us yet own and bless
this present double circle
as embodiment of our present path and promise.

- Keep a **low round table at the center of your plenary circle.** Ask participants to bring artifacts from their bio-region and to "dress" the table differently each half-day. (Add cloths from other nations, if needed as a base for the natural beauty of the table.) It can contain the candle, the bell, incense, the Scripture, depending on what you're ritualizing in that segment of the seminar.

In summary, use breath and bread, salt and water, earth and art . . . the stuff of our daily, sacred lives. Allow them each to speak through simple use. In combination with text and silence and song, they will image our struggles and breakthroughs, fire our imagination, enhance our ability to transcend ourselves in the crafting of the not-yet-possible: peace with justice.

Ceremonies are the outward expression of inward feeling.

Laotzu, sixth century B.C.
Chinese Philosopher

Sing of a Blessing

**Transpose Verse 4 up one-half step (D♭ Major).*
***Transpose Verse 5 up an additonal half step (D Major).*

WORDS and MUSIC: Miriam Therese Winter

Mother and God

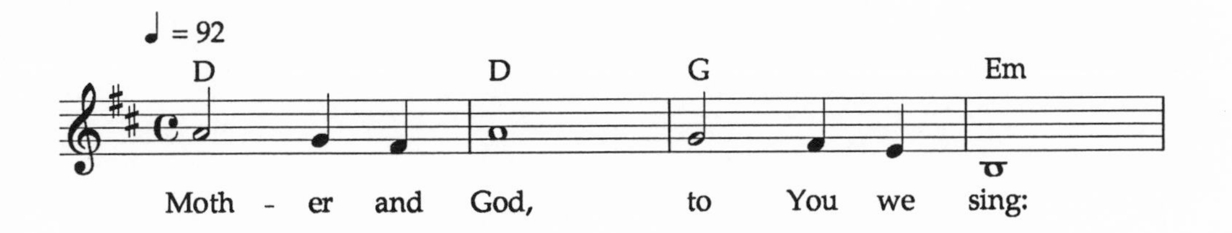

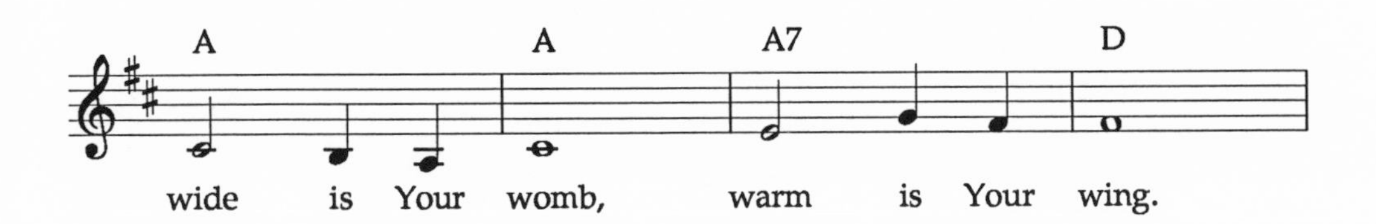

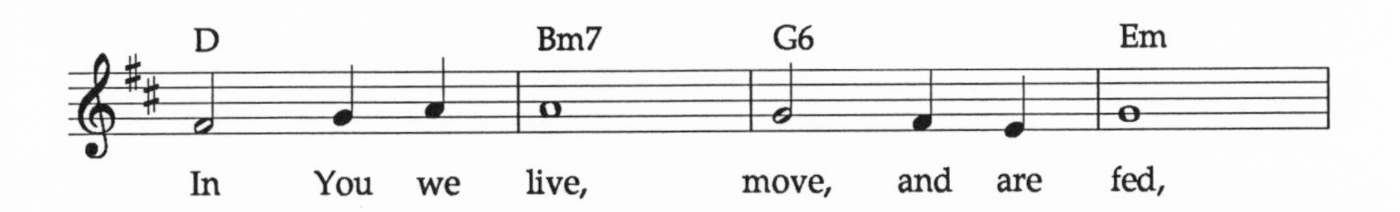

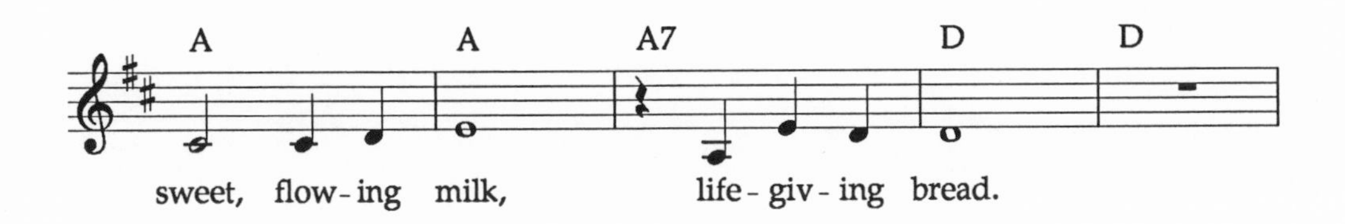

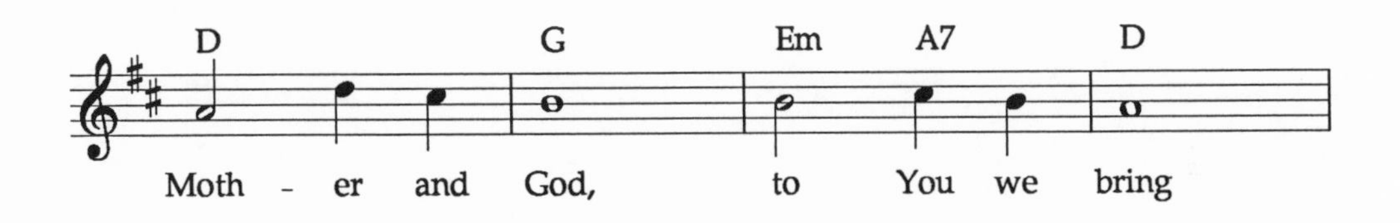

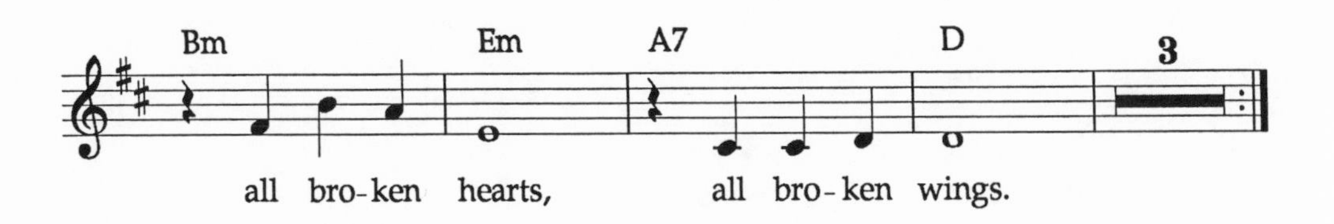

WORDS and MUSIC: Miriam Therese Winter

Blessing Song

WORDS and MUSIC: Miriam Therese Winter

How I Have Longed

WORDS and MUSIC: Miriam Therese Winter

Christ's Partners All Are We

MUSIC: MADRID, Source Unkown; harmonized by David Evans, 1927

Creator God, Creating Still

MUSIC: ST. ANNE, ascribed to William Croft, *Supplement to the New Version*, 1708

Live Into Hope

WORDS: Jane Parker Huber
MUSIC: MADRID, from the *Revised Church Hymnary, 1927,* by permission of Oxford University Press.

Creation's God, We Humbly Pause

WORDS: John W. Abbott
MUSIC: MELITA, John B. Dykes, ca. 1861

Hosea

WORDS: Based on Hosea
MUSIC: Weston Priory and Gregory Norbet, O.S.B.

G G G G
— In - teg - ri - ty ___ and jus - tice ___
G C C G
— with ten - der - ness ___ you shall know. —
G D D Em
— Long have I wait - ed for your com - ing
A G D7 G G
home to me and liv - ing deep - ly our new life. ___
G G G G G
You shall sleep ___ se - cure with peace; —
G C C G G
— faith - ful - ness ___ will be your joy. ___
D D Em A
Long have I wait - ed for your com - ing home to me and
liv - ing deep - ly our new life. ___

God Of This Great Creation

WORDS: Herbert O'Driscoll
MUSIC: Jim Strathdee

F(D)
C(A)
B♭(G)
Dm(Bm)
G(E)
ven - tion; Guide us in skills and arts:
cit - ies, Light - en our shad - owed skies;
boun - ty, Dwell - ing in worlds of need;
al - tar Come with Thy ho - ly fire;
C(A)
Gm7(Em7)
Dm7(Bm7)
E♭(C)
B♭(G)
God who be-queaths such beau - ty, Give us be - liev - ing
God who has made us wealth - y, Make us, we pray thee,
Grant us the grace of giv - ing, Guard us, O God, from
Make us and all things hu - man One with cre - a - tion's
1.-3.
C(A)
Gm7(Em7)
C(A)
Gm7(Em7)
4.
C(A)
hearts.
wise.
greed.
choir.

Dona Nobis Pacem

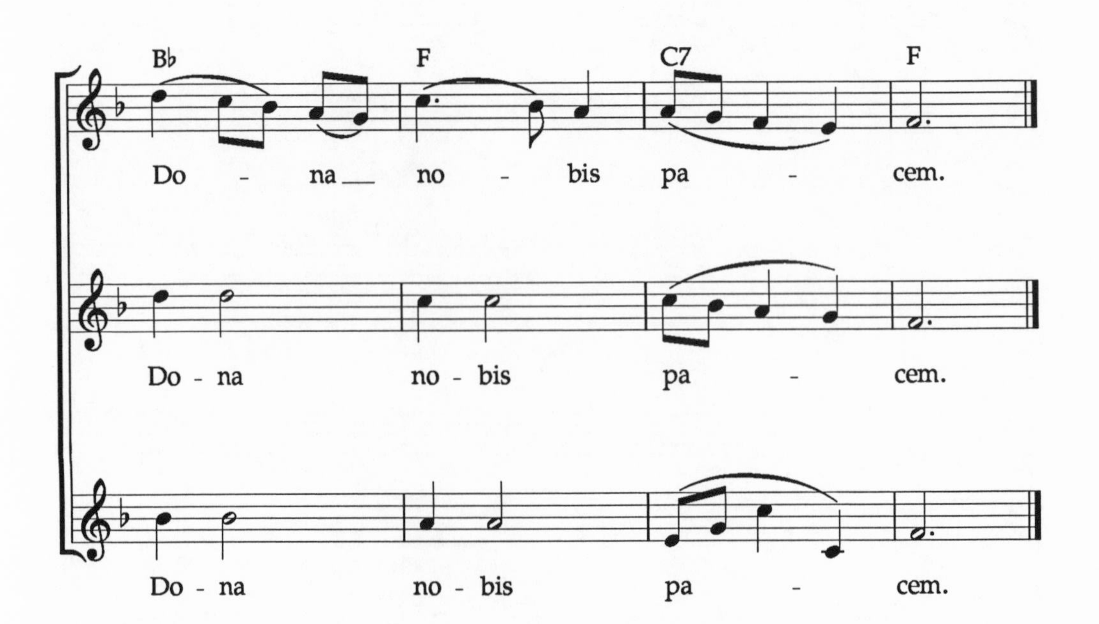

Source Unknown

In Christ There Is No East or West

WORDS: John Oxenham, 1852 - 1941; adapted by Grace Moore, Nancy Krody, and Ruth C. Duck.
MUSIC: McKEE, Negro Melody; adapted by Harry T. Burleigh, 1940

Were You There

5. Were you there when they laid Him in the tomb?
   Were you there when they laid Him in the tomb?
   O! Sometimes it causes me to tremble, tremble, tremble,
   Were you there when they laid Him in the tomb?

6. Were you there when they rolled the stone away?
   Were you there when they rolled the stone away?
   O! Sometimes it causes me to tremble, tremble, tremble,
   Were you there when they rolled the stone away?

WORDS: Afro-American Spiritual
MUSIC: WERE YOU THERE, Afro-American Spiritual

Sung Responses

THE FEAST OF LIFE, THE EUCHARIST AT THE SIXTH ASSEMBLY OF THE WORLD COUNCIL OF CHURCHES, VANCOUVER, 1983 World Council of Churches Publications, P.O.Box 2100, 1211 Geneva 2 Switzerland

Books of Worship Resources

Brinton, Henry G. (editor). *Banquet of Praise: A Book of Worship Resources, Hymns and Songs in the Spirit of Justice, Peace and Food for All.* Washington, D.C.:Bread for the World, 1990.

Carden, John (compiled by). *With All God's People The New Ecumenical Prayer Cycle.* Geneva: World Council of Churches Publications, 1989.

Cunningham, Nancy Brady. *Feeding the Spirit: How to Create Your Own Rites, Festivals and Celebrations.* San Jose, CA: Resource Publications, 1987.

Duck, Ruth C. (edited by). *Bread for the Journey: Resources for Worship.* New York: The Pilgrim Press, 1981.

Gjerding, Iben and Katherine Kinnamon. *No Longer Strangers: A Resource for Women and Worship.* Geneva: World Council of Churches Publications, 1983.

Johnson, Ann. *Miryam of Nazareth, Woman of Strength and Wisdom.* Notre Dame, IN: Ave Maria Press, 1984.

Johnson, Ann. *Miryam of Judah.* Notre Dame, IN: Ave Maria Press, 1987.

Miriam's Sisters Rejoice. Silver Spring, MD: Women's Alliance for Theology, Ethics and Ritual (WATER), 1988. (See Organizations for address.)

Schaffran, Janet, CDP and Pat Kozak, CSJ. *More Than Words: Prayer & Ritual for Inclusive Communities.* Oak Park, IL: Meyer Stone, 1988.

Winter, Miriam Therese. *WomanWord—A Feminist Lectionary and Psalter: Women of the New Testament.* New York: Crossroad, 1990.

Winter, Miriam Therese. *Woman Wisdom—A Feminist Lectionary and Psalter: Women of the Hebrew Scriptures, Part One.* New York: Crossroad, 1991.

Winter, Miriam Therese. *WomanPrayer, WomanSong: Resources for Ritual.* Oak Park, IL: Meyer Stone Books, 1987.

Women-Church Celebrations. Silver Spring, MD: Women's Alliance for Theology, Ethics and Ritual (WATER), 1989, 2nd edition. 8035 13th Street, Silver Spring, MD 20910.

Helpful Background

de Chardin, Teilhard. *Hymn of the Universe.* New York: Harper & Row, 1961.

Fox, Matthew. *Original Blessing.* Santa Fe, NM: Bear & Co., 1986.

Fox, Matthew. *A Spirituality Named Compassion and the Healing of the Global Village, Humpty Dumpty and Us.* Minneapolis, MN:, Winston Press, Inc., 1979.

Simos, Miriam. *Truth or Dare: Encounters with Power, Authority and Mystery.* New York: Harper & Row, 1987.

Organizing a Seminar

When we try
to pick out
something
by itself
we find
it hitched to
everything else
in the
universe.

John Muir

"Never doubt that a small group
of thoughtful, committed citizens
can change the world;
indeed, it's the only thing that ever has."
—*Margaret Mead*

". . . so you say.
Tell me old ones.
How did you do it?
How did you return the world
to a circle without fear?

And they smile

listen
hear what they say to you

We struggled
We held out our hands and touched each other
We remembered to laugh
We went to endless meetings
We said no
We put our bodies on the line
We said yes
We invented, we created
We walked straight through our fears
We formed the circle
We danced

We spoke the truth
We dared to live it."
—*Miriam Simos,* The Last Story

Meetings. Yes.

You have accepted one of the seminar's midwifery tasks. Bringing the whole to birth by giving structure, coherence, order to its myriad details.

Perhaps you're weary of hearing us say in these pages that **the medium is the message.** (There, we said it again!) It means, in this context, that your process together as a group can be a mirror of the kind of world we all work toward. Shared leadership, careful listening to diverse views, valuing time spent in getting to know each other, attention to detail, candor, inclusivity, the courage to do conflict resolution if needed among you, living up to commitments (there are no insignificant ones in group life), outreach across racial and ethnic (perhaps even religious) traditions.

May you enjoy each other and each present moment in this sacred segment of the peacemaking, justice-seeking task.

May you know together the joy of the fruition of your labors.

Having done it often, we know surprising pleasures await you. Blessings on your struggle toward a world that works for all . . . a struggle indeed "hitched to everything else in the universe."

BE PREPARED! Organizing a seminar will require substantial planning time (up to twelve months for a three-day event) and considerable energy. You will need help. A committed group of people working as a team can do it and in the process build community, competence, and new collaboration.

The following planning guide will lead you through the major organizational hurdles. It is divided into three sections:

- A Planning Timeline
- Steps in Organizing a Planning Committee
- Job Descriptions for Five Subcommittees

In the beginning you and two or three others must read this section of the Handbook and agree that a seminar is possible and worthwhile. You form the nucleus of the planning committee.

"Whoa! Are you kidding? This looks like too much work!" This section is long and detailed. It assumes you're planning a two or three-day global education seminar. However, other alternatives exist for employing this material which require substantially less preparation time. The sessions that make up the seminar can be used on their own, as well as in combination. Some alternatives:

Do an individual module (for example, **Coming to Our Senses in a Global Age**) as an element of some other event. Several of these modules have been presented at denominational educational gatherings, mission conferences, and in college and high-school classes.

Do a series of modules over a liturgical season. This is a particularly useful approach for a local church. See end of *Program Subcommittee* for a suggested outline.

Do a prayer service using the worship materials here in a conference or other setting dealing with global issues.

Whatever you can do, or dream you can, begin it. Boldness has genius, power and magic in it.

Johann Goethe

Don't agonize.
Organize.

Florynce Kennedy

Do a shorter seminar. The flexibility of the seminar material allows for a shortened version from a day to a day-and-a-half length. See *Program Subcommittee* for suggested designs. You will still need to organize a Planning Committee, but the number of folks required, as well as preparation time, are reduced. We list a reduced timeline (page 180). Keep in mind the following:

- This model assumes participants will not be staying overnight, significantly reducing cost and allowing for use of local meeting facilities (churches, schools, etc.).
- Because finances are less of an issue, the Logistics Subcommittee can take on these responsibilities. One additional task of this group will be to arrange for lunch and snacks.
- Your Subcommittees may only be one or two persons, but the Subcommittee worksheets will remain useful.
- In a local church setting, a brochure may not be necessary; posters and bulletin inserts may do as well.

These options demand less time, but no less care. Why bother? You're already overextended: who needs one more thing to do? You may be right. You do need to be realistic about what you take on. The country is littered with people committed to peace and justice who are at or near compassion fatigue because they have not mastered that simple, two-letter word "no."

To help you reflect, we summarize some hopes and accomplishments of your predecessors, the committees who planned the pilot seminars.

To explore connections between local and global situations

Each planning committee wished to make participants more aware of how global issues are related to the lives of people in their community. In Iowa, farm organizers talked with African exiles and local peace activists about the links between militarism, the Farm Crisis, and hunger in Africa. In North Carolina, the dynamics of racism in South Africa generated a spirited reflection on race relations in North Carolina. In Rochester, New York, a planning group designed a role-play that engaged refugees, bankers, businesspersons, pastors, and government officials in conversation on their common future. In Montreal, Quebec, women in ministry sought to dialogue with their refugee, ex-convict, and native-Canadian sisters.

To enhance global education skills
Planners wanted to help members of action networks increase their commitment to and skills in global education. In North Carolina, workshops in educational design, conflict resolution, and the use of media helped local Bread for the World groups and CROP Walk committees organize more effective global education events.

To support and nurture local activists
Many planners recognized the need to care for those who care. Attention to worship, reflection time, and experiences that tap the intuitive side of ourselves generated new energy and commitment.

> "[The seminar] awoke a new passion for justice I haven't had in years" (Union Theological Seminary, 1985).
>
> "The seminar raised one's consciousness about the connectedness of us all on this planet, and to start us on the road to sharing that consciousness with other people. It helped me to cope with the pain that is in the world, and to work through that pain to seek answers" (Rochester, NY, 1986).

To promote new collaboration between existing groups
Planners saw this event as a catalyst to spark new action for global peace and justice. Participants in every seminar were invited to caucus together. Sharing ideas, hopes, and plans led to a follow-up seminar led by participants in California, a new CROP walk in Iowa, new support for global education in the public schools of Illinois.

To allow our faith tradition to speak to our global condition
Planning groups felt it essential to sing, pray, and celebrate our hope as people of faith. Use of The Lima Liturgy (companion to the *Baptism, Eucharist, and Ministry* document from the World Council of Churches), as well as worship designed for each seminar, helped us see our hopes and fears for the world in light of God's word and work in the world.

An adventure is an inconvenience rightly considered.

G.K Chesterton

Seminar Timeline

(Note: Subcommittee tasks are to be done before the Planning Committee meeting listed for the month.)

	Planning Committee	Publicity/Recruitment
11 Months Before	Enlist and meet with Committee Establish Subcommittees Brainstorm seminar goals Read Seminar **Organizing** section	
10 Months Before	Finalize goals statement Determine audience/size dates preferred site Set future meeting dates	Develop preliminary suggestions for seminar audience
9 Months Before	Decide on Case Study Subcommittee Reports	Develop strategy for recruitment
8 Months Before	Determine cost/participant Subcommittee Reports Approve design	Check timelines for denominational, ecumenical newsletters, bulletin boards
7 Months Before	Approve resource people for Case Study Review budget Approve brochure Decide on scholarship monies	Design a brochure
6 Months Before		Distribute brochure Place ads in denominational/ecumenical newsletters Phone key inviters

Subcommittee Logistics	Program	Bookstore	Finances
Identify potential Sites	Hone seminar goals Read *Tales of the Heart* - **Introduction, Preface, Chapter Openings** and **Seminar Elements**		Open bank account Develop list of possible donors Brainstorm fund-raising ideas
Confirm reservations at seminar site	Consider possible options for Case Study	Identify bookstore that will sell on consignment	Place deposit on seminar site
	Present proposed design		
	Identify possible resource people for Case Study and other elements of program		Work up a basic budget for event
	Recruit and confirm dates with resource people	Contact resource people for suggested books	Prepare 2-5 Page description of seminar

Seminar Timeline
(continued)

	Planning Committee	Publicity/Recruitment
5 Months Before	Subcommittee reports	Follow-up call to inviters
4 Months Before	Subcommittee reports	2nd mailing of brochures if necessary
3 Months Before	Review registration, finances, program	Mailing to participants with instructions/ directions
1 Month Before		
Event Days		Carry out registration
After Event	Meeting for evaluation and follow-up	

Subcommittee			
Logistics	**Program**	**Bookstore**	**Finances**
Check with resource people on equipment requirements Confirm local logistic needs with seminar site	Order necessary films	Contact bookstore Submit orders	Arrange visit to donors Tally and deposit registration fees
	Design evaluation	Identify local/ international groups whose material you wish to display	
	Identify *Cameo* givers, facilitators		
Copy needed materials			
Setup, hospitality, cleanup	Distribute and collect. Evaluation	Setup and staff bookstore	At Registration Desk collect remaining registration funds
	Summarize evaluation for report to Planning Committee		Prepare Financial Report to Planning Committe Thank you notes to Funders

Reduced Timeline (For 1-1/2 Day Seminar)

(Note: Subcommittee tasks are to be done before the Planning Committee listed for the month.)

Time	Planning Committee	Logistics/ Finance
6 Months Before	Enlist and meet with Committee Establish Subcommittee Brainstorm seminar goals Read Seminar **Organizing** section	
5 Months Before	Finalize goals statement Determine audience /size/dates preferred site Set future meeting dates	Identify possible sites
4 Months Before	Decide on Case Study Approve design Subcommittee reports Determine leadership Agree on cost/person	Confirm site, place deposit Determine cost of event Arrange for food, snacks
3 Months Before		Check with leaders on material needs
2 Months Before	Assessment Reports by Subcommittee	
1 Month Before		Copy needed materials
Event 1 Month After	Meeting for evaluation and follow-up	Prepare Financial Report to Planning Committe

Subcommittee		
Program	**Publicity/ Recruitment**	**Bookstore**
Hone Goals Read *Tales*: **Introduction**, **Preface**, **Chaper Openings**, and **Seminar Elements**	Brainstorm promotion possibilities Check timelines for local denominational, ecumenical newsletters	Identify bookstore Place order
Develop Case Study Identify possible leadership	Begin initial promotion bulletin insiders, etc. Decide on need for brochures, posters, etc.	Contact local groups regarding display of materials
Order needed AV's Confirm dates and responsibilities with leaders	Place add in local newspapers	
Design the evaluation	Mailing to participants: Instructions Advance Reading	
Recruit facilitators *Cameo* givers		
Summarize Evaluation for report to Coordinating Committee		

If these goals speak to your own hopes for your community, then read on to learn the steps required to realize these goals.

TASKS: To initiate the seminar planning process you must do three things:
1. Locate a sponsor.
2. Recruit a planning committee.
3. Host the first planning committee meeting.

The remainder of this chapter will describe how to find a sponsor, create this group, and detail their tasks. Six workgroups will be needed:

The Planning Committee is composed of the chairpersons of the various Subcommittees, the Event Coordinator, and other interested parties. This committee coordinates the planning of the event and makes final decisions.

The Subcommittees will enlist additional individuals for more specialized tasks related to the seminar. The five subcommittees are:

- Publicity/Recruitment
- Logistics
- Program
- Bookstore
- Finances

I will act as if what I do makes a difference.

William James

To give you a sense of the responsibilities of these groups and to describe the overall planning scheme, we begin by looking at the Seminar Planning Timeline (page 176). You will note that the timeline begins with the first Planning Committee meeting, thus assuming you have already been at work.

STEPS IN ORGANIZING A PLANNING COMMITTEE

1. **Know the Process.** "The journey of a thousand miles begins with one step." The process outlined below has been developed over four years, one step at a time. It works. Look carefully at its shape. Before you begin to enlist others you must become familiar with the organizational design yourself. You may decide to modify the steps spelled out here if you are planning a shorter event, but you will need to do the same basic planning.

The meetings of the Planning Committee are themselves opportunities to experience the kinds of awareness and community that is the goal of the event. Following the suggested format will familiarize planners with elements of the seminar, enabling them to feel more confident if they act as leaders during the event.

2. **Enlist a Sponsor.** At least one organization needs to be identified as sponsoring the seminar. The sponsor might be a social action committee, a church, a judicatory task force, a CWS/CROP Committee, or a local ecumenical group. See below for more possibilities. This organization will convene the first planning meeting. If possible, enlist multiple sponsors to ensure wider commitment, publicity, and participation.

   - Local church or judicatory hunger, peace, mission education committees
   - Local/regional ecumenical groups (church and clergy councils and others), including
     - Church World Service Regional Offices/CROP Committee people
     - Church Women United
     - Bread for the World chapters
     - IMPACT groups
     - Clergy and Laity Concerned
     - Ten Days for World Development groups (Canada)
   - Local Community Organizations with Global Interests
     - American or Canadian Friends Service Committees
     - NAACP Chapters
     - Returned Peace Corps or CUSO groups
     - United Nation Association
     - YMCA/YWCA
     - League of Women Voters
     - Urban League
     - Local peace and justice advocacy groups
     - Campus ministry programs
     - Community colleges
     - Black sororities and fraternities
     - Local service organizations
     - for other organizations in the USA and Canada see **Resources**

This person called up and said, "You've got to come and take this seminar. It will completely change your life in just one weekend." And I said, "Well, I don't want to completely change my life this weekend. I've got a lot of things to do on Monday."

Rick Fields

3. Set a Date/Place for the First Meeting.

4. Recruit the Planning Committee. A committee of 6 to 10 persons is desirable (including the chairpersons of each Subcommittee and the Coordinator). Others may be enlisted for their expertise. All members should be also active on a Subcommittee.

In our experience, the diversity of the planning committee is the best indication of the diversity of those who will attend the event. So be "global" in your approach as well as in your content. Make every attempt to have your committee reflect the racial, ethnic and religious diversity of your community.

Particular abilities to look for include:

- Knowledge of the local community and church scene
- Past experience in organizing events, coordinating conferences
- Dependability and willingness to make time available
- Association with or leadership in an organization with a constituency you wish to attract to the seminar
- Expertise in education and/or fundraising

I slept and dreamt that life was pleasure, I woke and saw that life was service, I served and discovered that service was pleasure.

Rabindranath Tagore

The most effective way to entice persons to the initial planning meeting is by *personal invitation.* Once you've identified the persons you want to approach, divide the list among the two or three others with whom you are starting. In your personal invitation explain the purpose of the meeting and say why this person is needed. Be clear that the task of this meeting is to begin planning a global education event. Follow up your call or visit with a letter confirming the time and place of the meeting. In the letter reiterate the purpose of the meeting. Enclose a copy of the *Seminar Description* sheet (see end of this section).

5. Meeting Frequency. The timeline for a complete seminar is based on monthly meetings of the Planning Committee. Outlines for the first three meetings are provided below.

The first meeting date is set, a crucial moment in the planning process. We include here advice to enable enjoyable, productive meetings. Some of the most basic considerations to keep in mind include: clearly state the purpose of the meeting, announce beginning and ending times, take careful minutes. It is also helpful to display the agenda prominently on newsprint so everyone can see where you're heading. Finally, be sure to attend to the ideas and suggestions of the committee. Inviting their active participation in agenda setting and decision making will insure commitment to the tasks ahead.

In our experience, the way meetings proceed profoundly influences what they accomplish. Basic attitudes that are vital to the seminar itself are just as vital in planning: inclusivity, community, sensitivity, care of the environment. Here are a few ways to keep these in mind as your committee's work unfolds.

- Move meetings from one site to another so that a variety of denominational, economic, and racial "worlds" are touched. Make sure that sites are announced and directions provided.
- Insure that meeting sites are accessible for the differently-abled and are available by public transportation or that rides are arranged for those who need them.
- In larger buildings, a sign or two pointing to the meeting site can be very useful.
- Be sensitive to others when setting meeting times. For example, holding meetings during normal working hours (which clergy may prefer) will eliminate participation by many.
- Serve refreshments after the meeting. Encouraging a sense of community makes the work more fun and shows the environment you want to create at the seminar.
- Be sensitive to the environment in which the meeting takes place. Natural light, chair/table arrangements that allow all to see each other (preferably a circle), attention to beauty (music, flowers, a tablecloth) communicate an appreciation for those present and enhance your work together.
- Keep your meetings to a manageable length—no more than two hours. Review the agenda and meeting length at the beginning of each meeting. Then stick to it or seek the group's agreement to change it. Start on time, end on time.
- Have mercy on the bodies of those present: take a break mid-way through the meeting.

When it comes to the future, there are three kinds of people: those who let it happen, those who make it happen, and those who wonder what happened.

Anonymous

- Arrive at the meeting site in time to set up necessary materials.
- Set aside time at each meeting for some personal sharing as well as planning. Fostering a sense of shared community will ease some of the normal frustrations that accompany planning any event.
- Between meetings send out Minutes and upcoming agenda.

Agenda for First Three Planning Committee Meetings

To assist you in the planning process we provide detailed agendas for the first three meetings. Preparing for the first of those meetings will set the tone and direction for all that follows. You face two questions at the outset. Who among the instigators of this idea will convene and lead the first meeting? The Planning Committee can select a Coordinator at a future meetings if you or your colleagues don't want to take on this task. The second question: Who will be the recorder for the first meeting?

Our present acceptance of a widespread poverty, ignorance, and misery is a blight that can destroy all of us.

Margaret Mead

On the logistics side make copies of handout materials in advance of the meeting including: *Timeline, Seminar Description* (end of this section), the *Subcommittee Worksheets* (end of this section), and the "Prayer to Humankind" worship sheet (in **Worship**). Also be sure to order the suggested audiovisuals *well in advance.* These include *Big Island* or *No More Separate Futures,* and for the worship *Child of the Universe.* See the AV section of **Resources** for ordering information and a description of each. Finally, gather any materials needed: newsprint, Magic Markers, audiovisual equipment, refreshments.

Agenda for First Planning Committee Meeting

(Approximate time required is set in parenthesis)

1. Opening the meeting (15 minutes)

A. **Welcome the group.** Thank people for coming. Review the agenda (on newsprint) for the meeting. Remind them this will be a two-hour meeting. Circulate a sign-up sheet to collect names, group affiliation, addresses, phone numbers.

B. **Invite all present to introduce themselves** and to say why they came.

C. **Worship:** ***Prayer to Humankind.***

2. Introduce the seminar (30 minutes)

A. Explain that the slide show and worship are elements of a Global Education Seminar. Explain your desire to organize such an event in your community. What are your hopes? You may wish to refer to the opening section of this chapter that highlighted what other groups have been able to accomplish. Display this book, have copies for each member of the committee if possible. It helps in getting people onboard and dividing the tasks. Try to at least have a copy for each Subcommittee convenor.

B. **Hand out the one-sheet description of the seminar, pages 192-193 (the copies received in the mail may have been left at home).** Outline the description and seminar goals.

C. What reactions or questions do people have?

3. Seminar goals brainstorming (10 minutes)

Does this seminar reflect concerns within the group regarding global education? Possible approaches to this question:

- Why are we interested in global peace and justice?
- What are peace and justice issues in our own community?
- What more do we need to know about our own community?
- What do we need to learn about the rest of the world?
- How do we see our local problems (and solutions) linked to concerns in the rest of the world?
- What would success look like? What's the best case scenario?
  (Ask the recorder to write the main points of this last question on newsprint)

4. Illustrate the connections (15 minutes)

To illustrate the kinds of connections between local and global issues that the group has been making and the need for education regarding those issues, show either *The Big Island* or *No More Separate Futures.* Elicit reactions and observations.

5. Take a five-minute break.

6. Distribute copies of the timeline (10 minutes)

Outline the tasks of the Planning Committee and the five Subcommittees. Point out that each Subcommittee will be responsible for choosing a chairperson, setting meeting dates, adhering to the timeline, and staying in touch with the Coordinator.

7. Determine the group's interest (20 minutes)

A. Begin by recalling the images of success from the brainstorming session.
B. **In the light of these hopes, are we ready to begin planning such an event?** This moment is important. You may find interest matched by reluctance. If so allow that reluctance. Trying to force a decision can be an invitation to rejection. Listen carefully for agreements, hesitations.
C. Test for agreement as soon as a decision appears to be emerging. Do not assume silence is consent. Insist on a spoken response from those present.
D. If the group agrees to begin planning, proceed to step 8 (Subcommittee assignments). If only a few wish to proceed you may wish to hold on Subcommittee assignments until the next meeting and focus on step 9 (Who else should be involved?).

8. Obtain tentative commitments to serve on the Planning Committee and the five Subcommittees. (10 minutes)

Fear not those who argue but those who dodge.

Marie Ebner-Eschenbach

A. Identify one person as the convener for each Subcommittee. Distribute Subcommittee worksheets to their respective members.
B. If you do not wish to continue as Coordinator of the Planning Committee, you should ask who would be willing to take on this role.
C. Decide whether you will have a permanent recorder or rotate this role. If the latter, decide who will be recorders for the next two meetings.

9. Consider who else should be involved (5 minutes)

A. Who is missing from the group?
B. Are there persons you want to involved in a particular Subcommittee?
C. Confirm assignments for who will approach these people prior to the next meeting.

10. Set next several meeting dates and places (10 minutes)

11. Brief evaluation of the meeting (10 minutes)

A. What went well in the meeting? What could be improved? How?

12. Closing prayer or song (5 minutes)

13. Homework before next meeting

A. Read over organizational material in handouts.
B. Convene Subcommittees. They should meet at least once before the next Planning Committee meeting.
C. Think about potential participants for the seminar.
D. Ask the Logistics Subcommittee to develop a list of possible sites with description, costs, etc.

14. Hospitality time

Refreshments, socializing. During this time make it a point to talk with as many persons as possible, especially those who were quiet during the meeting. What are their reactions to the meeting? Make this a regular practice during the socializing time.

Agenda for Meeting #2

1. Re-do introductions (10 minutes)

Welcome any new people, circulate a sign-up sheet for name, organization, address and phone. Present agenda for meeting. Remind them this is a two-hour meeting.

2. Open (20 minutes)

A. Read this quote:
"Injustice anywhere is a threat to justice everywhere. We are caught in an inescapable network of mutuality tied in a single garment of destiny" Martin Luther King, Jr.
B. Lead the committee (divided into groups of three persons each) in the *First Experience of Injustice* exercise found in **Community Building.**
C. Point out that this exercise is one element in the seminar.

3. Review briefly the Minutes of the last meeting (10 minutes)

Go over Planning Committee and Subcommittee

Hard times ain't quit and we ain't quit.

Meridel Le Sueur

As you come to know the seriousness of our situation—the war, the racism, the poverty in the world—you come to realize it is not going to be changed just by words or demonstrations. It's a question of risking your life. It's a question of living your life in drastically different ways.

Dorothy Day

responsibilities. Are there any questions? Check in with Subcommittees. Have they met yet? Who's chair? At the break encourage new members to sign up for a Subcommittee.

4. **Review goals statement from Program Subcommittee (10 minutes)**

5. **Identify desired audience for seminars (30 min.)**

   Review list prepared by Recruitment Subcommittee. Brainstorm to see if there are others (groups or kinds of people) you'd like to see at the seminar. Be sure to record this list on paper or newsprint. From the list, select the three groups you are most interested in reaching. What are possible avenues of approach to these people? The Recruitment Subcommittee will be asked to plan a strategy for enlisting their participation.

6. **Break (5 minutes)**

7. **Consider possible sites generated by the Logistics Subcommittee. Pick first and second choice for site. (10 minutes)**

8. **Discuss possible dates, check for possible conflict with other events in the area. (15 minutes)**

9. **Confirm future meeting dates and sites. (5 minutes)**

10. **Evaluation of meeting (10 minutes)**

11. **Closing prayer or song (5 minutes)**

12. **Homework (see timeline)**

    Note: Before next meeting, type up a listing of the Planning Committee with names, organizations, addresses, and phone numbers for distribution to the committee.

13. **Hospitality time**

Agenda for Meeting #3

1. Begin with a brief period of **prayer/reflection** at this and subsequent meetings. The **Worship** section contains several possibilities. Following the prayer, ask one of the planners to present a *Cameo. Cameos* are described in **Community Building.** Before the meeting, ask someone to be prepared to offer a *Cameo*

and explain how it is done. Give them a copy of the *Cameo* description sheet. Point out that this activity is one of the elements of the seminar. (15 min.)

2. **Review the agenda (5 minutes)**
3. **Ask Program Subcommittee** to report on proposed Case Study. Following questions and discussion confirm Case Study topic. (45 **minutes)**
4. **Confirm site and seminar dates (10 minutes)**
5. **Hear from other Subcommittees (30 minutes)**

   Note: most of the meeting content from now on will be reports on the work of the Subcommittees. Before Planning Committee meetings, the Coordinator should get in touch with Subcommittee chairs to determine items for the agenda and the approximate length of time required for discussion.

6. **Evaluation of meeting (10 minutes)**
7. **Closing prayer/song (5 minutes)**
8. **Homework (see timeline)**
9. **Hospitality time**

By the end of your third meeting the planning process will be well on its way. Future meetings of the Planning Committee will be largely for sharing information and solving problems among the various Subcommittees. The last meeting of the Planning Committee will occur after the seminar to evaluate the seminar and the planning process.

Conspire, in its literal sense, means "to breathe together." Teilhard de Chardin urged "a conspiracy of love."

Marilyn Ferguson

Tales of the Heart Seminar

The *Tales of the Heart* seminar was developed over a period of four years by the Office on Global Education, Church World Service. Field-tested in communities across the USA, the seminar invites participants to **experience and celebrate their connection to the whole earth community (the Body of Christ) and to its global concerns.** The educational activities contained in *Tales* assumes that cultivating a global perspective involves the whole person: heart, head and hands.

SEMINAR GOALS: You'll note that these overlap and reinforce each other:

- **BUILD COMMUNITY:** The stories, experiences, passages of our own lives make apparent our oneness in the human community. Retelling those stories, revisiting their facts and feelings, helps us reclaim power, rekindle hope, cement new alliances. We are empowered and healed in the telling of the tale. We take heart.
- **CONSIDER OUR WORLDVIEW:** The story of a special witness—often a guest from another nation - illuminates and embodies one of the many issues engaging the human family. Our own view is nudged, perhaps altered. We spend time on notions of "the other," difference, relationship, "enemy," "us and them." We explore our own "frame of reference."
- **DISCERN OUR CALL:** We reflect on the God-word (theology) implicit in our deliberations. What is the worldview of a compassionate God? In specially designed worship we spend time with the Spirit and Wisdom of our own and other great faith traditions. We renew our thirst for truth and justice—within and without—in silence, prayer, text, image and song.
- **NAME NEXT STEPS:** Ah, the familiar territory of action! Perhaps as we craft personal and collective advocacy on global issues, we exit clearer on the starting point: the clarity and peace of our own hearts.

Seminar conversations might include:

- Why do we so resist change in our worldview?
- Today in Eastern Europe, old enemies seem to change before our eyes. Who's our enemy now? Can we live without one?
- What is burn-out? How do we recover a vision of the future that can nourish us?

Nuts and Bolts

HOW TO DO IT: The book *Tales of the Heart* contains careful step-by-step instructions on how to organize a seminar, detailed directions on how to lead its various segments, and worship materials—including handouts ready for duplication. It also thoroughly familiarizes the leaders/organizers with the sources from which the seminar is drawn.

LENGTH: 2-3 days is the norm. While it can be varied to suit a shorter period, at least an evening, overnight and full day is recommended. Another alternative: a series of weekly two-hour sessions.

AUDIENCE: All who care about the planet: junior high through adult learners. Despite its clearly Christian base, persons from quite different religious, ethnic and cultural traditions have found the seminar meaningful and empowering.

Comments from Former Participants:

- "The Seminar helped raise one's consciousness to the connectedness of all on this planet, and start us on the road to sharing that with others. It helped us to cope with the pain that is in the world, and to work through that pain to seek answers."

  Upstate New York

- "The first conference I have ever left and not felt burned out and drained."

  Ghost Ranch, New Mexico

- "The worship was a special treat—an integral part of living and growing."

  Springfield, Illinois

- "I greatly appreciated the balance of worship, lecture and discussion."

  Malibu, California

- "Really helped me to experience and articulate a global view. I'll be using these methods when I return home. Thanks."

  St. Simon's Island, Georgia

From *Tales of the Heart*, Hampson/Whalen, Friendship Press, 1991.

The new survival unit is no longer the individual nation; it's the entire human race and its environment. This new-found oneness is only a rediscovery of an ancient religious truth. Unity is not something we are called to create; it's something we are called to recognize.

William Sloan Coffin

I do not want

PUBLICITY/RECRUITMENT SUBCOMMITTEE

my house walled in on all sides and my windows stuffed.

I want the culture of all ands to be blown about my house as freely as possible.

Mohandas K. Gandhi

Major Tasks

1. Develop a strategy for recruiting seminar participants.
2. Develop and print needed materials (brochures, letters of invitation, etc.).
3. Contact identified inviters and assemble list of invitees.
4. Publicize the seminar through local/regional ecumenical and denominational leaders and newsletters, and other channels.
5. Coordinate advance mailings to participants.
6. Staff the registration at the seminar.
7. Maintain communication with Planning Committee and Coordinator.

A Strategy for Recruitment

Key questions to address:

- Who is the audience?
- What are they concerned about?
- Who can help us connect with these people personally?
- What is the best vehicle for communicating our invitation?

- **Who is our audience?**

  The Planning Committee will make the final decision regarding the audience. Your first task is to prepare some possibilities for the Planning Committee prior to its second meeting. Very likely, the audience will be constituents of groups whose representatives are on your Planning Committee. The audiences targeted during the field testing included pastors, mission educators, religious educators, hunger/peace/mission leaders in local churches and judicatories, and Church World Service/CROP volunteers.

- **What does the designated audience care about?**

  What information, skills, opportunities, will be attractive? Issues of local concern will emerge as the

Sample Registration Form

CHURCH WORLD SERVICE

CHURCH WORLD SERVICE is the relief, refugee resettlement and development agency of the National Council of Churches of Christ in the U.S.A. CWS cooperates with and acts on behalf of 31 Protestant and Orthodox communions. Its overseas work is undertaken by local agencies, usually church related, in 90 countries around the world. Thus, CWS is a link in a people-to-people network of U.S. churches and overseas colleague agencies working in partnership to help people help themselves.

The CWS OFFICE ON GLOBAL EDUCATION is mandated to inform and sensitize the U.S. public about the root causes of hunger, the limitations of global resources and the interdependence of all people. The Office works in a collaborative and cooperative style, animating and supporting existing initiatives in global education in the U.S., as well as providing educational programming.

GLOBAL EDUCATION: "A WORLD'S EYE-VIEW"

Global education or education for global justice is a process which helps people understand the conditions of hunger, poverty and oppression and why these conditions exist and persist. Global education arouses and nurtures in individuals a commitment to envision and actively promote a more just, sustainable, participatory and thus, human global environment.

What Will We Do?

explore

CONNECTIONS BETWEEN THE THIRD WORLD AND U.S. FARMERS

***Farmers moving beyond production**
***Connections with international cartels**
***U.S. farm and foreign policy**
***Educational approaches/resources**

RESOURCE PEOPLE

David Ostendorf. Director of Prairie Fire Rural Action, Des Moines, a rural education training and advocacy group. David is working nationally on issues related to the farm and rural crisis. He is also an ordained United Church of Christ minister and has written extensively on rural issues and the churches.

Loretta Whalen, Director Office on Global Education, educator, musician, liturgist.

Thomas L. Hampson, Associate Director, Office on Global Education, former high school teacher, curriculum writer.

*Other local resource persons to be announced.

PLEASE NOTE:

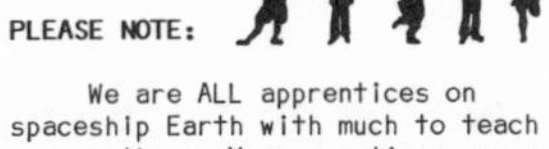

We are ALL apprentices on spaceship Earth with much to teach one another. Your questions, your stories and your struggles will be an important part of our time together.

"This we know, the earth does not belong to us, we belong to the earth. This we know, all things are connected, like the blood which unites one family. All things are connected. Whatever befalls the earth, befalls the children of the earth. We did not weave the web of life, we are merely a strand in it. Whatever we do to the web, we do to ourselves."

--Chief Seattle (1854)
(language modified to be inclusive)

SEMINAR:

EXPLORING OUR GLOBAL CONNECTIONS AND COMMITMENT

Front

EVERY DAY WE DINE WITH THE WORLD

Our tables are set by hands we never see. Yet the life of the farmer, whether in Illinois or the Philippines, is inextricably linked to ours.

Similarly, our tables tie us to the fate of the land that produces our food.

Every meal embodies the simple truth:

"There are no more separate futures."

WE INVITE YOU

to join us in exploring the challenge implied in this interconnectedness:

* the call to a GLOBAL PERSPECTIVE - a fresh understanding of ourselves, our community, our nation and our world.
* the call to a COVENANT embracing all of creation.

SPONSORS Church World Service Office on Global Education * Church World Service Downstate Illinois Regional Office

GOALS

1. To explore the meaning of a global perspective for our lives.
2. To investigate the connections between Third World and U.S. farmers.
3. To deepen the theological and scriptural roots of our peace and justice work.
4. To promote networking, ecumenical action and nurture of spirit.
5. To enhance skills in doing global education.
6. To sing and celebrate our gifted diversity.

SEMINAR FACTS

When: From 5:00 PM (dinner) Friday, November 20 to 7:00 PM Saturday, November 21, 1987.

Where: Lake Williamson Christian Center Carlinville, Illinois.

Cost: $37 including room and board (per person, double occupancy) if registered by October 10; $42 after October 10.

For Whom: Everyone involved in mission education, rural life issues, and CROP events.

This event will be limited to 50 participants. Consider this your invitation, and if you are able to attend, please return the form below promptly to:

Global Education Seminar, Church World Service/CROP,
909 S. 5th St., Suite B, Springfield, IL 62703

You may send full payment with this form, or, if you prefer, a deposit of $20.00 with the balance due at the Seminar. Make checks payable to Church World Service.

Name ____________

Address ____________

City ________ State ________ Zip ________

Phone (Business) ________ (Home) ________

Position/Institution ____________

Denomination ____________

****** DEADLINE FOR ALL APPLICATIONS IS NOVEMBER 1, 1987 ******

CWS USA CHURCH WORLD SERVICE

Back

Program Committee designs the local/global case study. The Publicity/Recruitment Subcommittee's job is to translate these to the designated audience in an engaging manner.

- **Who can help us connect with our audience?**

First, consider what groups you may wish to have represented on your committee. Broadening your membership base will encourage participation.

Second, identify key persons, "inviters" in your respective organizations and the larger community who *should know* about the event, even though they may not themselves participate (judicatory executives, media persons, etc.). Meet with them. Share promotional materials and your enthusiasm. Enlist them to alert their networks about the event by sending out brochures with personal letters of invitation. You do the same with your own networks.

Each small task of everyday life is part of the total harmony of the universe.

St. Theresa of Lisieux

- **What are the best vehicles for getting the word out?**

Newsletters—Prepare a list of newsletter deadlines from local/regional groups (denominational, ecumenical, community activists). Submit your announcements and articles to them in advance of those dates.

Brochures—In coordination with the Program Committee, create a flyer on the event with as much detail on program as possible. The brochure should have a pre-registration form to be returned with a non-refundable deposit (See Sample on previous page).

Some one organization/person must be identified as the point of contact for the seminar. Their address will appear on the brochure. They will be responsible for tracking advance registration and answering phone questions.

Posters—These are useful for church and library bulletin boards.

Phone Calls—Once the material has been sent out, follow-up phone calls by your group have proved most effective. Although time-consuming, the personal touch sets this event apart from the other activities clamoring for the attention of concerned people.

LOGISTICS SUBCOMMITTEE

Major Tasks

1. Locate and confirm seminar site.
2. Arrange for materials required by resource people.
3. Coordinate arrangements at the site:

   A. Liaison to seminar site.
   B. Attend to special needs of participants (diet, for example).
   C. If necessary coordinate room assignments.
   D. Collect and set up chairs, displays, audio-visual equipment, etc. (see *Materials Checklist*, p. 199.)
   E. Assemble registration packets, name tags.
   F. Set up and clean up "fests."
   G. Clean up at end of seminar.

4. Maintain contact with Planning Committee and Coordinator.

Site Considerations

- *Where* the seminar takes place can exert a powerful influence on *what* occurs during the seminar. Energy expended early to find a good site will pay substantial rewards later.
- Many facilities are booked months (even a year) in advance, so begin early.
- *If at all possible visit the site before making your final decision.*
- Three major issues arise in selecting a site: cost, accessibility, and attributes.

Cost:

The kind of site you choose and the length of the seminar will largely determine cost. Cost influences who is able or willing to participate. There are always trade-offs. Once the Planning Committee has determined the length of the seminar, compare the site you feel is affordable and the one that is most desirable (if there is a difference). In conjunction with the Finance Subcommittee, consider if funding other than participant fees may be available. Don't give up. Another strategy is to enlist people/staff in charge of the facility as collaborators in the seminar—fees may be then reduced.

It is great and there is no other greatness—to make one nook of God's creation worthy of God—to make some human heart a little more blessed, less accused.

Thomas Carlyle

Accessibility

In town or out of town—that is the question. In-town sites are easier to get to, but accessibility can tempt persons to drop in and out. Out-of-town sites tend to eliminate "drop-ins" but may pose transportation problems for some. We've never found the latter to be insurmountable, but they can add to the work. In general, for a more than 2-day seminar, out of town has proven better for us than in town. If transportation must be provided, the Logistics Subcommittee should research some options and related costs and report to the Planning Committee. You will be responsible for coordinating transportation.

Site Attributes to Consider

- Adequate space for small and large group work, ideally away from eating space and kitchen. Dishwashers can disturb a session.
- Rooms that can really be darkened (for audio-visual use). Anemic visuals weakened by too much light are much less effective.
- Availability of audiovisual and other equipment supports (see *Materials Checklist,* p. 199.) At what cost? Is a knowledgeable staff person available to assist in setting up equipment?
- A space for socializing away from the sleeping area.
- Furniture in the meeting space that is comfortable and easily moved.
- Sleeping arrangements. Number of persons per room, and per restroom.
- Space outside for walking, playing.
- Space for displays, bookstore.
- Distance between eating, meeting, and sleeping areas. This is particularly important if you anticipate participation by differently-abled persons. It's also an issue if the weather is inclement.
- Access to copying facilities.
- A Chapel or other appropriate space for worship.
- Piano.

Questions To Ask

- Is it possible to hang material on the walls with masking tape?
- Who will be the staff liaison at the center?
- How is registration handled? Room assignments?

- Is there a bookstore already at the site? If so, are they willing to handle consignment orders and staffing?
- Are there facilities for the differently-abled?
- Are there facilities for daycare?
- Are meal times convenient? Are there options for people on special or vegetarian diets? How are coffee breaks, evening refreshments dealt with?

Arrangements during the Seminar

You will be responsible for arranging the seminar site. If you are fortunate, a staff person will be on the site to help you. Either way, plan to arrive a minimum of three hours prior to the seminar to set up chairs, audio-visual equipment, displays, etc. (See **Seminar Elements** for clues on creating a welcoming environment.) Prior to the event, divide the tasks among your group to distribute work/worries evenly and clearly.

A Word about Fests

Fests are for relaxation and refreshments. These can be simple or elaborate at your discretion. Some sites will arrange them for you, others not. What to do about beer/wine? Some sites prohibit it. The nature of your group will also influence this decision. If you do have alcohol, be sure to have attractive alternatives: juice, soft drinks, punch, etc.

If I can't dance . . . I don't want to be part of your revolution.

Emma Goldman

Note: Logistics are the nuts and bolts of the seminar. This role is not the most glamorous—however in our experience it is often the most essential element in determining whether or not the seminar offers a welcoming and hospitable experience for participants.

Materials Checklist: Likely Equipment Required During Seminar

- Name tags
- 16MM projector
- VHS/VCR and monitor
- Screen (large and highly reflective)
- Plenty of extension cords
- At least three, 3-pronged adaptors
- Extra bulbs for all audio-visual equipment
- Cassette tape recorder
- Podium
- Projection table
- Newsprint

- Wide-tip marking pens of various colors
- Masking Tape
- Large batik or colored fabric for table covers
- Display table for bookstore and "freebies"
- Food and drink for fests and snacks if not provided by site
- Small medical kit
- Volleyballs, frisbees, and other outdoor equipment if not provided at site

PROGRAM SUBCOMMITTEE

Major Tasks

I hear, I forget, I see and I remember, I do, and I understand.

Suzanne Toton

1. Become familiar with seminar modules and design-options.
2. Hone seminar goals and present to Planning Committee.
3. Generate options for Case Study.
4. Design seminar and create a time schedule based on goals and length agreed to by the Planning Committee.
5. Estimate cost of program.
6. Recruit leadership for seminar (modules and worship).
7. Recruit and instruct facilitators.
8. Recruit *Cameo* presenters.
9. Design and distribute evaluation.
10. Summarize evaluations for Planning Committee consideration following the seminar.
11. Order films mentioned in modules.
12. Maintain contact with Planning Committee and Coordinator.

Note: The Program Subcommittee is responsible for the design and content of the seminar. While this book provides a wide array of activities, alternative designs, etc., a good deal of imagination and work will be required to make these plans come to life. Members of this Subcommittee should include experienced educators.

Becoming Familiar with the Seminar

Your first task will be to get acquainted with the seminar material. Begin with the **Preface, Introduction,** and the chapter openings that begin each major section to get a view of the overall approach to the seminar. Spend some time in the Subcommittee discussing this material.

Second, review the summary descriptions of the seminar modules and the possible combinations of these modules found in **Seminar Elements.**

Note: We highly recommend the committee view the video "Count Me In" early in your planning process. See **Resources** for description and ordering information.

You can plan events, but if they go according to your plan they are not an event.

John Berger

Goals (complete before the second Planning Committee meeting)

The initial conversation on goals will take place in the first Planning Committee meeting. Your job is to clarify the material developed in the brainstorming session. Work to identify goals that are clear and realistic. You may do this by writing a draft goal statement. Keep in mind that your goal statement should identify:

- WHAT you are trying to achieve
- with WHOM
- by what MEANS

Bring this statement to the next Planning Committee meeting for comment and ratification. Choose one or two people to present the draft statement and moderate a discussion about it. Develop your statement carefully, listening attentively to all points of view. Don't expect the Planning Committee simply to rubber stamp what you've created. Struggle with this statement demonstrates concern for the outcome. The result for the Planning Committee will be community, mutual ownership, and commitment to what the group has created. The growth and learning will be worth the struggle.

Developing the Case Study

(complete before the third Planning Committee meeting)

"Think globally, act locally," Rene Dubos tells us. While the modules in this manual seek to explore a global perspective, the *application* of a global perspective to a particular issue will be your task in the Case Study. Your approach can be simple or elaborate, brief or lengthy. The topic, design and leadership are yours to decide.

Choosing a Case Study Topic

You will present an option or series of options for the Case Study to the Planning Committee at their third meeting. A few suggestions on generating these options:

Be patient with all that is unsolved in your heart. Try to love the questions themselves, like locked rooms and like books that are written in a foreign tongue . . . Live the questions raw.

Rainer Maria Rilke

1. MAKING LOCAL-GLOBAL CONNECTIONS. To initiate this conversation in the Subcommittee, consider some of these questions:
   - Where do we see our lives being influenced by or influencing another part of the world?
   - Where are people suffering in our community?
   - What connections do we see between the suffering of people in our community and the lives of struggling people in other parts of the world?

   As the group reflects on and ties together responses to these questions, what patterns begin to emerge? Identify the three most promising topics and present them at the Planning Committee meeting.

2. PIGGY-BACKING EXISTING THEMES. An alternative to creating your own topic is to use a pre-existing one, for example, the Ecumenical Mission Study Themes, developed by Friendship Press. Friendship Press publishes a topical theme and geographical area theme each year. Written and audio-visual study resources linked to these themes offer materials useful not only for seminars, but for participants to study with their own groups and churches as well. If you pursue this approach, be sure the Bookstore Subcommittee orders samples from Friendship Press. For information on themes and related resources, write Friendship Press, Rm 772, 475 Riverside Dr., New York, NY 10115 or call (212) 870-2496.

   Consider focusing on *the annual themes of various "Weeks" or "Days"* observed in the US and Canada. Special study and promotional materials are prepared for these themes. If your event coincides with one of these dates (or if you want to prepare people to develop programs for these events), consider this option:

WORLD FOOD DAY, OCTOBER 16

World Food Day Office, 1001 22nd St., N.W., Washington, D.C. 20437 Phone (202) 653-2404

World Food Day Association, 255 Argyle Ave., Ottawa, Ontario K2P 1B8 Canada Phone (613) 233-9002

WORLD HEALTH DAY, APRIL 7

American Association for World Health, 2001 S Street, N.W.; Suite 530, Washington, DC 20009
Phone (202) 265-0286

PEACE WITH JUSTICE WEEK, OCTOBER 16-24

Peace with Justice Week Office, 777 U.N. Plaza, 11th flr.
New York, NY 10117 Phone (212) 682-3633

CENTRAL AMERICA WEEK,
falls during 3rd week in March

Interreligious Task Force on Central America,
475 Riverside Drive, Rm. 563, New York, NY 10115-0050
Phone (212) 870-3383

HUMAN RIGHTS WEEK,
begins Sunday prior to December 10

Human Rights Office,
National Council of Churches,
475 Riverside Drive, Rm 634, New York, NY 10115-0050
Phone (212) 870-2424

TEN DAYS FOR WORLD DEVELOPMENT,
dates set annually, usually the last week of January to first week in February.

Ten Days for World Development, 85 St. Clair Avenue
East, Toronto, Ontario M4T 1M8 Canada
Phone (416) 922-0591

Designing the Case Study

The Task: To craft an engaging encounter between your participants and the topic. Imagine the topic as a person you want to introduce rather than a set of facts you want people to know. Think about your own experience in high school, for example. Which do you remember more vividly—the teachers or the topics? To put it another way, how can you embody the topic, give it flesh, so people experience it as well as learn about it. Psychologist Rollo May speaks to this task:

> "Only the truth that is experienced at all levels of being has the power to change the human being."

Some Options:

Witnesses

What better way to embody a topic than to spend time with someone who has lived it? For example, in Southern California we explored the topic of Nicaragua/US Relations with Tomas Telez, Executive Secretary of the Baptist Convention of Nicaragua. His life story transformed headlines into lifelines.

Witnesses need not come from far away. We will never forget local people who shared their own struggles: farmers in Iowa, welfare mothers and refugees in New York, former Peace Corps volunteers in Ohio. Look to your own community for witnesses.

If you wish to have a speaker from another country as a witness, check with the mission office of your denomination, the local Church World Service regional office, your local Learner Centre in Canada, or your neighboring colleges to see who is already scheduled to visit your area. Agencies that can assist in locating speakers are listed in **Resources**.

Ideally, a witness or witnesses will be present for the entire seminar as a participant. Certainly she/he will make a presentation or two to the group as a whole, but presence at meals, fests, and breaks makes possible the beginning of a real relationship with this person.

> Those who trust us educate us.
>
> George Eliot

In our experience, establishing relationship is the most powerful stimulus to broadening and deepening participants' sense of connection to a larger world.

In a similar vein, we have frequently requested that in one presentation witnesses simply tell their life stories. "How did you get to be you?" This sharing often proves memorable for witnesses as well as participants. In sharing life stories we encounter the common hopes and fears of all persons on this fragile planet.

Dialogues between witnesses also offer a powerful educational opportunity. In Iowa, a farm organizer's conversation with a Liberian development expert revealed new connections between the debt/development dilemma of first- and third-world peoples.

Finally, *witnesses need not simply lecture.* Poets, musicians, and artists have revealed their stories through creative expressions that go beyond the "facts." For example, the beauty and power of the music of Jim and Jean Strathdee, witnesses in Southern California, challenged and nurtured participants in a way no lecture ever could. See **Resources** for a list of performers we've encountered along the way.

Drama

In Rochester, N.Y., planners wrote and performed an extended role play on their local/global connections. Creating the play was itself a collaborative adventure engaging such diverse elements of their community as unemployed workers, refugees, government officials, bankers, and local activists.

If designing your own play sounds too ambitious, consider other possibilities. For example, Bread for the World has produced "Lazarus," a musical on hunger and poverty. The score and instructions for performing are available. See **Resources** for information about this and other dramatic resources.

A final option. Inquire about "popular theater" groups in your area. Improvisational theater and other non-formal approaches to drama have proved very powerful for both educating and organizing. Check your local college drama department for leads.

Exposure Trips

"People learn with their feet," a colleague once advised us. Entering a new setting, or "making a plunge," as these trips are sometimes called, can be a very powerful experience. But the time, cost, and logistics of such a venture limit the usefulness of exposure trips for a brief seminar.

When the forms of an old culture are dying, the new culture is created by a few people who are not afraid to be insecure.

Rudolf Bahro

During a five-day seminar held at Ghost Ranch in New Mexico, participants spent an entire afternoon visiting the Santa Clara Pueblo and the Puye Cliff Dwellings. Response to this experience was very positive. Both morning and evening sessions were devoted to preparing for and evaluating the visit.

In Montreal, small groups of five to seven persons visited a variety of programs for women in the city. An entire day was set aside to reflect upon and analyze the experience.

A good review of several exposure-trip models can be found in *Pedagogies for the Non-Poor,* by Alice Frazer Evans, Robert A. Evans, and William Bean Kennedy. Maryknoll, NY: Orbis Books, 1987.

If you decide to make exposure trips, a few words of advice:

- Send small groups. Too often exposure trips overwhelm the sites they visit by their size and noise.
- Carefully explain the purpose of the event and your expectations to those you plan to visit. Don't assume they understand what you want.

- Take time to prepare participants for their visits and schedule adequate time to reflect on the experience afterwards.
- Triple-check all logistics: transportation, meals, expected times of arrival and departure. Arriving late to a site can mean finding an empty building.
- Be sure to have a back-up plan in case the trip has to be cancelled.

Simulations

Simulation games engage participants on a variety of levels at once—and can be fun. They can take from one to three hours (or more) to play and analyze. The **Resource** section lists a few of the more popular games. You will probably have to purchase a game unless you know someone who owns one.

Preparation is crucial to a successful simulation. Play the game at least once prior to the seminar itself—perhaps with the Planning Committee. Familiarity with the game from start to finish allows you to run the game more confidently during the seminar and frees you to be more observant of what happens in the group. It is useful to have at least two people leading the simulation so that they can observe group dynamics.

Media

An outstanding series of audio-visual resources on global peace and justice issues have been created in the last few years. **Resources** lists a few of our favorites available at no charge except return postage, from the Church World Service Film Library. Films/video/slide presentations can bring another part of the world to life, especially in our visually oriented culture.

Audio-visuals can also be used effectively in combination with other program elements. For example, in Illinois our conversation with a witness on the farms crisis was launched by looking at part of the videotape *Down and Out in America*. Part of the preparation for our Ghost Ranch field trip was watching *Chaco Legacy* (not available from CWS).

If I go as a Hindu, I will meet a Muslim or a Christian. If I go as a socialist, I'll meet a capitalist. If I go as a brown man, I'll meet a black man or a white man.

But if I go as a human being, I'll meet only human beings.

Satish Kumar

A Word about Process

Process, as distinguished from content, describes how participants relate to the topic and to one another. The energy and imagination you spend on the development of the Case Study must be matched with equal attention to how you engage participants. How will they bring their experiences to bear on what is presented?

A few possibilities:

- **Silence.** Allowing people time to dwell reflectively on what they have just experienced is itself a way of learning. Habituated as we are to constant noise and change, we rarely take time to notice how we feel emotionally and physically. Because such attention is unfamiliar, some initial instruction is often necessary, i.e., "Take a moment now to notice how you feel. What is your body telling you right now," or "Take a moment to be quiet. What image stands out for you from the last session? Spend some time with that image and the feelings that accompany it."
- **Grounding the Experience.** After a time of silence, we've found it is valuable to ask people to express the result of their reflections. Some ways we've used include:
  - Writing a note to yourself on what you noticed or learned, or drawing an image that captures the experience;
  - Forming pairs or small groups to share the fruit of this reflection.
- **Closure.** Bring the conversation back to the group as a whole for comments, observations, questions, next steps.

Note: Individual sessions have more specific instructions for small-group work.

Designing the seminar as whole
(complete before the fourth Planning Committee meeting)

Once you are clear on the Case Study begin to assemble the rest of your design. The modules in this book create a frame around the case study. **Seminar Elements** describes one design that we have field tested. Other possible combinations appear near the end of this section.

You will need to review the goals, Case Study, and the summary of the modules as you begin the process of crafting the event as a whole. By the time of the next

Planning Committee meeting you should have created your own seminar, identifying major elements: modules, Case Study, breaks, meals, worship, etc.

Once the design has been approved and leadership recruited print up a complete schedule with all responsibilities assigned.

Additional sources for help in designing your event:

- *Basics & Tools: A Collection of Popular Education Resources and Activities.* CUSO Education Department, 135 Rideau Street, Ottawa, Ontario, K1N 9K7, Canada, 1988.
- Arnold, Rick, Deborah Barndt and Bev Burke. *A New Weave: Popular Education in Canada and Central America.* Available from CUSO Education Department, see above for address, 1986.
- *Resource Manual for a Living Revolution.* New Society Publishers, P.O. Box 582, Santa Cruz, CA 95061-0582, 1978.
- *Make A World of Difference: Creative Activities for Global Learning.* Office on Global Education, Friendship Press, P.O. Box 37844, Cincinnati, OH, 45222-0844, 1989.
- *We Could Do That!.* One World Week, P.O. Box 100, London SE1 7RT, United Kingdom, 1989.

Program Costs
(Complete before the fifth Planning Committee meeting)

What will it cost? Estimate your total program cost for: honoraria, AV equipment rental, and other related costs. This information should be communicated to the Finance Subcommittee as they prepare the proposed budget for the seminar.

Creating Small Groups

Small groups are used several times in the seminar. We suggest that you create groups that continue throughout the course of the seminar. This promotes a sense of familiarity and safety, conducive to sharing sometimes difficult issues. We have created small groups in two ways:

- Assigned: Simple, efficient as long as the group designations are clearly communicated, colored dots on the name tags for example. We have employed assigned groups when we wanted to insure maximum variety in each small group (age, region, race, faith, etc.).

- Serendipity: Our major vehicle has been *Line of Least Acquaintance* found in **Community Building**. This method has the advantage of being more spontaneous, less controlling.

Finding Leaders

In addition to arranging for witnesses and Case Study presenters, the Program Committee must find leaders for three kinds of activities:

- leaders for seminar sessionsand worship
- facilitators for small groups
- presenters of *Cameos*

Those responsible for leading *Tales* sessions should be experienced educators, comfortable in front of groups and patient with the pace of group process. See **Resources** for some clues on locating leaders. Ideally, these people would be members of the Program Subcommittee. They should spend time becoming familiar with the design of the seminar and the particular module(s) they are responsible for leading. Be sure to also give them the *Leader's Guide* to assist their preparation (found at the end of this section). Teachers, religious educators, and pastors are all potential leaders for modules.

The distresses of choice are our chance to be blessed.

W.H. Auden

The **Worship** section contains finished worship designs as well as resources and suggestions for alternative activities. Those responsible for planning and leading worship should be given the task and the material well in advance. Be sure they are clear about the larger goals and focus of the seminar. Encourage them to read the **Preface, Introduction** and Chapter Openings. They may need to link to the Logistics Subcommittee to arrange for musical instruments.

Recruit session and worship leaders well in advance to allow adequate preparation time.

Small-Group Facilitators enable the process of the seminar to unfold. They should be good listeners and good watchers of group dynamics. **Seminar Elements** contains instructions for facilitators. Part of your task will be to introduce facilitators to their roles as well as to the seminar goals and overall design during a brief orientation session prior to the seminar. We recommend that the leaders of the major sessions also attend so that everyone is up to speed.

If you love it enough anything will talk with you.

George Washington Carver

We have recruited facilitators from the Planning Committee as well as participants. At the very latest, orientation of facilitators can take place immediately prior to the seminar. It's hectic, but it is possible.

For a description of *Cameos* see **Community Building.** This description can be used as a handout for those you recruit. The seminar is based on the power of story telling—not only the stories of "exotic" others but also our own "ordinary" stories. *Cameos* are one expression of this approach. *Cameo*-givers should be recruited before the seminar from among the participants to allow them time to prepare.

Emphasize that *Cameo*-givers are being asked to tell a story, not a biography or an advertisement or a political statement. The length of a *Cameo*, no more than five minutes, should also be emphasized. Even with these precautions you may find yourself listening to something that would be better said elsewhere or left unsaid. Despite the risk, in our experience, *Cameos* have yielded some of the most memorable, moving moments of the seminar.

Evaluation

How will you know if you achieved the goals set out when you began planning the seminar? Your task will not be complete unless you evaluate the results.

- **During the seminar:** Two forms of evaluation are included in the seminar design: daily informal evaluations called *Temperature Checks* (see **Community Building**), and a formal evaluation sheet distributed near the end of the seminar. A sample form follows this section. Be sure to include time in your design to have participants complete the evaluation before they leave.

  We also recommend that the Planning Committee and other leaders meet once or twice during the seminar to assess what is happening.

- **After the seminar:** Your last task will be to summarize the evaluations and report to the next meeting of the Planning Committee. Depending on your goals, you may wish to ask participants to complete a follow-up evaluation some months after the event.

Final Comment

The Program Subcommittee has a challenging and exciting job—to design a seminar that embodies your goals, employing local resource people to lead this adventure. You will meet new and people in the process. You will learn much about collaboration. Good luck.

DESIGN OPTIONS: items in bold below refer to specific sections of this book.

1 Day Design

8:30 AM	Registration, Coffee
9:00	Overview and Introductions
9:30	**Worship: *Prayer to Humankind***
10:00	**Coming to Our Senses in a Global Age**
11:45	Lunch
1:00 PM	Case Study
2:45	Break
3:00	**Theologos: The Theological Basis of Justice-Seeking**
4:45	Break
5:00	*Covenant* film, see AV section in **Resources**.

1 ½ DAY SEMINAR

Day I:

5:00 PM Registration/dinner

7:00 Opening

- Welcome, introduce leaders
- Logistics (location of phones, restrooms, meal times)
- Review seminar goals/agenda
- Leaders: ***"I Introduce Me"***
- ***Cameo***
- ***Demographics***
- ***Line of Least Acquaintance***

8:30 **Worship: *Prayer to Humankind***

9:00 Fest

Day II

8:45 AM ***Temperature Check***

Cameo

People say that what we're all seeking is a meaning for life. I don't think that's what we're really seeking.

I think that what we're seeking is an experience of being alive, so that our life experiences on the purely physical plane will have resonances within our own innermost being and reality, so that we actually feel the rapture of being alive.

Joseph Campbell

9:00 **Theologos: The Theological Basis for Justice-Seeking**
10:45 Break
11:00 **Coming to Our Senses in a Global Age**
12:00 Lunch
1:00 PM Case Study: *Connections between Third World and U.S. Farmers, Dave Ostendorf of "PrairieFire"*
- 1:00 Presentation
- 2:00 Response by selected "listeners"
- 2:15 Break
- 2:30 Questions
- 3:00 Small groups: develop possible actions of solidarity
- 3:20 Plenary: Collect ideas and note best opportunities for collective and individual action

4:15 Film: *Covenant* (see audio-visual listings in **Resources**)
5:00 Dinner/Departure

4 ½ DAY SEMINAR

Day I:

5:45 PM Dinner
7:00 Opening
- Introduce Seminar Goals/Agenda
- ***Demographics***
- ***Temperature Check***
- ***Line of Least Acquaintance***
- **Worship: *Prayer to Humankind***

9:15 Fest

Day II:

7:30 AM Breakfast
8:30 ***Temperature Check***
Cameo
Theologos: The Theological Basis of Justice-Seeking
12:00 Lunch
1:00 PM Workshops
3:00 Exploring Ghost Ranch
5:45 Dinner
7:00 ***Cameo***
Faces of the Enemy
9:15 Fest

Day III:

7:30 AM	Breakfast
8:30	***Cameo***
	Case Study: *Northern New Mexico and Forgotten Sacred Memories: A Case of Plenty in Poverty*
	Antonio Medina, Director, Mora Valley Health Clinic
10:00	Break
10:15 AM	Film: *Chaco Legacy*
11:00	Native American Intergenerational Changes: Spirituality, Natural Resources and Culture
	Stephen La Boueff and Family, Santa Clara Pueblo Potters
12:00	Lunch
1:00 PM	Field Trip: Puye Ruins, Santa Clara Pueblo
5:45	Dinner
7:00	***Cameo***
	Hispanic Poetry and Song
	Cipriano Vigil, Folklorist and Musician
9:15 PM	Fest

Day IV:

7:30 AM	Breakfast
8:30	***Temperature Check***
	Cameo
	Exploring Our Worldview
12:00	Lunch
1:00 PM	Workshops
3:00	Exploring Ghost Ranch
5:45	Dinner
7:00	***Cameo***
	Coming to Our Senses in a Global Age
9:15 PM	Fest

DAY V:

7:30 AM	Breakfast
8:30	**Temperature Check**
	Cameo
	Evaluation
	Worship
10:00 AM	Conclude

Alternative Format: Using elements of the seminar for a five-week series.

For a local church setting, a weekly study series may be the most convenient format. Here is a suggestion for a five-week series (assumes a weekly session of 1 hour 45 minutes. **In some cases this will require streamlining the module.**):

Week 1 **Coming to Our Senses in a Global Age**

Week 2 **Theologos: The Theological Basis for Justice-Seeking**

Week 3 "Witness." See Page 234 for clues for finding potential witnesses in your community.

Week 4 **Exploring Our Worldview,** part 1

Week 5 **Exploring Our Worldview,** part 2

Leader's Guide

As a person leading one or more of the major elements of the seminar you'll have much to think about. We provide this check list to assist your preparation and presentation.

- **Become familiar with the material.** Spending ample time reading through the session materials assures that you "have" the key points, diminishes anxiety, and enables a more spontaneous, lively presentation.
- **Make good copies of handouts well in advance.** Don't assume that the seminar site will be able to make duplicates for you.
- **Order and preview audio-visuals early.** Descriptions of the AV's we suggest and instructions for ordering are found in **Resources** section. Preview will assist in getting a sense of the entire session. Reduces surprises!
- **Become familiar with your equipment.** Confidence in setting up and running AV equipment at the seminar site will reduce hassles in the midst of your session. Leave about double the time for set up that you think you'll need. . . . Locate light switches and amplification system, and their foibles. Can the cassette player, for example, be connected to the room's sound system?
- **Review the design, and be present for the whole event.** Though you may lead only one element of the seminar, knowledge of what precedes and follows your portion will provide a helpful context for your remarks.
- **Care for recruitment in advance.** Some modules expect you to recruit readers or others to assist you. Caring for this early in the seminar spares you and others last-minute frenzy. Do you need a worship leader or musician?
- **Meet with facilitators.** If you work with small groups in your session, be sure to attend the facilitator orientation convened by the Program Subcommittee. Review with them the small-group task(s) for your session.
- **[Leader instructions appear in the session materials bolded and in brackets.]**
- **Attend to time.** You may want to pencil in time benchmarks for yourself in the margins of the leader's material. We find it very helpful to have a watch easily visible for frequent reference.
- **Leaven your presentation with stories.** Illustrations from your own life concretize your points and help participants know you a

bit better. Similarly, ask for illustrations, stories from the participants.

- **Remember the body.** Human tolerance of sitting is limited. Include stretch breaks. "Two-minute standup break, within three feet of your chair"!
- **Remember the room.** As you set up the room (even *between* sessions) attend to its beauty, chair arrangements, acoustics, lighting, ventilation.

In the world to come I shall not be asked,
"Why were you not Moses?" I shall be asked,
"Why were you not Zusya?"

Rabbi Zusya

From *Tales of the Heart,* Hampson/Whalen, Friendship Press, 1991.

Global Education Seminar Evaluation

A. Seminar Elements:

Please circle appropriate number and add any comments you care to make.

Thank you for your attention to this task.

	Excellent		Fair		Poor	
1. *Line of Least Acquaintance* Comment:	1	2	3	4	5	6
2. *Cameos* Comment:	1	2	3	4	5	6
3. **Worship** Comment:	1	2	3	4	5	6
4. **Theo-Logos** Comment:	1	2	3	4	5	6
5. **Coming to Our Senses** Comment:	1	2	3	4	5	6
6. Case Study Comment:	1	2	3	4	5	6
7. Advance Reading Comment:	1	2	3	4	5	6
8. Overall Design Comment:	1	2	3	4	5	6

B. Personal Reflections

1. What were your own goals for this time?

____

____

____

____

2. Were your goals realized?

____

____

____

____

3. The best moment for me in the Seminar was:

4. The worst moment in the Seminar for me was:

C. Logistics

1. Advance Information	1	2	3	4	5	6
Comment:						
2. Food/Lodging	1	2	3	4	5	6
Comment:						
3. Bookstore	1	2	3	4	5	7
Comment:						

D. Other Comments:

BOOKSTORE SUBCOMMITTEE

Major Tasks

1. Contract with local bookstore for consignment order of books.
2. Arrange transport of books to seminar site.
3. Set up display of books.
4. Order and display free sample materials.
5. Staff the display during seminar.
6. Return unsold books, monies to bookstore.
7. Maintain contact with Planning Committee and coordinator.

Finding a Bookstore

If the Seminar site has an existing bookstore your task lightens considerably. If one is not available, check local Cokesbury or Newman bookstores. In Canada consult your nearest Learner Centre. If these are not available and other local bookstores will not cooperate, then call the national offices of Cokesbury at 1-800-672-1789 to arrange for an order. Check with a bookstore whether you will need to collect and pay sales tax.

What Books?

A suggested list of titles appears below. These books are "classics" on aspects of global education. You will probably not order them all. Choose the ones that seem most appropriate to your group and program (probably no more than 4-5 copies per title).

Once the Case Study has been determined, ask the designated resource persons what materials they would like to have on sale.

Freebies

Many groups, magazines, etc., are happy to share promotional materials (and sometimes samples) at no charge. A few of our favorites, with addresses for ordering, are listed below. Don't forget to display materials from local organizations as well.

Have you ever seen an inchworm crawl on to a leaf or a twig, and then, clinging to the very end, revolve in the air, feeling for something, to reach something? That's like me. I am trying to find something out there beyond the place on which I have footing.

Albert P. Ryder

Source	What's Available
Seeds P.O. Box 6170 Wace, TX 76706 (817) 755-7745	"Test Your Hunger IQ"; back issues; subscription info
World Press Review The Stanley Foundation Office of Publication 200 Madison Avenue New York, NY 10016 (212) 889-5155	back issues; subscription info
The New Internationalist 175 Carlton Street Toronto, Ontario M5A 2K3 Canada (416) 923-9857	back issues; subscription info
Institute for Food and Development Policy 145 Ninth Street San Francisco, CA 94103 (415) 864-8555	current catalog and/or flyers
Global Pages Immaculate Heart College Center 10951 W. Pico Blvd., Suite 2021 Los Angeles, CA 90064 (213) 470-2293	back issues; subscription info
Global Education Associates Suite 456 475 Riverside Drive New York, NY 10015 (212) 870-3290	flyers
Syracuse Cultural Workers Box 6367 Syracuse, NY 13217 (315) 474-1132	current catalog
Bread for the World 802 Rhode Island Avenue, NE Washington, DC 20018 (202) 269-0200	current catalog
Office on global Education 2115 N. Charles St. Baltimore, MD 21218-5755 (301) 727-6106	resource order sheet samples of materials

Institute for Policy Studies Fifth Floor 1601 Connecticut Avenue, NW Washington, DC 20009 (202) 234-9382	current catalog
Center for Teaching International Relations, University of Denver Denver, CO 80208-0268 (303) 871-3106	current catalog
The Stanley Foundation 420 E. 3rd Street Muscatine, IA 52761 (319) 264-1500	sample materials "Teachable Moments" "World Press Review"

Display of materials

Pay attention to presentation. An attractive and orderly display invites people to browse and enhances sales. Be sure to have adequate space for display—don't crowd material together. This goes for the freebie table too! Consider using batik or other cloth material to set off the display. Place the display in an area where participants will be gathered already: meeting space, dining room, etc.

You must understand the whole of life, not just one little part of it. That is why you must read, that is why you must look at the skies, that is why you must sing, and understand, for all that is life.

J. Krishnamurti

Staffing the Table

Take a few minutes before the seminar to read the back flaps of the books ordered. You need not become an "expert," but it helps to have some familiarity with your stock. At the beginning of the seminar announce the location of the bookstore, your role as staff and the times you will be available. Check with the site to locate a secure place to keep the money received during times the display is not staffed.

Suggested Books for Display and Sale

Benjamin, Medea and Andrea Freedman. *Bridging the Global Gap: A Handbook on Linking Citizens of the First and Third Worlds.* Cabin John, MD: Seven Locks Press, 1989.

Berry, Wendell. *Home Economics.* San Francisco, CA: Northpoint Press, 1988.

Bobo, Kimberly. *Lives Matter: A Handbook for Christian Organizing.* Kansas City, MO: Sheed & Ward, 1986.

Bodner, Joan (ed.) *Taking Charge of Our Lives: Living Responsibly in the World.* San Francisco, CA: Harper & Row, 1984.

Brown, Lester. *The State of the World.* New York: W.W. Norton & Company, (issued annually).

Dass, Ram and Paul Gorman. *How Can I Help? Stories and Reflections on Service.* New York: Alfred A. Knopf, 1987.

Fox, Matthew. *Original Blessing.* Santa Fe, NM: Bear & Co., 1983.

Hamilton, John Maxwell. *Entangling Alliances: How the Third World Shapes Our Lives.* Cabin John, MD: Seven Locks Press, 1990.

Hamilton, John Maxwell. *Main Street America & the Third World.* Cabin John, MD: Seven Locks Press, 1986.

Keen, Sam. *Faces of the Enemy: The Psychology of Enmity.* San Francisco, CA: Harper & Row, 1986.

Larson, Jeanne and Madge Micheels-Cyrus (compiled by). *Seeds of Peace: A Catalogue of Quotations.* Philadelphia, PA: New Society Publishers, 1986.

Macy, Joanna. *Despair and Personal Power in the Nuclear Age.* Philadelphia, PA: New Society Publishers, 1983.

Neal, Marie Augusta, S.N.D. *The Just Demands of the Poor: Essays in Socio-Theology.* Mahwah, NJ: Paulist Press, 1987.

Schaef, Ann Wilson. *When Society Becomes an Addict.* San Francisco, Harper & Row, 1987.

Sivard, Ruth Leger. *World Military and Social Experiences.* Washington, D.C.: World Priorities, (issued annually).

FINANCES SUBCOMMITTEE

Major Tasks

1. Open a bank account.
2. Develop tentative budget.
3. Pay deposit on seminar site.
4. Bank incoming registration monies.
5. Develop fund-raising strategies, if necessary.

6. Make final financial report as part of evaluation and pay bills.
7. Maintain contact with Planning Committee and coordinator.

It is the art of mankind [sic] to polish the world, and everyone who works is scrubbing in some part.

Henry David Thoreau

How to Develop a Tentative Budget

To get estimated expense and income figures for your budget, check with representatives from the Subcommittees, especially the Program Subcommittee (travel expenses or honoraria for leaders, copying costs for program materials, audio-visual rental, etc.), the Logistics Subcommittee (site charges for lodging and meals, extra food and supplies needed), and the Publicity Subcommittee.

We include here a very helpful guide for building a budget taken from *Thinking Globally—Acting Locally: A Citizen's Guide to Community Education on Global Issues* by The League of Women Voters Education Fund to assist you:

A careful plan includes detailed budgeting of expenses. Start by dividing the seminar into major components that will require funds and break them down into specific functions or expenses. In designing a budget, the following guidelines may prove helpful.

1. Include adequate funds for publicity and promotion. This expense is often overlooked but it can be the most important in determining the success of your project.
2. Include more funds than you initially think necessary for mailing costs. Large mailings for invitations or a general announcement of an upcoming event can be expensive if sent first class. Third class mailings are cheaper but take two to three weeks to arrive. Time permitting, try to use the third-class bulk rate permit of a nonprofit organization (if you are mailing the minimum of 200 pieces).
3. Include a substantial "miscellaneous" category for emergencies.
4. Depending on your project, include budget line items for such things as delivery service, planning meetings, local transportation, child care and audio-visual equipment rental.
5. Add sufficient funds to cover miscellaneous expenses of participants and special guests such as funders or community leaders. Things to consider include an

extra night in the hotel for those who must arrive early, parking, and child-care expenses.

6. Consider including funds for speaking honoraria. In some cases, this won't be necessary—for example, government employees generally do not accept honoraria. In other cases, you may have to pay a fee to get a good speaker. Honoraria can range from $100 to thousands of dollars.
7. Accommodations and meal expenses vary greatly among regions of the country. When figuring room and meal charges, be sure to add in taxes and gratuities. Also consider whether you want to book single rooms or require that participants share a double room.

The following is an example of a project budget for an extensive project. You can adjust or delete line items depending on the kind and size of your project.

Facilities	
Meeting Space	$__________
Meals	__________
Accommodations	__________
Equipment Rental (VCR and TV, microphones and sound system)	__________
Subtotal:	$__________
Speakers	
Fees/Honoraria	__________
Travel/lodging/meals	__________
Subtotal:	$__________
Materials	
Invitation/Brochure and Program	__________
Design and typesetting	
Printing (500 copies)	
Conference Packet	__________
Films, games, resource material	__________
Subtotal:	$__________
Miscellaneous	$__________
Staff Salaries (or Expenses)	
Coordinator	__________
Support Staff	__________
Volunteer Expenses	__________
Child-Care Expenses for project volunteers	__________
Subtotal:	$__________

Administrative Costs	
Telephone	________
Postage	________
Supplies and Equipment (typewriter, paper, pens)	________
Copying, routine	________
Subtotal:	$________
Evaluation and Report	$________
TOTAL	$________

Once the budget is set up, a careful accounting of all income and expenses is essential for several reasons: 1) to keep tight control over the project; 2) to serve as a warning system when funds are becoming short, so that you can raise more money or cut expenses; 3) to use as a reference for judging budget requirements of future projects; and 4) to fulfill a donor's accounting requirements.

It's not the tragedies that kill us, it's the messes.

Dorothy Parker

The person charged with accounting duties should closely monitor all expenses and scrutinize the need for each expense. She or he should not be reluctant to tighten the financial reins when necessary and should be diligent in saving all receipts and keeping accurate records for all expenses.

About Money for Seminars

Previous seminars have been designed to be largely self-supporting events, which means that participants pay their own room and board. Upfront money will be required for the deposit on the seminar site. Generally this cost has been born by the sponsoring organization. Additional costs for materials, mailings, etc., will vary from program to program. Here is a draft budget from a seminar organized in Illinois.

DOWNSTATE ILLINOIS SEMINAR
Second Draft Budget

Expense	
Planning Committee Meetings (mileage & parking)	310
Resource Person (honorarium/travel)	600

Conference Center (overnight/3 meals)		
45 adults @ $40	1,800	overnight/ 3 meals
10 youths @ 40	400	
	$3,110	

Income

Church World Service IL.	$310
Registration Fees	
45 adults @ $55	2,475
10 youths @ $40	400
	$3,185

Notes:
1. UCC's will donate the brochure, Church World Service will do mailing, coordinate registration.
2. Conference Center requires $200 deposit. This has been forwarded by Church World Service to be returned at end of seminar.

Ideally, some items can be paid for with "in-kind" contributions from one of the co-sponsoring groups. For example, a sponsoring church could contribute use of its mimeograph or photocopier; another allows mailings to be done more cheaply on its non-profit permit. Some groups may lend audio-visual equipment.

Monies for Participant Scholarships and honoraria may require some fund raising. To attract people from diverse economic backgrounds, subsidizing of room and board costs will be useful. Similarly, your resource people may require some reimbursement for travel and lodging. Determine with the Planning Committee if the sponsoring organizations can sustain the costs or if they prefer to add these costs into the registration fee. If the Planning Committee decides that outside funding is necessary, attend to the guidelines below.

Guidelines on Fund Raising

1. Begin early. The money is available for your program.
2. Recruit assistance from those in your community who are experienced fund raisers and/or who have the potential for generating contributions from their own organizations and contacts.

3. Offer to list sponsors and contributors to the Seminar on the program.
4. Sources

   A. Contact local judicatory hunger/peace/justice task forces to seek possible funding and to enlist their support in promotion. Look to local Catholic religious communities, campus ministry programs.
   B. Contact Local/State/Regional Councils of Churches for information and early support for the event.
   C. Compile a card file of potential donors—foundations, banks, state agencies, churches, corporations—their past interests and present trends, and names of contact persons as well as proposal deadlines.

5. As soon as possible, prepare a two-to-five page description of the Seminar event: the purposes; how these purposes will be realized; anticipated activities, guests, participants; value to groups involved and the larger community; and a basic budget.
6. Send this description to potential donors. In a follow-up telephone call arrange a visit. If funds aren't forthcoming, request in-kind contributions.
7. Be sure to say "Thank you."

Helpful Resources

Mitigui, Nancy. *The Rich Get Richer and Poor Write Proposals.* Amherst, MA: University of Massachusetts, Citizenship Involvement Training Program (CITP). 138 Hasbrouck, University of Massachusetts, Amherst, MA 01003. $6.00 plus 50c postage.

Program Planning and Proposal Writing (A Step By Step Guide). The Grantsmanship Center, 1031 South Grand Avenue, Los Angeles, CA 90015.

The Foundation Directory. The Foundation Center, New York, NY, Library Reference Number: AS 911 A2 F65. Lists foundations in the U.S. by State and describes the grant requirements for each.

Flanagan, Joan. *The Grassroots Fundraising Book (How to Raise Money in Your Community).* Contemporary Books Inc., 1982.

Putting the Fun in Fundraising (500 Ways to Raise Money for Charity). Contemporary Books Inc., 1979.

The good we secure for ourselves is precarious and uncertain . . . until it is secured for all of us and incorporated into our common life.

Jane Addams

> I have to cast my lot with those
> who age after age, perversely,
>
> with no extraordinary power,
> reconstitute the world.
>
> Adrienne Rich

The persons, films, books, and organizations below represent a fraction of the vital network of individuals and groups engaged in the service of a more just and peaceful world. You are not alone.

We are particularly pleased with the listing of performing artists. To our knowledge this collection is unique.

We also list a number of Canadian references. We are grateful to Ten Days for World Development and the Development Education Center for their assistance in identifying these excellent resources. The analysis and methodology of global education efforts in Canada has much to offer U.S. educators. We hope that this book and the U.S. references listed will be of value to our Canadian colleagues as well.

Resources are grouped under the following headings:

- Locating Speakers
- Artistic Resources
- Simulation Games
- Audio-visuals

We have expended considerable energy to insure that addresses and other references are current. Be aware, however, that changes may occur over time in location, price, etc.

Locating Speakers

We list only a few of the many sources for international speakers, or those speakers with international experience. Those agencies that appear in **bold** are listed with their address and phone at the end of the section.

Through Your Denomination

Consult with the Mission Education and International Service offices of your denomination at the judicatory and national levels for possible international visitors or staff. Consider using persons who have returned from volunteer-in-mission experiences as well.

Ecumenical Resources

In the USA, the 26 regional offices of **Church World Service** offer an excellent source of speakers among the staff and their local networks. In Canada, **Ten Days for World Development** tours "Third World" visitors annually as a part of their program.

Campus-Based Resources

Local colleges and universities probably represent the richest source of people from abroad, including many with experience in the Third World. According to the Institute of International Education (IIE), there were almost 350,000 foreign students in the United States during the 1986-87 academic year, the overwhelming majority of them from the developing world. Most institutions have an international programs office of some kind (titles vary from campus to campus) that provides on-campus services to foreign students and scholars. The foreign student advisor can help to identify students and faculty from a country or region of your interest. Some institutions have even established formal speakers' bureaus.

The international programs office should also be able to advise you about American students returned from research, study, or service projects in many parts of the world who would be effective and often eager speakers for your organization or school.

International houses and dorms, and student groups with international or development agenda are other campus-based resources. One such group is the **Overseas Development Network,** which will know of students with hands-on development experience through internships in Third World countries.

Do not overlook U.S. faculty. Chances are that professors in relevant disciplines will have spent some time abroad in consulting, teaching, or research. Some schools have area study centers whose faculty (as well as graduate students) would also be excellent resources. Find out whether your local college or university has put together a directory of staff with international experience.

Community Organizations

Contact the headquarters of exchange programs such as **Youth for Understanding,** the **Experiment in International Living,** and **AFS International/Intercultural Programs** to put you in touch with their local alumni.

The **National Council of Returned Peace Corps Volunteers** supports and facilitates their members' efforts to share the Peace Corps experience with other Americans and maintains a listing of contacts across the country.

Several hundred mid-career international visitors come to the United States each year for short-term visits, from about three weeks' to several months' duration. Frequently, as they travel around the country, a local program of visits and appointments to colleagues in their field of interest is organized by one of the 100 chapters of the **National Council for International Visitors (NCIV).**

In Canada the network of "Learner Centres" across the country will know of international resources in their area.

Your town or city might be a "sister" to a municipality abroad and frequent host to its citizens. **Sister Cities International** administers this program and can be contacted about the over 800 local chapters. In addition, your state is likely a partner to a province or nation in Latin America through a program managed by **Partners of the Americas.** These organizations welcome opportunities to reach new audiences in affiliated communities.

For a business/trade angle, you might contact local industries that import from, export to, or have operational affiliates overseas. You will find there not only widely traveled Americans but their colleagues from abroad who visit regularly for business discussions or training.

Other community sources: churches whose members include returned missionaries, locally organized ethnic groups, veterans associations, World Affairs Councils, YM-YWCAs, scouting organizations, and consulates of foreign governments. Some colleges and universities also maintain a file of individuals in the community knowledgeable about things "international."

National Organizations

The Washington headquarters of the **Peace Corps** itself has initiated a program of "Volunteers in Development Education" through which newly returned volunteers spend six weeks as guests in a community, serving as resources to schools and local organizations.

In Canada **CUSO** can put you in touch with returned volunteers who have received excellent training in popular education, as well as periodic international visitors. The Public Affairs Branch of the **Canadian International Development Agency (CIDA)** can also be contacted as a source of speakers.

The **Council for International Exchange of Scholars (CIES)** administers the "Occasional Lecturer Program" to help colleges and community scholars from abroad who come to the United States each year under the Fulbright Scholar Program. Most scholars are willing to travel to participate in meetings if the costs of transportation, accommodations, and meals can be covered. Since the experience is more beneficial to the scholar if a visit lasts several days and includes a variety of activities, you might want to tap this resource in collaboration with a local college where the visitor could meet with faculty, lecture, conduct seminars, and the like. In some cases, some financial assistance for the transportation portion could be available from CIES.

No longer is woman's moral reasoning viewed as simply a different style; it has become a political necessity for the preservation of the world.

Dr. Dorothy Austin

The Third World Women's Project based at the Institute for Policy Studies brings excellent speakers to the USA every year. All speakers are women from Third World contexts. The women represent a variety of perspectives, economic class, and experience. Their travel to your event from Washington, D.C. must be covered by you along with a modest honorarium.

The American Association for World Health has created a speakers bureau to address health issues for professional and civic groups.

The **World Bank** has developed a "Speakers' Program" providing business, civic, and professional organizations with the opportunity to hear senior World Bank officials address global economic issues.

If you are organizing an event where a large or influential audience is anticipated, officials of government agencies in Washington will often accept a place on the program. The **Agency for International Development,** the **Departments of State, Commerce,** and **Agriculture,** and the **United States Information Agency** all have an interest in educating the American public about the international issues with which they deal.

The United Nations, of course, has a wealth of resources among its staff and their colleagues in the rest of the world. For the initial contact with this complex organization write the **U.N. Non-Governmental Liaison Service.** In your letter to them be as specific as you can about the kind of speaker your looking for, the topic to be addressed, and the audience for the event. They will assist you in locating the right person.

Learning about Speakers

Another of the ways to learn about the availability of speakers on international issues is to attend local conferences, meetings, etc. Campus activities, for example, are often open to the general public, and attendance at lectures, seminars, and even such student-run events as international fairs and concerts are good places to meet potential speakers. Contact the public affairs office of your local institution for information, and ask to be put on the mailing list to receive notices of specific events.

Looking around the community, you might seek out meetings of such public-education organizations as the United Nations Association, the League of Women Voters, the Foreign Policy Association, the Society for International Development, American Friends Service Committee, **Educators for Social Responsibility,** world trade councils of chambers of commerce, labor groups, and political committees. You might hear, for example, of "International Round Tables," where local people involved in international commerce invite participation by the public. Museums and area-specific cultural groups also often sponsor lectures and discussions.

FOR SPEAKERS, CONTACT:

AFS International/Intercultural Programs
313 East 43rd Street, New York, NY 10017, 212 949-4242

American Association for World Health
2001 "S" Street, N.W., Suite 530, Washington, DC 20009
202 265-0286

Church World Service (CWS)
PO Box 968, Elkhart, IN 46515-0968, 219 264-3102

Canadian International Development Agency (CIDA)
Speakers' Bureau, Public Affairs Branch
200 Promenade du Portage, Hull, Quebec K1A 0G4, CANADA
819 997-5456

Council for International Exchange of Scholars (CIES)
Eleven DuPont Circle, N.W., Suite 300,
Washington, DC 20036-1257, 202 939-5405

CUSO Education Department
135 Rideau Street, Ottawa, Ontario K1N 9K7, CANADA
613 563-1242

Educators for Social Responsibility (ESR)
23 Garden Street, Cambridge, MA 02138, 617 492-1764

Experiment in International Living (EIL)
Kipling Road, Brattleboro, VT 05301, 802 257-7751

National Council for International Visitors (NCIV)
1623 Belmont Street, NW, Washington, DC 20009, 202 332-1028

National Council of Returned Peace Corps Volunteers (NCRPCV)
PO Box 65294, Washington, DC 20035, 202 393-5501

Overseas Development Network (ODN)
PO Box 1430, Cambridge, MA 02238, 617 868-3002

Partners of the Americas
1424 K Street, N.W., Suite 700, Washington, DC 20005
202 628-3300

Peace Corps
Office of Development Education
Room 1107, Washington, DC 20526, 800 424-8580 ext 276

Sister Cities International
120 South Payne Avenue, Alexandria, VA 22314, 703 836-3535

Ten Days for World Development
85 St. Clair Avenue E, Toronto, Ontario M4T 1M8, CANADA
416 922-0591

Third World Women's Project
Institute for Policy Studies, 1601 Connecticut Avenue, N.W.
Washington, DC 20009, 202 234-9382

United Nations Non-Governmental Liaison Service (UN-NGLS)
11th floor of DC-2 Building, Rm DC2-1103

UN-NGLS *continued*
2 United Nations Plaza, 44th Street at First Avenue
New York, NY 10017, 212 754-3117

U.S. GOVERNMENT AGENCIES

U.S. Agency for International Development (AID)
Office of Public Inquiries, Bureau for External Affairs
Washington, DC 20523, 202 647-1850

U.S. Department of Agriculture
Information Division
Office of International Cooperation and Development
Washington, DC 20250, 202 653-7589

U.S. Department of Commerce
Office of Public Affairs, Washington, DC 20230
202 377-3263

U.S Department of State
Bureau of Public Affairs, Washington, DC 20520
202 647-2234

U.S. Information Agency (USIA)
Office of Public Liaison, 301 Fourth Street, S.W.
Washington, DC 20547, 202 485-2355

World Bank
Office of External Relations, 1818 H Street, N.W.
Washington, DC 20433, 202 477-8825

Youth for Understanding (YFU)
3501 Newark Street, N.W., Washington, DC 20016
202 966-6808

Adapted with permission from HUMAN RESOURCES FOR GLOBAL AND DEVELOPMENT EDUCATION
Consortium for International Cooperation in Higher Education (CICHE)
One DuPont Circle, Suite 616, Washington, DC 20036
202 857-1833

ARTISTIC RESOURCES

Art inspires, challenges, broadens our horizons— the heart of global education. We introduce here just a few of the many creative individuals and groups who have offered their talents in the service of a better world. They are educators in the fullest sense, persons who lead us to a new openness, a deeper appreciation of our selves and our beautiful, fragile planet.

Drama

Peri Aston: Solo Theatre
8 Wilton Crescent
Wimbledon
London SW19 3QZ
United Kingdom

Peri Aston: Solo Theatre *continued*

Peri Aston, a frequent visitor to the U.S., performs four solo shows of her own devising, richly varied in content and style:

"Joan of Arc": woman as agent of change weaves through the play in the symbolic elements of Earth, Air, Water, and Fire.

"Quest": The tramp woman is given a vision of her lost feminine roots. A universal search for self-understanding.

"Not Just a Pretty Face": A thought-provoking and humorous portrayal of aspects of a woman's life.

"Pierrot & Co.": Favorite characters from the commedia dell' arte—Harlequin, Pantaloon and Doctor, and of course, Pierrot himself.

Bread and Puppet Theatre

Peter Schumann
RD#2
Glover, VT 05839
525-6972

or

Trudi Cohen
539 West 112th St., #3B
New York, NY 10025 805/
212/316-0870

Bread and Puppet Theatre is known for its wondrous spectacles consisting of huge puppets, banners, slideshows, music, pageant and free sourdough rye bread. Bread and Puppet has toured the U.S., Central and South America, and Europe practicing the credo of its founder (Peter Schumann): "In spirit the arts are gods: they heal, revolutionize, fulfill, perfect."

Gould and Stearns

44 Hillcrest Terrace
Brattleboro, VT 05301
802/254-8355

"A Peasant of El Salvador": A play presented with a mix of mime, acting, and music. This is a political parable to give audiences an alternate point of view about the history of the civil war in El Salvador. Available for national touring and for local theater companies to produce. Inquire for permission and royalties.

Theatre is like bread,
a necessity.

Bread & Puppet Theatre

New York Street Theatre Caravan

c/o Marketta Kimnbrell
87005 Chelsea Street
Jamaica, NY 11432
212/454-8551

Founded in 1970, the Caravan is one of America's unique experimental theatres—a multi-racial company of professional actors devoted to bringing theatre of the highest quality to those outside of the cultural mainstream. Equipped with a modern-day "theatre wagon" (a flatbed truck) the Caravan has performed its plays and street corner cabarets for numerous grassroots organizations: unions, prisons, youth groups, Indian reservations, universities, and schools.

SMALL WORLD/WIDE WORLD:
A Theatrical Performance

Daisy Kabagarama
McPherson College
McPherson, KS

or

Kate Kasten
c/o E. Kasten-Ultang
67460 10 W. 34th Street
Des Moines, IA 50312

This humorous 45-minute play is about resolving cultural misunderstandings between a foreign and a native graduate student on a U.S. university campus. The actors lead a follow-up discussion providing an opportunity for participants to share and interpret their own experiences of cross-cultural misunderstandings. This script may also, for a fee, be used by others upon written permission of the authors.

Dance/Music

Center for the Dances of Universal Peace
114 Forrest Avenue
Fairfax, CA 94930
415/453-8159

A network and resource center: through music and dance, toward one world, within and without. The Center offers workshops, retreats and classes.

Ki Performance Group
c/o Ferne Bork
PO Box 203
Washington, VA 22747
703/987-3164

The members of each group come from diverse backgrounds in music, theater, and dance:

- **Ki Theatre (formerly Golden Key)**
  Multi-disciplinary theater inspired by stories. "Conference of the Birds" charts a journey to the heart of man's search for meaning. "Strange Consequences," a series of theatrical cameos interweaving the power of personal memories with the mystery of myths from ancient Africa, Asia, and the Americas.

- **Portman & Reisler**
  Bring the worlds of theater and music together in a seamless fusion of acting, movement and music that gives life, power, and passion to their stories. Speaks to the aspirations and the anxieties that live within.

- **WorldWind**
  Vocal duo singing "timely songs from a timeless tradition"—songs that communicate social and global concerns, lift the human spirit, and reinforce a sense of our interconnectedness. Repertoire includes eclectic variety of original, traditional, and international songs in fifteen languages.

Montana Logging and Ballet Company
Bob Fitzgerald
1515 Winne
Helena, MT 59601
406/443-1690

The Montana Logging and Ballet Company is a music and comedy group, spiced with topical political satire (formerly under the name The People Tree).

Peace Child Foundation
3977 Chain Bridge Road
Fairfax, VA 22030
703/385-4494

Peace Child is both a musical play and an international exchange project. The play was born in 1982 and tells the story of Peace Day in the year 2025—and how the nations of the world establish peace.

The Peace Child Foundation organizes exchanges of young people to perform the play every summer. A Peace Child study-pack for use in schools, communities, or churches is available.

Jim and Jean Strathdee
Desert Flower Music
PO Box 1735
1332 Porter Street
Ridgecrest, CA 93555
619/375-2320

The Strathdees write and perform music that speaks to the pain of our world with passion, hope, and humor. They are powerful, energetic leaders for conference and worship.

ARTISTS' ORGANIZATIONS

Alliance for Cultural Democracy
c/o Bob Feldman
PO Box 2478, Station A
Champaign, IL 61820
217/352-2421

Nationwide, nonprofit organization for community-based arts programs and activist artists. The Alliance's members are visual artists, theatre workers, musicians, media artists, dancers, arts administrators, and others involved in community and cultural work in urban, suburban, and rural settings.

Christians in the Arts Networking, Inc.
PO Box 1941
Cambridge, MA 02238-1941
61/ 783-5667

Provides networking services for Christians worldwide in the visual arts, music, theatre, or dance. Annual membership includes subscription to CANews.

Lutheran Alternative Musicians and Artists for Justice (LAMAJ)
c/o Lucy Kolin
215 Ridgeway
Oakland, CA 94611
415/655-2422

LAMAJ is a network in the beginning stages of formation; currently it is eighty-members strong. It is being created to locate and link together musicians, artists, and dramatists nationwide who are working or would like to be working within the Lutheran community.

Simulation Games

Bafa Bafa (Rafa Rafa for Grade Five to Grade Eight students) participants live and cope in a "foreign" culture and then discuss and analyze the experience. During the discussion, the mysteries of each culture are revealed and perceptions compared. 12-40 participants. One 2-3 hour session. $90.00 for **Bafa Bafa;** $39.00 for **Rafa Rafa.** Available from SIMILE II, PO Box 910, Del Mar, CA 92014 (619) 755-0272.

Death of a Dissident deals with economic development including foreign investment, civil unrest, social justice, and human rights in a Caribbean dictatorship. 39 participants for four 1-hour sessions. $69.95. Available from The American Forum, 45 John Street, Suite 1200, New York, NY 10038 (212) 732-8606.

The Debt Game helps us understand the links between hunger at home and abroad. Participants see the human impact of the international debt crisis by playing the roles of developing and developed countries and banks. 7-15 participants for one 2-hour session. Available from the American Friends Service Committee, New York Metropolitan Region, 15 Rutherford Place, New York, NY 10003 (212) 598-0950.

Ecopolis recreates the 150-year evolutionary process in a large city, with reference to the international ecological impact. 15-35 participants. 10-15 hours. $18.00. Available from INTERACT, PO Box 997-S90, Lakeside, CA 92040 (800) 359-0961 or (619) 448-1474.

Fire in the Forest is set in the Amazonian Rain Forest with conflicting claims to the land and its use by environmentalists, settlers, and native tribes. Themes include environmental protection, respect for indigenous cultures, social justice, economic development, and poverty. 40 participants for four 1-hour sessions. $69.95. Available from The American Forum, 45 John Street, Suite 1200, New York, NY 10038 (212) 732-8606.

Hostage Crisis deals with Middle Eastern nationalism, terrorism, justice issues, survival skills, and cross-cultural understanding. Kit contains an introductory video, booklets for 43 roles, 2 texts, and a facilitator's manual. Four 1-hour sessions. $150. Available from The American Forum, 45 John Street, Suite 1200, New York, NY 10038 (212) 732-8606.

Star Power participants progress from one level of society to another by acquiring wealth through trading with other participants. Once the society is established, the group with the most wealth is given the right to make the rules for the game. The power group generally makes rules which maintain or increase its power and which those being governed consider to be unfair. This generally results in some sort of rebellion by the other members of the society and sparks animated discussion of economic justice. 18-35 participants. Preparation: 1/2 hour. 2 hours for Star Power. $79.00. Available from SIMILE II, PO Box 910, Del Mar, CA 92014 (619) 755-0272.

AV Resources

Films offer a powerful medium to bridge different worlds of place, culture, experience. We feature below the Church World Service film library whose collection of over 400 titles makes it the largest free lending library of films on justice and peace issues in the USA. *A catalogue of films is available on request.* Following a sample of the titles available from CWS, we list other sources of films in Canada.

Church World Service Film Library
PO Box 968
Elkhart, IN 46515-0968
219 264-3102

Using the Film Library

You or your group can arrange to borrow an audiovisual from the Church World Service Film Library by either phoning or writing. Please make your reservation as early as possible. We suggest a month to six weeks lead time. You will receive written confirmation of your reservation.

It's Free
The only cost to you when you borrow an audio-visual from the CWS Film Library is the shipping or postage you pay to return it. Since audio-visuals are often tightly scheduled, ship back the audio-visual no later than the next business day after the showing.

Some Restrictions Apply
Audio-visuals available on loan from the Church World Service Film Library may not be duplicated, edited, or exhibited for a fee. Except where noted, AVs may not be broadcast via television or cable without written permission from the producer or distributor.

Selected Titles

The Big Island (8 minutes/VHS), MacNeil/Lehrer NewsHour. Aaron Freeman takes an ironic, at times satiric, view of difficulties as citizens understanding our global village.

Child of the Universe (4 minutes/VHS), Office on Global Education/CWS. A beautiful photographic portrait of the oneness and diversity of the human family. Lively song-text, "Desiderata". Upbeat, moving, meditative.

Children of Apartheid (49 minutes/VHS). Walter Cronkite reports on the fate of thousands of black children under South Africa's state of emergency. Interviews with Rosanne, daughter of President P.W. Botha, and Zinzi, daughter of Nelson and Winnie Mandela, reveal vastly differing experiences and differing perspectives on apartheid.

Count Me In: A Guide for Planning Participatory Learning Events (19 minutes/VHS), Ten Days for World Development/ Inter-Church Coalition on Africa, CANADA. An engaging, practical and at times humorous training video for groups concerned with how people learn. It seeks to inspire groups to carry out learning events that are participatory and that will empower people to be critical, free, active citizens of the world. A helpful study guide is included.

Covenant (30 minutes/16mm film/U-matic), World Council of Churches. Promises, symbols and stories from the Sixth Assembly of the World Council of Churches. Images of the Assembly explore diversity, participation, challenge, eucharist, and covenant as integral pieces of ecumenical fellowship. The Assembly exemplifies the model of Church that confesses, celebrates, and covenants together to cross divisions that separate God's people from each other.

The Cry of Reason: Beyers Naude—An Afrikaner Speaks Out (56 minutes/VHS), South Africa. A moving chronicle of the life of Beyers Naude, from trusted pastor to the white Afrikaner elite to staunch supporter of the freedom movement.

Hope Is the Last Thing to Die (26 minutes/VHS), Church World Service. The stories and struggles of Brazil's street children to survive in a hostile, sometimes violent environment. Describes their daily routine, also examines the larger economic issues that push families to the edge, and beyond.

No More Separate Futures (9 minutes/SS), Office on Global Education/CWS. An exploration of the nature of global education and of issues that demand a global perspective: peace, militarism, the farm crisis, global hunger, women, water, population. Factual data presented through thought-provoking questions.

Women—for America, for the World (29 minutes/VHS, BETA), Vivienne Verdon-Roe. With common sense and compassion, women from various fields call for an end to the arms race and a change in our national priorities. Academy award recipient.

In Canada consult the Learner Centre in your area or one of the offices of the National Film Board of Canada listed below:

This is a present from a small distant world. . . . We are attempting to survive our time so we may live into yours.

Recorded Message
on board the
Voyager space probe

Mackenzie Building
1 Lombard St.
Toronto, Ontario
M5C 1J6
CANADA
416 973-9110

Complexe Guy Favreau
East Tower, Rm 005
200 Dorchester W.
Montreal, Quebec
H2Z 1X4
CANADA
514 283-4823

Permissions

We acknowledge with thanks the following permissions to reprint:

Coming To Our Senses

Cartoons

"Hard Hats," Jules Feiffer, Universal Press Syndicate, Promotion Dept., 4900 Main St. 9th Fl., Kansas City, MO 64112.

"Dinosaurs," Graham Wilson; "What's Wrong," Mulligan; "Just Tell Him," aDan Fradon, *New Yorker Magazine*, 25 W. 43rd St., NY NY 10036

"That's an Excellent Suggestion," *World Press Review*, May '88, © *Punch*/Rothco

"Ozone," *World Press Review* & Liebermann of Sueddeutsche Zeiting, Munich.

"Yes, God said 'Love . . .,'' *Baptist Peacemaker*, Deer Park Baptist Church, 1733 Bardtown Road, Louisville, KY 40205.

"Before we Demand," "I see Creeping Socialism," from *Between the Lines* by Eleanor MacLean, Black Rose Books, 3981 Boulevard St.-Laurent, Montreal, H2W 1Y5, Quebec, Canada.

"SOS," Unesco Sources, 7, Place de Fontenoy, 75700 Paris, France.

"Globe w/missiles," Wm. Gardner, *War Heads*, reprinted by Permission of UFS, Inc., United Features Syndicate, 200 Park Ave., NY 10166.

"Peanuts," Charles Schultz, Reprinted by permission of UFS, Inc., United Features Syndicate, 200 Park Ave., NY 10166.

"Herman," Universal Press Syndicate, 4900 Main St., Kansas City, MO 64112.

"It Kills me . . .," reprinted by Permission of NEA, Newspaper Enterprise Association, Inc., United Media Enterprises, 200 Park Ave., Suite 602, NY 10166.

"The undecideds have it . . .," reprinted with permission from *Seeds Magazine*, Copyright © 1987.

"What Can One Man/Woman Do?," ELCA, Hunger Program, 8765 W. Higgings Road, Chicago, IL 60631

Drawings

Drawing of Woman, *Education for Justice*, Tom Fenton, Orbis Books, Maryknoll Fathers, Maryknoll, NY 10545.

World Map: Peters Projection by Arno Peters, Distributed by Friendship Press, New York, copyright Akademische Veriagsanstalt. Used by permission.

Drawing (with Chief Seattle quote)—used with permission of *Creation Magazine*, Friends of Creation Spirituality, PO Box 19216, Oakland, CA 94619

Drawing (with Martin Luther King quote) Artwork by Miriam Therese MacGillis, OP, reprinted with permission of Global Education Associates, Suite 456, 475 Riverside Dr., NY 10155 from their publication *The Whole Earth Papers*, No. 16.

Drawing (with Levertov quote), Jane Pitz, CSJ, South Bend, IN.

Quotes

Excerpts from *The Search for Signs of Intelligent Life in the Universe* by Jane Wagner. Copyright © 1986 by Jane Wagner, Inc. Reprinted by permission of HarperCollins Publishers.

"Please Call Me by My True Names," by Thich Nhat Hanh. Poem is from the book *Being Peace*, published by Parallax Press.

"We have only begun . . .," Denise Levertov: *Candles in Babylon*. Copyright © 1982 by Denise Levertov, Reprinted by permission of New Directions Publishing Co.

"Breathing Through," *Despair & Personal Power in the Nuclear Age*, Joanna Rogers Macy, New Society Publishers, Phila., PA, Santa Cruz, CA, and Gabriola Island, BC Canada. (800) 333-9093.

Images **of the Enemy**

Excerpts from *Who Dies?* by Stephen Levine, © 1982 by Stephen Levine. Used by permission of Doubleday, division of Bantam Doubleday Dell Publishing Group, Inc.

"To Create an Enemy," from *Faces of the Enemy* by Sam Keen. Copyright © 1986 by Sam Keen. Reprinted by permission of Harper & Row Publishers, Inc.

"Christmas 1914," A. Clutton-Brock, *In a Dark Time*, ed. Robert Jay Lifton & Nicolas Humphrey, Harvard Univ. Press, 1984.

"ERA's story," from *How Can I Help* by Ram Dass and Paul Gorman. Copyright © 1985 by Ram Dass and Paul Gorman. Reprinted by permission of Alfred A. Knopf, Inc.

"Perhaps this sounds very . . .," *Modern Man in Search of a Soul*, Carl Jung, Harcourt Brace Jovanovich, Inc., Orlando, Florida 32887.

"Spanish Brute" A Cartoon History of US Foreign Policy, Wm. Morrow & Co., 105 Madison Ave., New York, NY 10016

Worship

"We must be loved into roundness. . .," by Chuck Lathrop. Cited in *A Spirituality Named Compassion*, by Matthew Fox. Copyright © 1979 by Matthew Fox. Reprinted by permission of HarperCollins Publishers.

"My Lord God, I have no idea . . .," Prayer from *Thoughts in Solitude* by Thomas Merton. Copyright © 1958 by The Abbey of Our Lady of Gethsemani. Renewal copyright © 1986 by the Trustees of the Thomas Merton Legacy Trust. Reprinted by permission of Farrar, Straus and Giroux, Inc.

"A Prayer for the Church," Madonna Kolbenschlag, 105 Webster Ave., Morgantown, WV 26505.

"A blessing," This poem from *Four Winds* by Gene Meany Hodge is used with the kind permission of Sunstone Press, Box 2321, Sante Fe., MN 87504.

"You know, oh God . . .," "Oh Lord, I do not know . . .," "The blessing of the God," "As the earth keeps turning . . .," "Affirmation of Peace & Justice," "Litany of Gratitude," *With All God's People, The New Ecumenical Prayer Cycle*, World Council of Churches, 150 Route de Ferney, PO Box 2100, 1211 Geneva 2, Switzerland.

"Bakerwoman God," Alla Renee Bozarth, reprinted with permission from *Womanpriest: A Personal Odyssey*, 2nd ed. Luramedia, 1988, and *Stars in Your Bones: Emerging Signposts on Our Spiritual Journeys*, North Star Press of St. Cloud, 1990. Also performed by the poet on *Water Women*, audio cassette, Wisdom House, 1990.

"Oh God, we are persons . . .," *Bread for the Journey: Resources for Worship*, edited by Ruth Duck, Pilgrim Press, reprinted by permission of the publishers, copyright 1981.

"And so the times comes, . . .," Miriam Simos, *Truth or Dare*, HarperCollins, 10 East 53rd St., New York, NY 10022.

"Mother God, Father God," Adapted from *More Than Words*, Janet Schaffran, Pat Kozak, copyright © 1986, 1988, reprinted by permission of The Crossroad Publishing Company.

"Our Mother, Our Father," *WomanPrayer WomanSong*, Miriam Therese Winter, copyright © 1987 Medical Mission Sisters.

Psalm 126, from *"Why, O Lord?"* by Rev. Zephania Kameeta, published by World Council of Churches, 1986.

"Songs of the Tewa," This poem courtesy of Sunstone Press, PO Box 2321, Sante Fe, NM 87504-2321.

Resources

"I have to cast my lot . . .," excerpt from *Natural Resources*, poem by Adrienne Rich, in *The Dream of a Common Language, Poems 1974-1977*. Used by permission, W. W. Norton & Co., Inc.